Writers of the 21st Century

URSULA K. LE GUIN

Also available in the Writers of the 21st Century Series:

ISAAC ASIMOV
ARTHUR C. CLARKE
RAY BRADBURY
ROBERT A. HEINLEIN
PHILIP K. DICK *(in preparation)*
STANISLAW LEM *(in preparation)*
ROBERT SILVERBERG *(in preparation)*

Also co-edited by Joseph D. Olander and Martin Harry Greenberg:

Time of Passage: SF Stories about Death and Dying
Tomorrow, Inc.: SF Stories about Big Business
Run to Starlight: Sports through Science Fiction *(with Patricia Warrick)*
The City 2000 A.D.: Urban Problems through Science Fiction *(with Ralph Clem)*
The New Awareness: Religion through Science Fiction *(with Patricia Warrick)*

Edited by

JOSEPH D. OLANDER

and

MARTIN HARRY GREENBERG

TAPLINGER PUBLISHING COMPANY / NEW YORK

Dedication

This book is respectfully and gratefully dedicated to Roy E. Thomas, editor at Taplinger Publishing Company, who, through his vision, hard work, skills—and, most of all, his patience—has been responsible for bringing to the science fiction community additional and needed perspectives of this fascinating literature. Like all editors, his has also been a labor of love.

First Edition

Published in the United States in 1979 by
TAPLINGER PUBLISHING CO., INC.
New York, New York

Library of Congress Cataloging in Publication Data
Main entry under title:
Ursula K. Le Guin.

(Writers of the 21st Century)
Bibliography: p.
Includes index.
1. Le Guin, Ursula K., 1919. —Criticism and interpretation —Essays. 2. Science fiction, American—History and criticism —Essays. I. Olander, Joseph D. II. Greenberg, Martin Harry. III. Series

PS3562.E42Z95 813'.5'4 77-76722
ISBN 0-8008-7943-0
ISBN 0-8008-7942-2 pbk.

Designed by Manuel Weinstein

CONTENTS

Acknowledgments

Grateful acknowledgment is made for permission to quote brief passages from the following works by Ursula K. Le Guin:

CITY OF ILLUSIONS. Copyright © 1967 by Ursula K. Le Guin. Used by permission of Grosset & Dunlap, Inc.

THE DISPOSSESSED. Copyright © 1974 by Ursula K. Le Guin. Used by permission of the author and her agent, Virginia Kidd, and by permission of Harper & Row, Publishers, Inc.

THE FARTHEST SHORE. Copyright © 1972 by Ursula K. Le Guin. Used by permission of the author and her agent, Virginia Kidd, and by permission of Atheneum Publishers and Victor Gollancz, Ltd.

THE LEFT HAND OF DARKNESS. Copyright © 1969 by Ursula K. Le Guin. Used by permission of the author and her agent, Virginia Kidd.

PLANET OF EXILE. Copyright © 1966 by Ursula K. Le Guin. Used by permission of Grosset & Dunlap, Inc.

ROCANNON'S WORLD. Copyright © 1966 by Ursula K. Le Guin. Used by permission of Grosset & Dunlap, Inc.

THE TOMBS OF ATUAN. Copyright © 1970, 1971 by Ursula K. Le Guin. Used by permission of the author and her agent, Virginia Kidd, and by permission of Atheneum Publishers and Victor Gollancz, Ltd.

WILD ANGELS. Copyright © 1975 by Ursula K. Le Guin. Used by permission of Capra Press.

THE WIND'S TWELVE QUARTERS. Copyright © 1975 by Ursula K. Le Guin. Used by permission of the author and her agent, Virginia Kidd.

A WIZARD OF EARTHSEA. Copyright © 1968 by Ursula K. Le Guin. Used by permission of Houghton Mifflin Company.

Introduction

Joseph D. Olander and Martin Harry Greenberg

FOR APPROXIMATELY SIXTEEN years Ursula K. Le Guin has provided readers of science fiction and fantasy with stories and novels which have enriched their lives and expanded the horizons of the field. Her contributions to the literature have been measured only partly by awards she has received (see page 247). Her impact may also partly be measured by the critical attention her fiction is receiving, as this book of critical essays demonstrates. Some of these essays offer perspectives for perceiving the artistic "ordering vision" in her fiction; others here deal with important subjects and themes in her work. But they all attempt to help us better understand her fiction and her contributions.

For Le Guin, science fiction represents an "open system," where the potential for thinking about ideas and patterns exists relatively unfettered by imposed or inherited systems of society and thought. Indeed, for her, science fiction and those who write it are characterized by a "dislike of, and restlessness within, the closed system."* Whether science fiction is an "open" or "closed" system will continue to receive much debate. If an "open" system represents diversity, then Ursula K. Le Guin's fiction qualifies as "open." Her work is filled with different kinds of beings and societies which are portrayed, for the most part, in almost totally consistent alternative world settings. It is this aspect of her work that encourages many people to refer to her as the natural successor to Tolkien.

Unlike most science fiction writers, Le Guin projects the essence

---

*Ursula K. Le Guin, "Surveying the Battlefield," in "Change, SF, and Marxism: Open or Closed Universes?" in *Science-Fiction Studies,* I (Fall 1973), 88–90.

of life not as unlimited change or process, but as quietude, stillness, and mystical union with Being. Her fiction tantalizes us with a mythic vision that is deftly used to bridge human order and the order of nature. Whereas many science fiction writers start with man in order to make him godlike, Le Guin starts with nature in order to reach man. Man's imperfect nature and the necessity of coping with the problems such a nature implies are threads woven throughout her fiction.

Moreover, much science fiction takes a decidedly secular view of the world. Le Guin's fiction, on the other hand, suggests an almost sacred (but not sentimental) view of the world. In her work events appear to affect humans—and other kinds of beings as well—in the form of fate or grace. Certain terms and conditions of nature seem immutable. She often portrays the world as providing circumstances which beings should accept, while consistently painting a picture of man whose responsibility and accountability must be an integral part of these events—phenomena to be worked with, not against.

The continued emphasis in Le Guin's fiction on balance, on equilibrium, on being "in touch," has led some persons to speculate on whether her family's relationships with the culture and lives of American Indians are significantly related to major themes in her fiction. There does seem to be a parallel, but whether or not this can be established, it remains clear that Le Guin's focus on man–nature relationships is a hallmark of her writing. In this connection her fiction seems to infer an ethical theory. In a natural state man is basically good, but the violation or abandonment of this natural order leads to turmoil, injustice, and political conflict. Le Guin offers us a profoundly deep awareness of man's context in nature that takes us beyond mundane human conventions, hypocrisies, and customs. Her protagonist is often the uncommited individual, that is, the non–acting or contemplative individual. This runs counter to the Hobbesian hero of much science fiction—the competent individual who may be physically, morally, and intellectually superior to others and for whom right action is self–actualizing.

Furthermore, most science fiction writers tend to concern themselves with the "outer realm"—the vast cosmos or the superior technological society—whereas Le Guin is clearly chiefly concerned with the "inner realm," the arena of the psyche. A familiar science fiction scenario portrays an individual who sets out to change the world—to conquer it or shape it—for his own survival or for the survival of the group to which he belongs. Le Guin allows her characters to enter an inner world—often one of pain and mental anguish—to achieve wholeness, an almost mystic union, with the universe. This striving for union, or balance, with the universe—Le Guin's natural world—is not naively romantic. For Le Guin the world is composed of both good and evil, and the solutions to the problems which humans and other beings face must take into account the interdependency of these two forces.

Finally, Le Guin's fiction may be filled with wizards, aliens, and clones, but the vision contained in her stories and novels is, above all, concerned with what is most permanent about the human condition. When one enters the world of her fiction, one encounters a distinctive universe of discourse. Both the critic and the science fiction fan are well advised to start with this perspective.

1. The Master Pattern: The Psychological Journey in the Earthsea Triology

MARGARET P. ESMONDE

THE DENIZENS of ivory towers owe a debt of gratitude to Ursula K. Le Guin for taking up the career of writer. Her science fiction novels provide grist for an increasing number of scholarly mills. Serious science fiction critic Robert Scholes has called her "probably the best writer of speculative fabulation working in this country today."[1] The critical journal, *Science Fiction Studies,* has devoted an entire issue to her work.[2] In all this serious critical attention, there is only one serious omission: practically no one has taken her Earthsea trilogy seriously!

There are two possible reasons. First, the trilogy is "pure" fantasy. In "This Fear of Dragons," Le Guin herself remarks that a moral disapproval of fantasy, intense and very aggressive, is an integral part of the American character. We have been brainwashed to see fantasy as "childish, or effeminate, unprofitable, and probably sinful."[3] A more serious obstacle arises from the fact that the trilogy was originally published as "juvenile fiction." What serious critic is willing to admit in print that he or she reads children's books, and fantasy to boot!?

With the exception of book reviews in journals devoted to children's literature, criticism of the Earthsea trilogy consists of a few brief analyses of the first book, *A Wizard of Earthsea*. Scholes gives it four pages, two of which are quotations from the book itself. The second and third books are either ignored entirely or dismissed with a casual remark that *The Tombs of Atuan* concerns female maturation and *The Farthest Shore* is about death.

The only discussion of the complete trilogy to date is George

Slusser's recent study of Le Guin's work, *The Farthest Shores of Ursula K. Le Guin.* Of necessity limited in his analysis of the individual books, Slusser devotes his discussion to the thesis that the Earthsea trilogy cannot be separated from the Hainish novels which it parallels because in the trilogy, "major themes are not simply mirrored or reflected, but carried forward and developed in new ways."[4] His argument is excellent and convincing.

Le Guin employs the same pervasive light-and-shadow imagery in both her science fiction and her fantasy; the significance of true names, the touching of hands, and the circle journey are important in both. The nature of evil and the preservation of the Equilibrium are her concern in Earthsea as well as in the Hainish novels. Specific images are repeated almost exactly. In *A Wizard of Earthsea,* Le Guin's description of the boy Ioeth running fast and far ahead of Ged down a dark slope into the Dry Lands of Death calls to mind the vivid image of Estraven skiing down hill in a long curving descent through the shadows over the snow to the border and death, with Genly Ai powerless to save him. "Tormer's Lay," which Estraven recites to Genly Ai in *The Left Hand of Darkness,* might easily be the second stanza of the song, "The Creation of Éa." Taoism is a major philosophical influence in both, and both reflect her interest in dreams and deep understanding of anthropology.

But more important than any of these analogies—and basic to the achievement of her primary purpose in both the Earthsea trilogy and the Hainish novels—is Le Guin's use of the psychological journey toward the integration of personality that Carl Jung wrote about. The progression of an ego from uncertainty and self-doubt to assurance and fulfillment is a process to which Jung devoted a great deal of attention. So, too, has Le Guin; in one form or another, the theme appears in all her novels.

In the Earthsea trilogy we have the best opportunity to see how she uses it. The protagonist of each volume undertakes a journey of personality that culminates in the integration of his self. Since these straightforward stories deal in strong colors and plain fabrics, we can readily detect the design the master patterner has woven, not just in Earthsea but throughout the entire fabric of her work.

Le Guin discusses this psychological journey at considerable length in "The Child and the Shadow." She explains her symbolism in general terms of Jungian psychology, according to which there is imposed on every individual both the urge and the necessity to become conscious of himself, to develop that human awareness which distinguishes the mature personality from the infantile one. In *Aion,* Jung identifies the conscious personality as the "ego" and the personal unconscious as the "shadow," stating that the shadow is a moral problem which challenges the whole ego personality.[5] To become conscious of this shadow takes considerable moral effort, since it involves recognizing the dark aspects of one's own personality as being present and real. This act of recognition is essential to achieving any kind of self-knowledge. Though it is a difficult task, with insight and goodwill, the shadow can to some extent be assimilated into the conscious personality.

Jung further describes the shadow as "the dark half of the human totality," warning that one cannot omit the shadow that belongs to the light figure; for without it, this figure lacks body and humanity. He concludes that in the empirical self, light and shadow form a paradoxical unity, and speaks of the process whereby a person achieves the integration of ego and shadow as "individuation."

Le Guin has also written much about the function of this Jungian shadow, calling it the dark brother of the conscious mind whom we must follow if we are to enter the collective unconscious. She goes on to say that the shadow is all we do not want to admit, or cannot admit, into our conscious self. It is all the qualities and tendencies within us that have been repressed, denied, or neglected. She cites Jung's statement that everyone carries a shadow; the less it is embodied in the individual's conscious life, the blacker and denser it is. "The less you look at it, in other words, the stronger it grows, until it can become a menace, an intolerable load, a threat within the soul." [6] She concludes that this shadow stands on the threshold. We can let it bar the way to the creative depths of the unconscious, or we can let it lead us to them. "It is inferior, primitive, awkward, animal-like, childlike; powerful, vital, spontaneous. It's not weak and decent...it's dark and hairy and unseemly; but, without it, the person is nothing." [7] For Le Guin, the Jungian shadow is the guide on the journey to self-knowledge, to adulthood, to the light, a journey which, Jung says, is every individual's imperative need and duty. For Le Guin, "most of the great works of fantasy are about that journey." Furthermore, "fantasy is the medium best suited to a description of that journey, its perils and rewards."[8] When we examine Earthsea, that is exactly what we see demonstrated.

Of the three books in question, the first, *A Wizard of Earthsea,* is most clearly patterned after the journey toward selfhood. Le Guin's hero, Ged (the Jungian ego) is an adolescent, self-centered person possessed of the innate ability to perform great feats of wizardry but lacking in the discipline necessary to use the raw talent responsibly. Chafing under the patient training of Ogion, his master, Ged first glimpses his shadow through a temptation natural to adolescence. Seeking to impress an attractive young girl with his prowess, he attempts a feat of wizardry beyond his ability to control. He is only just saved by the intervention of the fatherly Ogion; but he has felt a dawning awareness of the presence of the shadow—the dark self within, the shadow of sexual desires, the shadow of desire for power, the shadow of his own mortality—which he cannot yet accept.

Refusing to be guided by Ogion's wisdom, Ged "goes off to college," to the school for mages at Roke. He learns too easily to develop his powers. As a student, though, he is solitary, quick-tempered, and proud. Trying to put himself on an equal social footing with Jasper, a sophisticated fellow student, Ged again works a great spell, one that is beyond his control: he summons the dead. Psychologically unable to accept the idea of his own death, however, Ged cannot sustain the spell and nearly destroys himself in the process. Of this period of adolescence Le Guin remarks:

> I think that when in pre-adolescence and adolescence the conscious sense of self emerges, often quite overwhelmingly, the shadow darkens right with it. . . . He [the adolescent] begins to take responsibility for his acts and feelings. And with it he often shoulders a terrible load of guilt. He sees his shadow as much blacker, more wholly evil, than it is. The only way for a youngster to get past the paralyzing self-blame and self-disgust of this stage is really to look at that shadow, to face it, warts and fangs and pimples and claws and all—to accept it as himself—as *part* of himself. The ugliest part, but not the weakest. For the shadow is the guide. . . . The guide of the journey to self-knowledge, to adulthood, to the light.[9]

After this encounter with his shadow, Ged is scarred, crippled, and mentally paralyzed. The condition lasts many months, and recovery is slow and painful. Ged's confidence is gone, his facility lost. Terrified by the glimpse of his darker self which can no longer be denied, a humbler Ged hesitates to go forward, instead, preferring the safety of Roke and the paternal protection of the Archmage.

As it must to all adolescents, though, graduation arrives, and

Ged accepts a post protecting a small village. There he meets his first major test on the road to maturity. He is promised mastery over his shadow if he will betray the village to the wily dragon, Yevaud. Though powerfully tempted, Ged puts the welfare of the people above his own and manages to resist his fear of the shadow.

A second and harder test involves both his desire for safety and for power. Serret, the young girl who tempted him on Gont, now promises great power if Ged will make a Faustian alliance with the Terrenon Stone. She promises that, by means of its amoral power, he can overcome his shadow. Ged barely escapes the temptation. Changing to a hawk, he returns to Ogion who restores him to human form only with great difficulty. So fearful does Ged become of his shadow that he loses his ego almost completely.

Ogion, the great wizard of Gont, is himself the perfect Jungian archetype of the "wise old man" often found in fairy tales and dreams, who leads the young hero back to unity of self. In his essay, "The Phenomenology of the Spirit in Fairy Tales," [10] Jung points out that the archetype he calls the wise old man often appears in the guise of a magician, a teacher, or some other person possessing authority. The old man always appears when the hero is in a hopeless or desperate situation from which only profound reflection or timely idea can extricate him. Since, for both internal and external reasons, the hero can't accomplish this himself, the knowlege needed to compensate for the deficiency comes in the form of a personified thought, that is, in the shape of the sagacious and helpful old man.

The old man frequently asks questions for the purpose of inducing self-reflection and mobilizing moral forces. Psychologically this is a purposeful process whose aim it is to gather together the assets of the entire personality at the critical moment when all one's spiritual and physical forces are challenged and with this united strength to fling open the door of the future. The wise old man shows the boy that he must rely entirely on himself, that there is no turning back. When the boy realizes this, his course of action is clear.

After Jung's old man has brought the boy around to the proper frame of mind, he gives him some advice which the boy can put to use in solving his dilemma. He often urges the boy to "sleep on" it. Frequently, too, he gives the boy something tangible that will assist him on his quest.

Ged's return to Ogion fits every particular of Jung's analysis.

As Ged and Ogion sit before the fire, Ged relates to his master all his adventures since he set sail from the isle of Gont, eventually confessing that he has no strength against the shadow that pursues him. Like Jung's archetype, Ogion points out all the times when Ged has demonstrated his strength against evil. While Ged reflects on this, the old man offers advice, pointing out what Ged already knows but cannot yet accept. He tells Ged there is no safe place to hide from the shadow and counsels him to turn around and face it. "If you go ahead, if you keep running, wherever you run you will meet danger and evil, for it drives you, it chooses the way you go. You must choose. You must seek what seeks you. You must hunt the hunter" (*WE,* VII). Again like Jung's old man, Ogion fashions a wizard's staff from a piece of yew wood and presents it to Ged to aid him on his journey. They lie down to sleep, and when Ogion awakens, he discovers a runic message on the hearth: "Master, I go hunting" (*WE,* VII).

As Ged pursues the shadow over land and sea, it grows more and more like him until at last, in the Jungian act of recognition, Ged sees it as a part of himself and gives it his own name. "Ged reached out his hands, dropping his staff, and took hold of his shadow, of the black self that reached out to him. Light and darkness met, and joined, and were one" (*WE,* X). Ged turns to his friend, Estarriol, and says: "Look, it is done. It is over. The wound is healed... I am whole, I am free" (*WE,* X). His friend understands "... that Ged had neither lost nor won but, naming the shadow of his death with his own name, had made himself whole: a man..." (*WE,* X). Thus Le Guin's hero achieves the goal of Jung's individuation process—maturity and self-knowledge.

In *The Tombs of Atuan,* the second book of the trilogy, ten or fifteen years have passed since Ged achieved psychological wholeness. Now free to act on behalf of others, he undertakes the dangerous mission of recovering the missing half of the ring of Erreth-Akbe from the Tombs of Atuan. By joining it with the half already in his possession, he hopes to learn the forgotten "Bond-Rune" that will restore peace and unity to all Earthsea.

Although reclaiming and reforging the ring are central to the external action of the plot, Ged himself does not appear until over a third of the way into the book, to the considerable disappointment of readers eager to learn more of the adventures of the young mage. Reclamation of the ring is almost anticlimactic; again, Le Guin is more interested in the Jungian journey toward integration than in external heroic adventures. She has explained that the subject of *Tombs* is, in a word, sex. "More exactly, you could call it a feminine coming of age," she says.[11] Her protagonist is Tenar who, as Arha the Eaten, the One Priestess of the Nameless Ones, must achieve her own integration of ego and shadow by symbolically reclaiming her true name.

The novel opens with a short prologue in which the five-year-old Tenar is introduced with compelling black-and-white imagery. We see her running through a blossoming apple orchard in the spring twilight. Above her the evening star pierces the black sky as she runs, like thistledown on the darkening grass, her black hair framing her small white face. Tenar makes a long circle through the orchard before turning toward home where her golden-haired mother waits patiently, outlined against the firelight of the cottage hearth.

This imagery of life and natural balance is in sharp contrast to the unnatural imagery of the Hall of the Tombs introduced later. There the six-year-old child is dedicated as Arha (whose name is taken from her by the nameless gods of darkness and death). The dead and frozen weeds of the Tombs, the black-robed priestesses, and the cold decaying buildings surrounded by stone walls and endless desert convey the spiritual and psychological aridity of those in the service of the powers that war against life.

In *The Tombs of Atuan* the mythological basis of Le Guin's plot is the story of the Greek hero Theseus who braved the labyrinth of King Minos of Crete to rescue Athens from oppression. With the help of Ariadne—the king's daughter, who gives him weapons and a ball of thread to help him find his way back—he successfully completes his task. In the various interpretations of this tale as a nature myth, Theseus' escape from the labyrinth is usually associated with the escape of the Sun-king from the ritual death of winter. Some have suggested that Ariadne was originally a pre-Hellenic goddess whose identity was merged with Aphrodite, goddess of love and fertility.

At any rate, in *Tombs,* the myth works well at both levels. Ged, the hero, comes to the labyrinth of Atuan seeking to free Earthsea from civil turmoil. He succeeds only with the help of Arha (Ariadne) who often uses "a ball of fine yarn" in exploring the labyrinth of Atuan. Like a sun-king of nature myth, Ged brings the light of his staff to illuminate the nameless dark and perpetual winter of the Tombs; like Ariadne (Aphrodite), Tenar nourishes and loves Ged. Together they escape to bring peace and fertility to the archipelago.

By connecting the goddess Aphrodite with the apple, a fruit sacred to her, Le Guin provides a symbol that is both apt and important. From the fertile apple orchard of her childhood, Tenar is taken to the apple orchard of the Place of the Tombs, whose meager harvest of yellow apples is always preserved by drying. One day she is given eight perfect, undried apples by Penthe, an unwilling novice who tells Tenar that she would rather marry a pigherd and live in a ditch than stay buried alive with "a mess of women in a perishing old desert." Although Tenar doesn't eat the apples Penthe gives her (Penthe does), the novice's frank conversation forces Tenar to consider her own life for the first time. "She felt that she had never seen Penthe before, never looked at her and seen her, round and full of life and juice as one of her golden apples, beautiful to see" *(TA,* "Dreams).

In his *The Uses of Enchantment,* Bruno Bettelheim points out that, in myth and fairy tales, the apple represents love and sex in both its benevolent and its dangerous aspects. By eating the Biblical apple, man exchanged innocence for knowledge and sexuality. In religious iconography, Bettelheim says, the apple also symobilizes the mother's breast,[12] while, in European literature it is a symbol of consummation as well as immortality.

The parallel goes deeper than the popular symbolism of the apple, though. The Biblical Eve could have remained safe and secure, forever a child in her garden, free of the pain of life and death. The only price was blind obedience. When she chose to eat the fruit of "the tree of the knowledge of good and evil," she forfeited the fruit of the second tree in the garden—the tree of immortality. With this choice (sometimes called by theologians, the *felix culpa,* the fortunate fault), she knew good and evil for the first time. By knowing both good and evil, any subsequent choice of good over evil reflected greater glory on her Creator and greater virtue in herself. When there is no opportunity to do otherwise, however, there is little merit in choosing good. Just as Eve in the Garden was forced into a pattern of goodness, in the Tombs, Tenar is forced into a pattern of service to the dark gods. When she disobeys and chooses knowledge and sexuality, she too is shut out of her "garden." Like Eve's, Tenar's choice comes at a price: she must sacrifice the security, prestige, and immortality of the One Priestess and learn the burden of freedom.

The presence of apples also suggests the fairy tale of Snow White, a classic of female maturation. Like Snow White, Tenar has hair as black as ebony and skin as white as snow. In addition, Tenar "loses" her real mother who is replaced by a jealous "stepmother," in this case, Kossil, high-priestess of the God-king. Kossil is filled with jealousy and envy of Tenar, for, Kossil knows, when Tenar comes of age, she will hold a superior position as the One Priestess of the Tombs of Atuan.

At fourteen, Tenar makes the transition to womanhood and becomes the One Priestess, with all its attendant powers. A year later, however, nothing has changed. The routine of her life is as boring and rigid as it was when she was five. At times she is nearly overwhelmed by the terror of the boredom. In Le Guin's description of the labyrinth—with its dead air, stifling darkness, and endless windings—the boredom is almost palpable.

Tenar is trapped in this female world, isolated from male society; thus her feminine instincts are subverted. But because she is priestess of a religion in which the night, the moon, and the nameless powers of darkness and death are worshipped, she learns the secrets of the labyrinth lying beneath the Tombs like a great dark city, a labyrinth filled with gold, crowns, bones, the swords of dead heroes, and years of silence. In the process she becomes mistress of the silence and the dark, rather than of life and light.

In her first act as priestess, Tenar is forced by Kossil to order the execution of three male prisoners by denying them food and water (the perversion of the female role as nourisher and preserver of life.) Cut off from life and tormented by dreams about the executions, Tenar turns more and more to the labyrinth that only she can know. There she finds pleasure in the solitude and darkness.

Into this sterile world comes Ged, the male principle, bearing light into the Undertomb by means of his wizard's staff, an obvious phallic symbol. He violates the domain of Tenar and the powers she serves, seeking, like the male chromosome seeking the female, to join his half of the ring of Erreth-Akbe to the half in the Treasure Room of the Tombs. With the union of the two halves, Tenar begins a new life. She easily imprisons the mage in her labyrinth. While deciding what she will do with him, Tenar experiences, not a sense of outrage at the violation, but a disquieting curiosity about her prisoner. A sexual awakening has begun.

The Undertomb itself symbolizes full sexual knowledge. Tenar had been forbidden to take a light there. Thus she didn't know what it looked like until Ged arrives with his glowing wizard's staff. "To have seen the Undertomb confused her; she was bewildered. She had known it only as...a mystery, never to be seen. She had seen it, and the mystery had given place, not to horror, but to beauty, a mystery deeper even than that of the dark" (*TA,* "Light").

A symbolic courtship ensues. Tenar blushes when she confronts Ged, and forbids him to look at her. But his gentle behavior flusters her until, stammering, she flees from the room. Yet she can't get him out of her mind. The rites and duties of the temple seem petty; the life of a priestess appears to her as "a secret brangle of jealousies and miseries and small ambitions and wasted passions. . ." (*TA,* "Great Treasure").

Having become a woman physically, Tenar experiences sexual desires; subconsciously, however, she fears the intellectual and emotional demands of her newfound womanhood. Again and again she retreats to the safety and ignorance of the dark. But she has seen the Undertomb in the light of the mage's staff; she has taken a bite of the apple. Her sexual curiosity and hunger for life beyond the labyrinth draw her back to her prisoner. When she demands that he demonstrate his magic, he clothes her in the illusion of a beautiful silken gown. "You told me to show you something worth seeing," Ged tells her. "I show you yourself" (*TA,* "Great Treasure"). But Tenar cannot yet accept her emerging female self yet and orders him to make it go away.

At this point they are discovered by a jealous Kossil who has been looking for an excuse to put her young rival to death. Tenar's eunuch, like Snow White's dwarves, can no longer protect her from the hatred of the rival. Tenar has made her choice.

Desperate to save Ged from Kossil, Tenar leads him to the Treasure Room, the sacred place where, until now, no man was allowed. She promises to return as soon as she can. In return for Tenar's trust, Ged symbolically expresses his affection for her by speaking her real name.

Seeking escape from the sexual desire that both thrills and frightens her, Tenar, like Snow White in the crystal coffin, falls asleep. In her dreams her long-forgotten mother appears and calls to her. When she awakens in the morning, Tenar makes the first tentative commitment to the full implications of sexual maturity. In the clear golden light of morning, a hawk circles in the empty sky. Shaking with cold, terror, and exultation, she speaks her name: "I have my name back. I am Tenar!" (*TA,* "Names").

Le Guin uses images of light and life to describe Tenar's growing awareness of who she is. The hawk's flight, recalling the creation hymn of Éa, is appropriate for the rebirth of Tenar, for which Ged, who is also called Sparrowhawk, is responsible.

In this rebirth, Tenar finds the strength to defy the "wicked stepmother," Kossil. But her confidence is easily shaken; she lacks the experience of the older woman and is torn with self-doubt. Returning to Ged, as he had returned to Ogion, Tenar despairs of achieving the freedom of maturity. "I am not Tenar. I am not Arha. The gods are dead, the gods are dead" (*TA,* "Ring"). In the classic gesture of comfort and trust, Ged puts his hand on hers and listens while she tells him about her confrontation with Kossil and her loss of faith in all that she once believed.

In a passionate speech which contains the central idea of *Tombs,* Ged reassures Tenar just as he had been reassured by Ogion in his darkest hour. Ged affirms the reality of the shadow against which a lone man has no hope. "I was dying of thirst when you gave me water," he tells her; "yet it was not the water alone that saved me. It was the strength of the hands that gave it" (*TA,* "Ring"). As he speaks to Tenar he turns her hand upward on his own and gazes at it for a moment. In a moving summary of the paradox of human existence, he continues:

> The Earth is beautiful, and bright, and kindly, but that is not all. The Earth is also terrible, and dark, and cruel. The rabbit shrieks dying in the green meadows. The mountains clench their great hands full of hidden fire. There are sharks in the sea, and there is cruelty in men's eyes. And where men worship these things and abase themselves before them, there evil breeds; there places are made in the world where darkness gathers, places given over wholly to the Ones whom we call Nameless, the ancient and holy Powers of the Earth before the Light, the powers of the dark, of ruin, of madness. . . . They exist. But they are not your Masters. They never were. You are free, Tenar. You were taught to be a slave, but you have broken free " (*TA,* "Ring")

Like Jung's wise old man, Ged says: "You must make a choice. . . .You must be Arha, or you must be Tenar. You cannot be both" (*TA*, "Ring"). She must accept her shadow as Ged did, or be overwhelmed by it. To encourage her, Ged reminds Tenar that there is a bond of trust between them. To demonstrate his complete trust in her, he tells Tenar his real name and gives her both halves of the ring of Erreth-Akbe, the most powerful talisman of Earthsea. It is a symbolic wedding ring. Buoyed by his trust, Tenar finds the courage to choose life, and in an act of faith and hope agrees to go with him. "When she said that, the man named Ged put his hand over hers. . . . She looked up startled, and saw him flushed with life and triumph, smiling. She was dismayed and frightened of him" (*TA,* "Anger").

Ged makes the broken ring whole as Tenar's choice fills him and gives him the power to defeat the forces of un-life. Male and female principle are joined as the ring is made whole, not with an illusion but with a great pattern. As Snow White is brought from death-in-life by her prince, Ged leads Tenar from the darkness toward the light. Still timid and shy, she responds to his plea to trust him as he has trusted her.

But Tenar is reluctant to abandon all the security she has ever known. Besieged by the dark power she has always served, she is consumed by guilt at her betrayal of her priesthood. Still, she follows him as Ged breaks through the Red Rock door while behind them the tombs and labyrinth convulse in an orgasmic earthquake. Again, on the threshold of freedom, Tenar cries out: 'No! No! Don't touch me—leave me—Go!" (*TA*, "Anger"). And Ged replies: " 'By the bond you wear I bid you come, Tenar,' " and in symbolic consummation, "she put her hand in his, and came with him" (*TA,* "Anger").

On their honeymoon journey west, images of light and joy prevail. Tenar looks at the sleeping man (Ged's name is not mentioned, so that Le Guin can make the experience universal). Through her feelings of love for him, she experiences the glory and joy of all life. "There was a joy in her that no thought nor dread could darken, the same sure joy that had risen in her, waking in the golden light" (*TA,* "Western Mountains").

Just as Le Guin is not satisfied with giving us the traditional heroic adventure tale, however, neither is she satisfied with the traditional "and they lived happily ever after." Real life isn't that simple, nor are human emotions immutable. Tenar's initial joy over her new life and freedom is soon tempered by the reality of her situation. Guilty over her past deeds and frightened by the prospect of an unknown life ahead, she tells Ged that she wants to stay in the mountains forever. But when he considers the possibility of staying where they are, Tenar admits that she is being foolish. Although there is no turning back, going forward is still very difficult for her.

When Tenar asks Ged if he will stay with her when they reach Havnor, and he promises to do so only as long as she needs him, her love for him quickly turns to feelings of betrayal and abandonment. He has made her afraid, and she wants to punish him for it. In short, she cannot yet accept the full responsibility for her actions. For the last time, Tenar faces the choice between death and life. Still the priestess, she takes from Ged the sacrificial knife she had given him but doesn't strike. This time Tenar makes the right choice: she chooses life—with all its uncertainty and pain.

As they sail away from the island, Tenar is symbolically freed from her old self. Her guilt and fear haven't been erased, but she is beginning to accept them as part of herself, as her shadow.

> A dark hand had let go its lifelong hold upon her heart. But she did not feel joy, as she had in the mountains. She put her head down in her arms and cried, and her cheeks were salt and wet. She cried for the waste of her years in bondage to a useless evil. She wept in pain, because she was free.
>
> What she had begun to learn was the weight of liberty. Freedom is a heavy load, a great and strange burden for the spirit to undertake. It is not easy. It is not a gift given, but a choice made, and the choice may be a hard one. (*TA,* ''Voyage'')

As the novel ends, Tenar fully accepts herself. She and Ged sail across a winter sea to the city of Havnor, white and radiant in the snow, contrasting sharply with the dark underground city that she had once been mistress of. When they arrive she walks through the streets of Havnor, the city of light, not alone as she did in the labyrinth, but reborn, holding Ged's hand like a child coming home. Tenar, who began the long circle voyage at the beginning of the novel, through the apple orchard and twilight, has finally come home. The psychological journey through the labyrinth of her own mind, filled with darkness and guilt, has ended in freedom and light. Maturation as a woman is complete; now she, too, is whole and free.

In *Wizard,* Le Guin presents clearly and simply, and in pure Jungian terms, the process of integrating the male ego with its shadow. By adding one phrase, the acceptance of personal mortality, she foreshadows the main theme of *The Farthest Shore,* the last book of the trilogy. When Ged achieves personal integration, the shadow for the first time is labeled as ''the shadow of his death.'' Now it isn't just Jung's shadow, but Le Guin's as well.

Tenar's coming of age in *Tombs* is expressed more passively than is Ged's pursuit and struggle; for Tenar is shadow, scarcely conscious of her ego. The need to accept mortality is no less strong, though. As the reborn Priestess of the Nameless Ones, Tenar believes that she will live forever. But this immortality comes at the price of her own identity; Tenar's true name must be "eaten." She achieves selfhood by relinquishing her everlasting life. The rightness of this choice is confirmed in *The Farthest Shore* as Le Guin graphically demonstrates the fate of those who disrupt the Balance by refusing to accept their own mortality.

This psychological journey toward wholeness through acceptance of personal mortality is the main pattern of *The Farthest Shore.* Arren, Prince of Enlad, is sent to Roke by his father to report on the failure of wizardry in the northern and western Reaches of Earthsea. Rumors of such failure have also come from the southern and eastern Reaches. At the Council of the Mages of Roke, Ged, now between forty and fifty and for the last five years Archmage of Roke, is determined to find the evil that is causing the imbalance and threatening the survival of Earthsea. Repeating the words of the Master Patterner, he chooses Arren to sail with him: "Not by chance does any man come to the shores of Roke. Not by chance is a son of Morred the bearer of this news" (*FS,* "Masters").

Their voyage eventually takes them to Selidor, "the last shore of the world," where they confront the evil sorcerer who has opened the door between life and death. Projecting their spirits, Ged and Arren pursue the sorcerer through the Dry Land of Death where Ged heals the breach in the Equilibrium. In a terrible test of endurance Arren brings an exhausted Ged and himself back from the Dry Land over the Mountains of Pain, to the sunlight and sea of the Farthest Shore, Selidor.

In *The Farthest Shore,* Le Guin undertakes the difficult task of expressing in concrete images, experiences that are purely metaphysical. Most readers are familiar with male or female integration and the sometimes stormy passage through adolescence, but death and immortality are another matter. As the author admits, *The Farthest Shore* is not as well constructed, not as sound and complete as the other two books, since it is about an experience no one survives. At the same time, however, she argues that it is about coming of age in a larger context, because "the hour when a child realizes, not that that [sic] death exists ... but that he/she, personally, is mortal, will die, is the hour when childhood ends, and the new life begins."[13]

If we can't relate wholly to the symbolic journey through the Dry Lands and back, we can to Arren's personal reactions to the dawning awareness of his own mortality. To further humanize her hero, Le Guin weaves the themes of moral and social integration into the stark pattern of life and death. We recognize as our own, Arren's struggle with the problem of evil and his development from a self-centered youth to a compassionate human being.

To further acclimate the reader, Le Guin draws more heavily on the heroic epic tradition in this book than in the earlier ones. On the surface, *The Farthest Shore* seems familiar, the tale of a young prince who will be ruler of all Earthsea if he survives a perilous quest. Appropriately, he is named Arren, which means "sword," and he carries an ancestral blade, the Sword of Serriadh, of which Le Guin writes: "there was none older in the world except the sword of Erreth-Akbe, which was set atop the Tower of the Kings in Havnor. The sword of Serriadh had never been laid away or hoarded up, but worn; yet was unworn by the centuries, unweakened, because it had been forged with a great power of enchantment" (*FS,* "Masters").

In addition to the enchanted sword, Arren has the advice and council of a wizard; he walks the paths of the dead; he must contend with an evil sorcerer; and is the fulfillment of a prophecy: he will unite his kingdom and rule long and well. But unlike epic heroes such as Tolkien's Aragorn, Arren will not achieve throne and crown by overcoming vast hordes of evil orcs, but by subduing his own desire for immortality, by conquering the "traitor, the self; the self that cries *I want to live; let the world burn so long as I can live!"* (*FS,* "Orm Embar"). His victory comes not at his coronation at Havnor but earlier on Selidor where, grasping a stone brought back from his conquest of the Mountains of Pain, he knows he has achieved a true victory over self, although there is no one to praise him.

Since it deals with death, *The Farthest Shore* is necessarily a philosophical book. In the exchange between Ged and Arren, between master and pupil, we are reminded of the Socratic dialogues or of Aristotle instructing Alexander. Though wizardy plays a vital part in saving Earthsea, Ged realizes that his most important function is to instruct the future king. Looking at Arren, he says aloud to the sleeping boy: "I have found none to follow in my way.... None but thee. And thou must go thy way, not mine. Yet will thy kingship be, in part, my own. For I knew thee first. I knew thee first! They will praise me more for that in afterdays than for any thing I did of magery. . ." (*FS,* "Dragon's Run").

The first and hardest lesson Arren learns is acceptance of personal mortality. Ged warns him that men upset the Great Balance when they indulge an unmeasured desire for life. When Arren asks why it is wrong to want to live, Ged replies that all men want to live, but when they begin to desire power over life as expressed in endless wealth, unassailable safety, and immortality, then desire becomes greed. If such men possess the knowledge or power to implement this greed, evil enters in and the balance of the world is upset and ruin threatens.

Ged and Arren's voyage to seek out the evil that is threatening Earthsea brings them first to Hort Town where, as in a dream, Arren first encounters the "tall lord of shadows" who holds out to him a tiny flame no larger than a pearl, offering him life. In his trance Arren takes a step toward him, following, and goes a little way into the "darkness" of which the wizards speak. It frightens him so much that afterward he is afraid to sleep because he sees the dark lord in his dreams holding out the pearl and whispering, "Come."

As the voyage proceeds, Arren dreams constantly of death and its horror, his fear growing to suffocating proportions. Always in the dreams, he sees a shadowy figure standing in a doorway, holding the pearl, "the glimmer of immortal life."

Although Arren doesn't tell Ged about his dreams, he often questions the mage about death and the Lore of Paln, the spells that summon the dead. When Arren asks if it is wicked to summon the dead, Ged replies that it is, rather, a misunderstanding of life. He compares death and life to his hand, noting that although the palm and the back are one hand, they aren't the same. To either separate or mix them is to destroy the hand.

So obsessed does Arren become with his fear of death and his desire to live forever that he does not heed Ged's counsel. Gradually Arren turns against Ged, supposing him jealous because the shadow figure has offered immortality only to Arren. Arren is so weakened by his anguish that, when Ged is wounded at Obehol and Arren is confronted by the physical reality of death, his will and courage are completely paralyzed. Thus he neglects Ged and allows their boat to drift.

When they are rescued, Arren confesses to the recuperating

Ged: "I was afraid of you. I was afraid of death. I was so afraid of it I would not look at you, because you might be dying. I could think of nothing, except that there was—there was a way of not dying for me, if I could find it. . . . And I did nothing, nothing, but try to hide from the horror of dying" (*FS,* "Children").

Ged does not attempt to temper Arren's fear with promises of a glorious paradise waiting after this life. Le Guin's land of death seems much like the classical Greek concept: dry, barren, without emotion. Arren's acceptance of mortality will not be eased by descriptions of an afterlife of bliss and perfection. Instead, Ged reaches out to take Arren's hand so that "by eye and by flesh they touched." He calls Arren by his true name—Lebannen, the Rowan Tree (in Celtic mythology, the tree of life)—and says: "Lebannen, this is. And thou art. There is no safety, and there is no end. The word must be heard in silence; there must be darkness to see the stars" (*FS,* "Children").

Ged assures Arren that he has the strength to face the reality of death, adding that to refuse death is to refuse life. In an impassioned speech that is the heart of the book, Ged says while still grasping Arren's hand:

> "Listen to me, Arren. You will die. You will not live forever. Nor will any man or any thing. Nothing is immortal. but only to us is it given to know that we must die. And that is a great gift: the gift of selfhood. For we have only what we know we must lose, what we are willing to lose. . . . That selfhood which is our torment, and our treasure, and our humanity, does not endure. It changes; it is gone, a wave on the sea. Would you have the sea grow still and the tides cease, to save one wave, to save yourself? Would you give up the craft of your hands, and the passion of your heart, and the light of sunrise and sunset, to buy safety for yourself—safety forever?" (*FS,* "Children")

Ged, who has long since accepted the inevitability of his own death, must depend on Arren's terror to lead them to the place "where joy runs out". Asked if he will continue the quest, Arren hesitates. He is doubtful; in his terror he fears that he will again betray Ged. But Ged quietly assures him: "I will trust you, son of Morred" (*FS,* "Children"). It is this act of trust in another human being that is a turning point in each book of the trilogy. With Ged's act of trust, restoration of the balance begins.

When Ged despairs in *Wizard,* his friend Vetch shows how much he trusts Ged by telling him his true name. Of this gesture Le Guin writes: "Who knows a man's name, holds that man's life in his keeping. Thus to Ged who had lost faith in himself, Vetch had given that gift only a friend can give, the proof of unshaken, unshakable trust'' (*WE*, ''Loosing''). Because of this act of trust, Ged regains faith in himself and knows, after a ''long, bitter, wasted time'' who he is.

In *Tombs*, Ged gives Tenar his true name, telling her that trust is what makes people strong, that it is what helps them overcome the powers of darkness. In this mutual trust Tenar finds the will to leave the Tombs, thus setting both herself and Ged free from the darkness.

Out of the mutual trust that exists between Ged and Arren in *The Farthest Shore* arises the strength that enables them to complete the ultimate quest. As they sail toward the fateful encounter, Ged tests Arren one last time, asking him if it is not better to be oneself forever. Arren says he knows the answer should be that it is not better, but that he still does not wholly agree. He tells Ged that when they set out, he was a child, but that he is a child no longer. He has learned that death exists and that he will die. Arren concludes that because he loves life, he can't welcome the thought of death, and again asks why he should not desire immortality. Ged replies that all men desire immortality, that the health of the soul depends on this desire. But he goes on to explain that life and death are part of the balance, that they continuously give birth to one another, forever. Offered this final chance to turn back from the face of death, Arren says simply: ''I will go with you.'' There are no more lessons to be learned. Ged says, ''You enter your manhood at the gate of death'' (*FS*, ''Selidor'').

By crossing the symbolic stone wall, their spirits begin the journey through the land of the dead, the Dry Lands. When Arren sees the silent shadows in the city of the dead, he is filled not with fear but great pity. A mother and child who died together ignore each other. In the silent streets lovers pass each other by. The potter's wheel doesn't turn; the loom is empty. There is only a vast silence and the unmoving stars.

The only relief offered from this gloomy prospect of life after death is a cryptic allusion to some form of reincarnation. Arren is told that the great hero, Erreth-Akbe, whose shadow dwells in the Dry Land, isn't really there. Instead, Ged describes him as earth and sunlight, as leaves on the trees and the eagle's flight. Without further explanation Ged concludes that all whoever died, live; they are reborn and have no end; nor will there ever be an end.

Although Le Guin's concept of future existence isn't clearly realized, her grim characterization of the afterlife is consistent with her purpose of showing that life is to be lived in the service of life, and that by lusting after immortality we lose the great gift of the present. Arren is reminded that his kingdom is the kingdom of life, where each living thing is beautiful and unique. In the great pattern of being that is more than life or death, nothing is repeated.

In the final confrontation with Cob, the evil sorcerer who has used his wizardry to upset the Balance, Arren sees the awful consequence of refusing to accept the Equilibrium between life and death. Without hesitation he tells Ged to shut the door between life and death. He has chosen mortality freely.

While Arren masters his fear of death, it is only one of several shadows he must overcome. He must also come to terms with evil as part of the process of moral integration. Ged is again the teacher as he points out that one creature alone can do evil: man. When Arren expresses the naive belief that good will always triumph over evil, Ged tells him that, whereas wizardry which serves a good end may be stronger than evil, this is by no means certain; man can only hope it is. Not really believing this, however, Arren asserts that surely one man would not be allowed to wreck the Balance of the whole world. But Ged asks him: Who allows? Who forbids? When Arren says he doesn't know, Ged replies that, except for the example of how much evil one man can do, he has no answers either.

For Arren, "the bleakness in finding hope where one expected certainty" is part of a moral integration as necessary as the psychological integration of his personality. He must reconcile himself to living in the hope of man's goodness, not in the security of believing absolutely in the triumph of virtue. This, too, is an essential part of coming of age. He who desires absolute security will never achieve selfhood.

Arren's moral and psychological integration are paralleled by his social integration. His ability to love truly and feel compassion for others grows as he sails with Ged. In *The Farthest Shore,* at his first meeting with Ged in the Court of the Fountain on Roke, Arren, who has never made a serious commitment to anything, "who had played at loving," is changed; "but now the depths of him were wakened, not by a game or dream, but by honor, danger, wisdom, by a scarred face and a quiet voice and a dark hand holding, careless of its power, the staff of yew.... So the first step out of childhood is made all at once, without looking before or behind, without caution, and nothing held in reserve" (*FS,* "Rowan Tree").

When their voyage brings them to the island of Lorbanery, Arren is deeply moved by Ged's grief for the lost talents of Akaren, the silk-dyer. The ardor of his hero worship deepens to "compassion: without which love is untempered, and is not whole, and does not last" (*FS,* "Lorbanery"). But when his pride is wounded, Arren's still fragile love gives way to anger. He is assailed by doubt in Ged's ability. His love for Ged turns to something resembling hate, so that when Ged is wounded, Arren, in his own depression and fear of death, feels nothing at all for him.

Ged's response to Arren's failure of love is to express again his trust in Arren. Thus their relationship is tempered and strengthened by trial and, based on this trust, grows to maturity. Arren has no remaining illusions. Even the childish hope that in the blackest hour of their voyage he would save his lord and all the world from the enemy now seems to him only a childish daydream. So he offers what he has, his service and a steady love.

As they are about to enter the Dry Lands of Selidor, Ged looks out on the world with a profound, wordless love of life shining on his dark face. Finally understanding Ged's love, Arren "saw him for the first time whole, as he was" (*FS,* "Selidor"). Arren remembers their first meeting at Roke, and joy wells up within him: "I have given my love to what is worthy of love. Is that not the kingdom and the unperishing spring?" (*FS*, "Selidor"). Faithful in friendship, hopeful of man's goodness, and loving life because he has accepted the shadow of his own mortality, Arren (Lebannen) returns to Roke whole and free, bringing healing and ready to restore wholeness to all of Earthsea.

The psychological journey through pain and fear to integration is a journey each of Le Guin's protagonists makes. Rocannon crosses his own mountains of pain to heal a world (*Rocannon's World*); Jakob Agat struggles to integrate Farborn and Hilf so a world may survive (*Planet of Exile*); Falk journeys across a continent to reintegrate his primitive self with Rammarren and thereby saves the Known Worlds from the Shing *(City of Illusions).* In *The Left Hand of Darkness,* Genly Ai and Estraven, his symbolic shadow, travel the "silent vastness of fire and ice" to integrate Gethen with the Ekumen; in doing so, Genly Ai is integrated with Estraven. And Shevek makes a painful trip between worlds to integrate Urras and Anarres (*The Dispossessed*). In mythic terms the psychological journey is the journey of Ged, scarred and suffering, to face his own shadow. It is Tenar's journey from the nameless powers of life. But most of all, it is Arren's journey through the Mountains of Pain with an endurance that outlasts his hope of achieving wholeness.

All of these journeys symbolize the journey every human being must make, one through pain and fear, aided only by trust in the goodness of man, hand holding hand, to the acceptance of mortality. Although Le Guin may embroider the design with the myriad ideas that her art inspires, Jung's archetypal journey toward integration—so clearly outlined in her Earthsea trilogy—provides the master pattern of her fiction.

2. The Archetype of the Journey in Ursula K. Le Guin's Fiction

PETER BRIGG

Unless physical action reflects psychic action, unless the deeds express the person, I get very bored with adventure stories; often it seems that the more action there is, the less happens. Obviously my interest is in what goes on inside. (Introduction to "Vaster than Empires and More Slow," in *The Wind's Twelve Quarters*)

BECAUSE OF its characteristic summing up of the human condition, the *journey* is one of literature's great archetypal patterns. Man searches for a knowledge of and a way to reach the goal of life's voyage. The process of traveling toward this goal provides the acute traveler with the experiential information that illuminates the goal. "True journey is return," the Odonian maxim governing *The Dispossessed,* is an expression of the process Jung described as "individuation," the finding of the answers to existence within the self from whence the conscious ego emerged and to which it must return in order to achieve psychic wholeness. When a writer externalizes that journey of the soul as fiction, the landscape of the journey has the metaphorical significance of myth and the learning it engenders in both traveler and reader stands as a paradigm of all human experience. Casting those paradigms into science fiction, Ursula K. Le Guin has developed and sophisticated her journey novels from the first, *Rocannon's World* (1966), to her most recent, *The Left Hand of Darkness* (1969) and *The Dispossessed* (1974). It is my purpose in this chapter to elucidate these journeys and illuminate the changes in presentation.

The general sense of development from one novel to the next is that of a movement inward from the geography of a physical journey, perhaps across a metaphorical landscape, to that of a journey of mind and soul, where discovery takes place as an ongoing process against a background of physical movement. In *The Left Hand of Darkness* and *The Dispossessed* there is a growing awareness and consideration of the very meanings of journeys as the concept itself becomes a preoccupation in the minds of the travelers. Mythic fiction in the journey mode is forceful and positive, picturing even the traveler's doubts as clearly marked watersheds to be met and conquered at the end of a chapter or section. Le Guin moves away from this simplicity to very real worlds where uncertain humans study their own movement through the traditional pattern, bringing to the surface the multifaceted meaning of the experience. This leads to a rich, complex, somewhat intellectual examination of the human voyage; but Le Guin wraps her insights in the sensuous fabric of creation to stymie any tendency to dryness, and produces instead an energetic and striking picture of the learning traveler.

To see the growth of Le Guin's representation of the journey, in this chapter we will investigate three particular aspects of journeys: destinations, travelers, and landscapes. Although it may seem perverse at first glance, the starting point of the investigation must be the study of destinations. Travelers relate to their surroundings insofar as the surroundings hamper their reaching the goal or —importantly in Le Guin—as surroundings provide a context in which to clarify the goal itself.

Destinations

In *Rocannon's World* Gaveral Rocannon begins his journey with a clear and intentional goal, to warn the League of All Worlds of the treachery that has destroyed his comrades and threatens the league. This initial casting of his intentions, with its subsidiary motive of revenge for the deaths of Rocannon's friends, is in the straightforward Romantic tradition of good and evil, a hero seeking a physical goal against great obstacles. In early scenes in the book, this is strongly reinforced, reaching a notable climax after Rocannon has been bloodied in battle: "Rocannon sat drunk and contented, riding the river of song, feeling himself now wholly committed, sealed by his shed blood to this world to which he had come a stranger across the gulfs of night" (*RW,* III).

But even in this, the first of her "journey" novels, Le Guin moves to complicate the goal in a way that will stress its internal nature. Rocannon "knows" his intentions in purely physical terms, but he is brought to a full understanding of the price that must be paid for the heroic act and the ambiguous nature of the "good" that he sees himself as serving. In the crucial final chapters of *Rocannon's World* he pays with Mogien's life for the gift of mind-speech that allows him to defeat the Faradayans. That mysterious gift costs him an even greater price when their base is actually destroyed, for his gift of empathy causes him to suffer the simultaneous agony of his thousand dying enemies. Thus Le Guin complicates the traditional conquest at the end of a journey into a reality where the triumph leaves the victor a broken man. This internalizes Rocannon's experience in a novel which is otherwise set in the external feudal-heroic style. Rocannon has reached the physical goal of his journey, overcoming both men and monsters along the way; but the goal has become more than he bargained for. Unlike the hero of romance, Rocannon is left alone and exhausted amongst near-strangers to live out his days after he has fulfilled his journey.

Genly Ai, the main traveler in *The Left Hand of Darkness*, is on a journey that from the start has more complex intentions than Rocannon's. Seeking to bring Gethen into the Ekumen has brought Genly Ai across light years from Terra but the journey in the novel is restricted to Gethen. It is not a physical journey from point to point but a series of trips in various directions, leading finally to the great trek across the Gobrin Ice. Genly is not traveling to a place but a situation, and he does not know how to get there. Gone is Rocannon's essential confidence in the rightness of the path. It has been replaced by a spirit more of quest than of journey. Also, the quest is largely an internal one, for no matter where Genly is on Gethen, his goal of achieving trust with the Gethenians is the same. He "knows" the mechanical aim of his quest without knowing the route. As the envoy, he must establish proper contact. But in the alien societies of Gethen, the mere ability to speak to people isn't quite the same thing as a genuine contact. So Genly, who represents a union of planets which itself is not altogether clear as to its ultimate intentions, finds his goal shifting; he must now search for contact in the social and mental universes. When this contact is finally achieved, though, Genly's rewards are complex, for he gains his practical goal at the cost of Estraven's life and a change in his own reality. Genly changes when he realizes that his real goal lies within the context of human-to-Gethenian contact on a personal level. In discovering his true purpose and the price of achieving it, he becomes a creature who partakes of two realities, yet is not completely either. The change Le Guin briefly and symbolically represents for Rocannon in the *agon* brought on by mindspeech is made more explicit for Genly as he comes to grips with the sense of duality that governs the light and dark world of Gethen, where the Foretellers of the Handdara know that simple answers come only to unimportant questions. The romantic confusion surrounding Mogien's sacrifice for the near-mystical gift of mindspeech is replaced by the clear cost paid by Estraven at the effective climax of *The Left Hand of Darkness.* Genly understands that he has changed and grown in the novel and that this was, after all, the aim of his quest. At the cost of a friendship beyond price and a change in the self, he achieves his goal.

If Rocannon's journey is aimed consciously at a goal that suddenly expands when it is reached, and if Genly's journey is a quest in which the goals are ultimately very different from those originally perceived, then Shevek's journey in *The Dispossessed* is a further step, for it is a quest in which final goals cannot exist. The act of becoming dominates Odonian philosophy. Thus the only goal one may have is to remain open to change. At the beginning of the novel, which is a climactic moment in Shevek's adult life, he has three goals: the creation of a General Temporal Theory; the unification of Anarres and Urras; and a goal that is common to every Odonian—preserving a society in which there is an ongoing revolution. Yet, alternating as it does between the events of Shevek's youth and those of the continuing and chronological present, the structure of the book reveals an overriding commitment to states of mind, to an understanding of the unique anarchic frame of Shevek's powerful mind and to the way events can be understood by this mind. Shevek is unusually open to experience. As his journey moves from infancy to his return to Anarres, he shows himself far more capable of understanding this journey through time than either Rocannon or Genly understand theirs. It's as though the earlier voyagers were blinded by goals, whereas Shevek, meditating on time and Odo's "true journey is return," sees that *process* is everything. This is reflected in the fact that Shevek, even in the excitement of arriving at the General Temporal Theory, sees at the same moment its implications for his political and personal selves. In addition, he is fully aware that this apparent "progress" or "discovery" is, in reality, a coming to terms with the ongoing process aspects of knowledge:

> He had been groping and grabbing after certainty, as if it were something he could possess. He had been demanding a security, a guarantee, which is not granted, and which, if granted, would become a prison.
> . . . . .
> There would be no trouble at all in going on. Indeed, he had already gone on. He was there. (*TD,* IX)

Shevek's quest for the second goal, the unification of Anarres and Urras, comes to a conculsion which parallels the General Temporal Theory. Shevek realizes that unification is not desirable and aims instead for a coexistence of Anarres, the planet of Simultaneity, and Urras, the planet of Sequency. Although the original goal is not reached, in its place emerges a redefined one, a yang-yin of divergent parts. In the political and scientific spheres, Shevek's discoveries don't change existing relationships; they clarify by throwing brilliant light on them, so that all may see the meaning that was always there.

Shevek's arrival at these partial, ever-incomplete goals is a manifestation of the Odonian mind at work. In this way, his third goal is realized: to preserve a society undergoing continual revolution. This goal is the basis of the logic for studying the journey. Shevek examines it as the exoskeleton of reality, the path along which both anarchy and time are realized and revealed. It is a vast change from the romantic action of *Rocannon's World,* with its implicit goals, to Shevek's patient, painstaking, and completely uncompromising examination of why, where, and how he is journeying. Through him, the concept of the journey is redefined. Its organic, always developing nature is the energy of Odonianism, Shevek, and the novel. There can be no more fascinating journey than Shevek's journey into journeys, the intricate examination of mythic structure even as the myth itself takes place.

In addition to the goals the characters set themselves or which they discover during their voyages, there is, in all three "journey" novels, an overriding theme of the need for communication. Rocannon, given mindspeech as well as the lives of Mogien, Iot, and Raho on Fomalhaut II, gains an understanding of the world which later bears his name. Genly Ai seeks to have a sincere message understood, but he must first overcome *shifgrethor* and the loss of sexual orientation in communication. When he finally mindspeaks Estraven, it is brought home by the latter's certainty that he hears the voice of his kemmering Arek, that even in the most intimate of speech forms, Estraven and Genly have only partially bridged a great gap. With Estraven's trust and sacrifice, however, Genly does begin to communicate with Gethen. Shevek fights a different battle for communication, one that is symbolized by the *ansible* which will emerge from his General Temporal Theory. He wants to overcome the difference between men so that ideas and aid can flow freely, bringing benefits for all. What mind-speech accomplishes in a paraverbal sense, and what the ansible accomplishes in the physical sciences, remain the symbolic representations of the emotional and rational communication between thinking human beings that is Shevek's goal.

In the three novels the destinations of the journeys become progressively more complex and elusive, moving from the external and morally clear to the internal and imprecise. It is my intention here to examine next the characters of the men who journey, to show how they perceive, learn, and change as they move toward these ever-deepening goals.

Travelers

As Donald Theall has pointed out, "Le Guin seems to have quite consciously developed some aspects of this utopian tradition [down to Thoreau and Morris], and in particular the role of *the stranger visiting a new world*" (emphasis mine).[1] Le Guin modifies the traditional utopian motif by placing a great deal of emphasis on the personality of the traveler and his reaction to the journey. She turns the handling of his adventures into a metaphor of the loneliness of human existence, stressing that man is constantly at risk, both physically and morally. Thus, instead of merely gaining a human perspective on a strange environment, we are presented with an analogy of those rare and terrifying moments in anyone's life when his integrity is his only resource, when the self is hermetically separated from the normal security of the social, political, and domestic context from which it naturally draws support. Though not articulated extensively in *Rocannon's World,* this position is established for Rocannon by the deaths of the members of his survey team. Right from the beginning of his story, Genly Ai's awareness of his isolation is considered: "Of course that [being noticed in a crowd, due to his size] was part of my job, but it was a part that got harder not easier as time went on; more and more often I longed for anonymity, for sameness. I craved to be like everybody else" (*LHD*, I).

For Shevek, the isolation is twofold. In the first instance it stems from his personal nature as the true and absolute Odonian on Anarres, and in the second, from his acute perception of the difference between himself and his fellow Cetians on Urras. Each traveler appears as a small foreground object against a panoramic background, a reduction achieved partly by the use of an omniscient narrator. The reader is thus in a position to evaluate the perceptions and responses of the travelers, to watch as they come to change worlds only to be changed by these worlds.

Because Gaveral Rocannon comes to Fomalhaut II as a fully trained professional investigator, it's somewhat surprising that he misinterprets so much of what he sees and that, until it is thrust upon him, he misses the central secret of the planet: paraverbal mindspeech. His position is analogous to that of the anthropologist who studies a culture in the belief that such study will reveal similarities to the anthropologist's own culture. Thus, despite his goodwill and apparent consideration of the sensibilities of others, Rocannon has a faintly superior attitude toward the races he encounters on Fomalhaut II. The League of All Worlds has come to the planet to bring technology and collect taxes, and Rocannon is a socio-scientific missionary following in the wake of this scientific imperialism. His feeling of superiority appears in the prologue in his private idea of greeting Semley thus: "...he bowed down very deeply, going right down to the floor on one knee, his head bowed and his eyes shut. This was what he called his All-purpose Intercultural Curtsey, and he performed it with some grace" (*RW*, "Prologue"). The same attitude appears when Rocannon obeys the professional requirement of keeping the host's cultural rules in the context of the Hallan society.

Several misunderstandings arise from Rocannon's attitude toward the planet. Because he doesn't clarify the relationship between myth and history, he does not trust the strength of the perceptions of Kyo and Mogien. Rocannon's failure to observe that the Fiia have chosen to obliterate the dark side of their past results in his failure to see the danger from the Winged Ones. A similar failure—failure to integrate the fragments of myth in an understanding that Mogien is part of the same stock as the Fiia—causes Rocannon to overlook the power of Mogien's prophecy of his own death after seeing the shadow in the moonlight. But Rocannon's response to Mogien's certainty looks both ways, to the aspect of professional and cultural blindness as well as the changed man who sees a new reality. "Summoning to his aid the last shreds of common sense, of scientific moderation, of the old life's rules, Rocannon tried to speak authoritatively: 'Don't be absurd,' he said" (*RW,* VIII).

Despite his failure to perceive the full situation on Fomalhaut II because he doesn't see the historical truths behind the myths, Rocannon's forced and intensive interaction with the planet and its races leads to a major change within himself: he begins to understand himself and Fomalhaut II better. Early in the novel he is also shown as being sympathetic to the very special gifts of the planet's people. "But Rocannon the hilfer, whose job was learning, not teaching, and who had lived on quite a few backward worlds, doubted the wisdom of staking everything on weapons and the uses of machines. Dominated by the aggressive, tool-making humanoid species of Centaurus, Earth, and the Cetians, the League had slighted certain skills and powers and potentialities of intelligent life, and judged by too narrow a standard" (*RW,* II). In keeping with the feudal-heroic cultural pattern of the planet, the change in Rocannon is large and mythic, symbolic rather than realistic. Although the style of this novel lacks the subtlety of genuine, complex human experience found in *The Left Hand of Darkness* and *The Dispossessed,* it does have the energy of change and the archetypal journey as well as some of the dreamlike inevitability of events that is typical of mythic tales. Some indication of the change in Rocannon is his dream that his old life is being burned away, dreamt while he actually stands in the fire as Zgama's captive: "Nothing came to him from all his earlier life, though he had lived many years on many worlds, learned much, done much. It was all burnt away. He thought he stood in Hallan, in the long hall hung with tapestries of men fighting giants, and that Yahan was offering him a bowl of water." (*RW,* IV).

This purging of Rocannon's former self is emphasized by his meeting with the Ancient One. Recovering at Lady Gayne's castle, Rocannon is viewed with awe, not because he is a Starlord but because he has survived the experience in the mountain. Rocannon himself is extremely aware of the change: ". . .anyway he had seen her [Semley] only once, on a planet eight lightyears away, a long time ago when he had been a man named Rocannon" (*RW,* IX).

His refusal to take Yahan with him highlights the change: "Vows break when names are lost. You swore your services to Rokanan, on the other side of the mountains. In this land there are no serfs, and there is no man named Rokanan" (*RW,* IX).

To replace what has been lost, Rocannon is given a new symbolic name—Olhor, the Wanderer—and with it, gains a place in the mythology of Fomalhaut II, in addition to a knowledge of the planet's secrets. He becomes a blood member of a questing band and is entrusted with the loyalty, wisdom, and lives of his companions. The most basic change, however, comes in the heart of the mountain where the characteristics of two of the planet's races are blended in the Ancient One (who has a special gift for Rocannon). While this event is presented as a moment of magic, in the psychology of myth it is the planet showing its acceptance of Rocannon by presenting him with a gift with which to save both the planet and the League. By becoming part of the world that is to be named after him, Rocannon is changed. The planet saves itself, something that will occur more subtly in *The Word for World Is Forest* and "Vaster than Empires and More Slow," and Rocannon, who will never be a true native, is maneuvered into the almost tragic position of being a double exile.

Although Rocannon's journey technically ends with the destruction of his enemies, his real achievement is the fuller understanding of Fomalhaut II that is thrust on him. The impact of this cannot be known abstractly; Rocannon must be transformed by the Ancient One so he can know the full agony of the enemies he kills and understand Kyo's and Mogien's gift. In the *agon* of the loss of Mogien and the deaths of a thousand men, Rocannon passes through a dangerous part of his journey and makes the discoveries about himself, which, in myth, are earned by the learning traveler.

Rocannon's growth is a qualified one, limited partly by the style of the book and partly by what I see as Le Guin's perception that he cannot come fully to grips with an alien reality. In the first place, the heroic role isn't fully suited to the ethnologist. Rocannon must lie to Mogien about his reason for turning back in despair. Moreover, the journey is forced on him by his enemies. When he has finally gone through the rigors of travel, the learning of the cave, and the struggle to overcome his enemies, Rocannon—or rather, the man he has become—completes his life journey, not by leaving Fomalhaut II but by staying to die as an exile in a culture he is only partially adapted to. Some of the conventional reward comes from Lady Gwyne and the peace in which to spend his last days; but she isn't the Semley who first attracted him. In addition, his refusal of the gift of mindspeech necessarily limits his contact with the culture of Fomalhaut II. In Le Guin's description of mindspeech, this passage stands out:

> Clinging to his humanity, he had drawn back from the totality of the power that the guardian of the well possessed and offered. He had learned to listen to the minds of one race, one kind of creature, among all the voices of all the worlds one voice: that of his enemy.
>
> With Kyo he had had some beginnings of mindspeech; but he did not want to know his companions' minds when they were ignorant of his. Understanding must be mutual, when loyalty was, and love. (*RW,* VIII)

Beneath Rocannon's seemingly considerate attitude of not wishing a one-way communication lies the truth: he would not be able to sustain its full impact. This defensiveness comes about because he doesn't recognize the extent of the commitment of Mogien, Yahan, and Kyo, nor how they "know his mind" without being able to weigh his thoughts. The limited empathy which Rocannon chooses functions as a weapon rather than as a marvelous gift with which to heal the division between men and races. His journey ends with the death of his enemies, for which Rocannon pays the price of isolation. In symbolism suggested by the story's mythic style, the gift has been "true" to Rocannon in a way that is restricted by his own flaw, that of having too narrow a goal. When the Ancient One asks Rocannon for his wish, his answer is: " 'I do not know,' the man said aloud in terror, but his set will answered silently for him: *I will go south and find my enemy and destroy him*" (*RW,* VIII). This answer—coming, as it does, from the dark and vengeful side of human nature which is so often masked by "practical," "necessary" ends—fixes the limits of Rocannon's achievement. In the context of magic and a psychological parallel with the energy released by the psychic self, the most dangerous act of all is to call upon the darkness to serve some specific end. Had Rocannon been humble so that he didn't know what to wish, the dark energy of the Ancient One—that of the psyche—would have given him all the gifts, including a wholeness that would have embraced the limited gifts of necessity and the greater gift of integration, both within the self and with all external reality. Rocannon ends up, however, only with the "real" achievements of having destroyed his enemies and gained insight into the genealogy of the peoples he is studying. What he fails to achieve is a psychic wholeness, something that would truly have been a pearl beyond price. For Le Guin, the traveler must let himself go where he is driven, or he will miss the true objective of his selfhood.

The shaping of Genly Ai's character is a major step forward in opening the metaphor of the journey to a consideration of the relationship between the journey, its purpose, and the development that occurs within it. Genly differs from Rocannon in that he is aware of the complications implicit in Rocannon's attempt to establish formal relations with aliens. Genly has been trained for the task which he has been put on Gethen to carry out. At his disposal are the records of previous investigators. Yet, as is the case with Rocannon, there seems to be a strange gap between the theory of intercultural relationships and putting them into practice.

In choosing a realistic mode for *The Left Hand of Darkness,* as opposed to the romantic mode of *Rocannon's World,* Le Guin has created a situation in which Genly can contemplate questions about the meaning of the journey for the traveler, and in so doing she accentuates the process of coping with the unknown in a way no other method of writing will allow. Before reality can be understood, the lone investigator must stand exposed to reality.

Among Genly's failures of perception, one predominates—his inability to negotiate with the Gethenians as whole, real beings. He can't escape the feeling that there is something wrong with them. Undoubtedly, Le Guin is setting up an analogy between the Gethenians and the "Others," an analogy she discusses elsewhere.

> The question involved here [of American science fiction] is the question of The Other—the being who is different from yourself. This being can be different from you in its sex; or in its annual income; or in its way of speaking and dressing and doing things; or in the color of its skin, or the number of its legs and heads.
>
> . . . . .
>
> If you deny any affinity with another person or kind of person, if you declare it to be wholly different from yourself—as men have done to women, and class has done to class, and nation has done to nation—you may hate it, or deify it; but in either case you have denied its spiritual equality, and its human reality.[2]

That Genly is aware of his failure to view the Gethenians properly, the reader knows from his description of Estraven early in the novel: ". . . I was still far from being able to see the people of the planet through their own eyes. I tried to, but my efforts took the form of self-consciously seeing a Gethenian first as a man, then as a woman, forcing him into those categories so irrelevant to his nature and so essential to my own'' (*LHD,* I). Yet, even despite this knowledge Genly blithely continues forward, on the presumption that the areas he hasn't penetrated are to be dealt with by assuming that they have been circumscribed, that their importance is known. Perhaps this is due partly to the physical resemblance between humans and Gethenians that lulls Genly into believing he understands. It's perfectly in character for him to discover late in the novel one of the differences—the resources of drothe strength.

Genly's fantastic professionalism, his sense that he knows the rules of the Envoy game and has only to follow through to win, is only and finally broken through on the physical and personal levels in his imprisonment and the arduous trek across Gobrin Ice with Estraven. In this respect Genly resembles Rocannon. Both must be divorced from the security of their fellows and their technologies in order to be truly open. In both novels the journeys function reductively, beginning when the travelers seem to have little or nothing and going on until they have even less. Also, in *The Left Hand of Darkness* much is made in the early scene with the king, as well as when Genly is in Orgota, of the fact that he can call for help at any moment. It is only as he faces death on the ice that he understands how the purpose of his mission is being realized on the journey he is taking with Estraven, in being-to-being communication which transcends politics.

> Alone, I cannot change your world. But I can be changed by it. Alone, I must listen, as well as speak. Alone, the relationship I finally make, if I make one, is not impersonal and not only political: it is individual, it is personal, it is both more and less than political. Not We and They; not I and It; but I and Thou. Not political, not pragmatic, but mystical. (*LHD,* XVIII)

In this contemplation Genly grasps the essence of his role and purpose. He can achieve it, though, only because he has already been trying to understand it, trying to find a course of action that will lead to his stated goal of furthering political cooperation between the two worlds. He has been trained to be far less active than Rocannon, to study and wait for events that will help bring his goal to him. In this respect he is better prepared for the collapse of the barriers, as in learning by doing he doesn't restrict himself to a rigid goal, as Rocannon did, but can see the meaning of what is given to him, what his role is within the context of his mission. Although

The Left Hand of Darkness doesn't recommend itself to a reading as psychomyth as readily as does *Rocannon's World,* it is still clear that Genly allows the energy of the other part of his duality, Estraven, to flood his own understanding and bring him into full communion with Gethen. Among Genly's achievements—which precede, but which also contribute to, the final revelation—are his acceptance of Argaven's resentment of the invasion of traditional Gethenian nationalism, an understanding of the myths he collects and puts in his report (each of which bears directly on the events in the main narrative), and his experience with the Foretellers of the Handdara. To see how Genly uses his observations to get to the truth of his need for personal integration with Gethen, it is useful to study his encounter with the Foretellers and his final adventure on the Gobrin Ice where, as is also true of *Rocannon's World,* the actual climax of the journey occurs before its practical aim has been achieved.

Genly's motive in journeying to the Foretellers is a limited one of satisfying his skepticism. Naturally, he distrusts the idea of prediction. Nor does he foresee that a knowledge of the Handdara can produce something vital to his goal of penetrating and understanding Gethen. But unlike Rocannon, who recoiled from Kyo's powers and rejected the larger potential of the gift of mind-speech, Genly is impressed with Faxe the Weaver. He quickly grasps the importance of the Handdarata on Gethen, although he merely glimpses its implication. "But," he says, "I began to understand Karhide better, after a halfmonth in Otherhord. Under that nation's politics and parades and passions runs an old darkness, passive, anarchic, silent, the fecund darkness of the Handdara" (*LHD,* V). Later, when Genly puts a question to the Foretellers and sees the answer come out of the dark mental chaos of the group, he is profoundly moved by both their sincerity and the effectiveness of the procedure. We realize that Genly has the ability to contact the Gethenians because he has the skill of mind-speech (Le Guin's metaphor for empathy) and because he finds in the Gethenian religion a lack of concern for ends, in relation to means and processes, something which heretofore has been for him just a theoretical teaching of the Ekumen. The profound truth left with Genly by Faxe and the foretelling is an attitude of openness to whatever influences life as it is expressed in the deliberate shying away from knowing the future that lies at the heart of the Handdara. The incident of the foretelling causes Genly to want Gethen to affect him.

When Genly and Estraven cross the Gobrin Ice on their journey to the heart of the planet Genly has long been trying to reach, they are also on a condensed journey into each other's heart. This journey has been brought on by a lack of effective communication which, in turn, has caused Estraven not to warn Genly, and by Estraven's genuine regard for the strange, perverted envoy. The journey begins with Estraven saving the life of someone who is practically his enemy and progresses through a stripping away of their resources, a process that reduces them to the bare essentials as individuals. It begins, too, in the shadow of the myths Genly relates. The first myth, "The Place Inside the Blizzard," tells of the separation of brothers on the ice when love fails, while the second, "Estraven, the Traitor," is about an ancestor of Estraven who is accused of being a traitor because of his love for an enemy. Everything preceding the journey over the ice is preparation for Genly's slow realization that he cannot successfully make contact with Gethen through the political world any more than he can count on the power of his offworld supporters. The trip across the ice parallels Genly's attempts to contact Gethen (which end with his arrival at the Voluntary Farm) and what he has learned from the Foretellers: to let Gethen come to him. When they first see the ice, Genly is receptive, aware that in experience itself lies a meaning he could not grasp no matter how much he studied Gethen. "It is good to have an end to journey towards; but it is the journey that matters, in end" (*LHD,* XVI).

Although Le Guin vividly describes the physical hardships and adventure of the journey across the ice, it is clear that the real movement lies in the emotional exchanges which develop into a deep intimacy between the two beings. In a situation where they are escaping from one group of enemies and heading toward another, the totality of their isolation together is stressed not by Genly, who has been alone throughout the novel, but by Estraven, who sees that he must face Genly without *shifgrethor*: "...up here on the Ice each of us is singular, isolate, I as cut off from those like me, from my society and its rules, as he from his" (*LHD,* XVI).

In this isolation both see the other fully for the first time, a fact underlined structurally by the split in what up to now has been a strict first-person narrative. Early in the journey, Estraven refuses

Genly's offer to use informal names; to do so would force him to admit Genly as a friend. But the sheer physical necessity of the trek forces them to cooperate, they begin to understand each other. When Estraven is in kemmer, Genly suddenly sees that he has refused to face the truly bisexual nature of the other: "Any need to explain the sources of that fear vanished with the fear; what I was left with was, at last, acceptance of him as he was. Until then I had rejected him, refused him his own reality" (*LHD,* XVIII). Here, the reader recognizes the merit of having the novel told in retrospect; for immediately after this realization, Genly adds his view of the experience, a view that is possible only long afterward. He recognizes that the energy of their growing love came from a knowledge of the difference between them, a knowledge brought into focus by the gap that prevents any meaningful sexual relationship. Their isolation breaks down as both cooperate in an endeavor on which their lives depend and in which they aren't prevented from understanding each other by the wall created by each one's pride—Genly's expressed in sexual expectations, and Estraven's in *shifgrethor.* It is in action and interaction on a journey fulfilling Le Guin's criterion of being both inner and outer movement that the answer to private and public problems is found.

Genly can be viewed as the hero of his journey and the novel only if it is granted that there can be no more difficult achievement than opening oneself to another, than surrendering to the unknown and accepting the outcome, whatever it is. But whereas Rocannon, for the most part, rejects the opportunity offered him, Genly has the strength and ability to learn from experience, to enter fully into the risk and accept the inevitable change. His inner journey, without which the outer journey across the ice to success would have been impossible, exacts the terrible price of Estraven's life and of Genly's security in his own identity. Later, when the spaceship has brought Genly's companions to Gethen, he realizes he is upset by their sexuality, that he is no longer one of them. But neither is it possible for him to be accepted at last by Estraven's father and son at the Hearth of Estre.

The moving conclusion of *The Left Hand of Darkness* grows out of a paradox: that the cost of the journey exceeds the reward of reaching its destination. At the same time, it helps the reader realize that the true reward was the *the journey*—as Genly remembers: "In such fortunate moments as I fall asleep I know beyond doubt what the real center of my own life is, that time which is past and lost and yet is permanent, the enduring moment, the heart of warmth'' (*LHD,* XVIII). The nearly overwhelming problem of human communication that is the heart of Genly's journey is clearly expressed in a novel where one human can learn to love another as a brother, even if it costs him his selfhood. The dying Estraven ambiguously calls out the name of his familial brother and, in doing so, leaves us wondering whether he means Genly, whose mindspeech was in the brother's voice, or the true Arek, for whom Genly can be only a shadow. But Genly is in no doubt as to the center of his own life; it is personal and private. It is his deep and abiding love for Estraven, not as an object or a curiosity but as a fellow being. Genly's true goal was that of his journey. Now the goal has found him, open and able to embrace it.

Moving from Genly's deeply emotional, driven nature—which attains the union of his self with Estraven—to the cool rational light of Shevek, the physicist-envoy of *The Dispossessed,* would at first seem to be movement away from the concept of total commitment by the traveler. But in creating the character of Shevek, Le Guin seems to be reaching for a more difficult course, that of integrating a razor-sharp intellect capable of evaluating the most minute action with a man driven by a great humane goal. Genly suggests to Argavan that Estraven served mankind above all; but he admits that he cannot know this. He is confident only of the private exchange of trust between them. Due to Shevek's special Odonian awareness, though, he is a sufferer who knows the extent of the pain he is causing while recognizing the rights of others at all times. His is the dilemma of being overly aware of the intricacy of human society and human motives, of knowing from his studies of time that in the web of existence, every moment bears on every other.

Clearly, Genly Ai's situation in *The Left Hand of Darkness* is best expressed at the moment when the problem of contact with Gethen is reduced to contact with Estraven during the blizzard. This situation is clarified and simplified, thus giving it great dramatic strength; but it is also limited in the way in which it is realistic and the way it takes into account the complex problems caused by Genly's contact with Estraven. These limits are absent from *The Dispossessed.* There the focus is always on the complexities of experience as they are perceived by Shevek's acute probing mind. Gone, too, is the limiting role of the envoy, for Shevek hasn't been trained for a task in a strange world. When he does arrive on Urras, he finds no clear path to follow. His life journey is broken up into the portions on Anarres and those on Urras. This way, the reader can share with him the experience of looking for the meaning of each incident and placing it in relation to his other actions. Thus such childhood experiences as experimental imprisonment make it possible for him to perceive mature situations. (The principle of self-determination that is at the core of Odonianism is in accord with Le Guin's intention of trying to reveal the meaning of experience.) Relieved of the role of envoy, Shevek defines his reality in the open, free of nearly all preconceptions.

In the complex worlds of *The Dispossessed*—where a utopian system is described in detail, from cradle education to mature group functioning in relation to a specific environment, and a second world (clearly an extrapolation of our present-day Earth) is described for contrast—Shevek stands out from the landscape in a way neither Rocannon nor Genly before him do. His ability to examine reality and reason about it—whether physics, politics, or society—is awesome, just as are his absolute moral integrity, his willingness to put his own life in peril for his beliefs, and his refusal to be the tool of any man. He isn't perfect, however. The mistakes of publishing under Sabul, of being seduced briefly by the luxury of Urras, and of mistaking Vea's intentions, are human errors; but Shevek's judgment of his own actions, a judgment that leads not to guilt but understanding and action, demonstrates the efficacy of Odo's philosophy.

Part of Shevek's equipment for the journey is his training in the system where every man is made responsible for his actions and is trained to evaluate them. What makes the character of Shevek so awe-inspiring is his sureness in pursuing his own judgments. To understand how such a person is possible requires a grasp of the potential of an education system that refuses to teach moral judgments, *as far as this is humanly possible.* Shevek is the ideal product of such a system. The extent of the system's failure can be measured by how Shevek comes into conflict with it. In a broad sense, his education occupies all the portions of the book that are flashbacks set on Anarres. These flashbacks reveal over and over again Shevek's refusal to compromise himself, whether he is refusing to send men to their deaths or demanding the right to fulfill his organic function and "do physics." With some initial help from Benap and Takver, Shevek overcomes the most difficult presupposition that must be questioned, the assumption that the un-state is itself the model of right action, that no one need question the growing number of inflexible constrictions imposed on the Anarresti in the name of survival. In the chapters set on Anarres we follow Shevek's life journey step by step, constantly aware that he is proving many times over the wisdom of Odo's original conceptions about the essential reasonableness of the educated and freed human mind.

When the mature Shevek goes to Urras, in the act that most clearly defines his refusal to bend his Odonian conscience even for the general will of the Odonian society, he brings the power of this remarkable training to bear upon his own actions, as well as the Urrasti society, like a powerful searchlight whose unremitting beam won't leave a shadow to hide the lie. In the chapters dealing with the voyage to Urras and with Shevek's early days there, we find his acuity almost unbelievable, as though the author were giving overly omniscient perception to the voyager. But the Anarresti chapters gradually dissipate this doubt, replacing it with the realization that the traveler who is fully open, who knows the wellsprings of his own actions, can come to terms with other realities in a way not even Genly, as sensitive as he tries to be in a "professional" manner, can achieve. What Genly slowly perceives Shevek *knows:* how to flow with the current of events. Shevek also has the confidence to strike out against that current, to act to change reality. The enormous risk of a journey away from a home he may never return to strikes Shevek and Takvar with its gravity, but both know it must be done, that the moral imperatives they have chosen as Odonians bind them to action in such a situation.

So, while Shevek protests that he goes to Urras empty-handed, he takes along the keen tool of his intellect. The novel, whose structure enunciates the temporal theory of the static coexistent with the dynamic that Shevek later develops, stops moving in the physical sense once Shevek is ensconced in his rooms on Urras. The major portion of the journey's action in the middle section is mental, as Shevek explores Urrasti society with his mind and gradually learns that what is blocking his understanding is similar to what he encountered on Anarres. When he realizes that he has been packaged, he can advance again. It is then that his mind makes the breakthrough in physics that is analogous to the action he chooses in the political sphere. His breakthrough is triggered by the incident with Vea, when he finds—at the real and physical level symbolized by his wasted seed—that he is pushing against an inflexible reality. He had once thought to change the relationship between Anarres and Urras; now he finds the Urrasti reality as fixed as the one Benap shows him on Anarres. In making this discovery Shevek sheds the naivete bred of believing the Urrasti to be like himself in openness, and accepts the difference. Once the problem becomes one of establishing a relationship rather than an identity between the two worlds, he sees the way forward just as he sees the aspect of relativity as the key to working on. Although he could see the intellectual lies inherent in Urrasti thought from the moment he stepped aboard the *Mindful,* he hadn't felt the full emotional meaning of the difference until the incident with Vea. After that, when the real world of Urras suddenly presses in upon Shevek as he participates in the demonstration and has to flee to the embassy of Terra, he can understand these events and choose his actions accordingly. As always, he turns his keen intellect on a situation and acts on the basis of reason collaborating with comprehended feeling.

We can think of Shevek as "conquering" both Anarres and Urras, if *conquest* is taken as meaning that a man comes to a full understanding of the personal and political landscapes of his journey and then plays an active part in shaping its ends. His mind can even embrace the similarities between the physics on which he works and the world situation he faces, without falling into the trap of understanding reality by making it fit his professional view of the world. From his Odonian training, in which Shevek sees the organic function of doing physics in relation to society as a whole, he has received the priceless gift of balance. This training is the basis of Le Guin's fictional logic for creating a character who is far better equipped to understand his actions and role in the world than is Rocannon, with his narrow goal of revenge and loyalty, or Genly, with his confused willingness to learn yet his failure to perceive his weaknesses.

Rocannon participates in the journey myth without being aware of the myth, and Genly can grasp the importance of the journey only in the midst of the blizzard. Shevek, however, provides a continuous critique of the *idea* of journeys. Thus Le Guin is able to achieve the double feat of illustrating the isolating, educative, inner and outer journey with Shevek's story, while at the same time creating a major character who is very much aware of the meaning of what he is doing, who is constantly evaluating what is happening within the special framework of the journey myth. The specific version of the myth Shevek is conscious of is the one derived from Odo's "true journey is return" and the accompanying philosophy concerning the relationship between means and ends, in which means, or process, are seen as dominant. Shevek's awareness of this all-important predominance of action, which progresses toward a goal without betraying the goal in a specific deed, is expressed in *true journey is return*. Action must always be returned to intention. When Shevek decides to found the Syndicate of Initiative on Anarres, he sees that, unlike the temporary satisfaction of pleasure, "fulfillment is a function of time."

> It [the circular search for pleasure] has an end. It comes to the end and has to start over. It is not a journey and return, but a closed cycle, a locked room, a cell.
>
> Outside the locked room is the landscape of time, in which the spirit may, with luck and courage, construct the fragile, makeshift, improbable roads and cities of fidelity: a landscape inhabitable by human beings. (*TD,* X).

If he is to make the journey, Shevek must act in "the landscape of time," always with an eye to the still center of moral right on which all rightness is based. In the fruitful yet painful process of keeping ends and means in constant tension with each other lies the meaning of Shevek's journey. The character of this voyager is profoundly confident exactly because Shevek understands the purpose of the journey: to fulfill an end that is always changing, yet which is forever rooted in the same demands, demands which, in the end, can only be articulated from within the traveler, no matter how much an external system may have freed him to face them squarely. In the character of Shevek, the voyager, Le Guin gives us the paradigm of the ideal voyager—always willing to learn and change, confident of his movement because it is based on an emotional and logical understanding of the self. Keng's reaction to Shevek's personality is very much Le Guin's voicing of what she is trying to accomplish, what she *has* accomplished in this portrait of a knowledgeable traveler:

> The strength of Shevek's personality, unchecked by any self-consciousness or consideration of self-defense, was formidable. She was shaken by him, and looked at him with compassion and a certain awe.
>
> "What is it like," she said, "what can it be like, the society that made you? I heard you speak of Anarres, in the square, and I wept listening to you, but I didn't really believe you. Men always speak so of their homes, of the absent land. . . But you are *not* like other men. There is a difference in you." (*TD,* XI)

Shevek's voyage has become as lonely as that of Rocannon or Genly, but he carries with him the protection and guidance of the self known and the self learning, and this makes the light of his perception shine everywhere. Although he doesn't solve a final, complex political problem at the conclusion of the novel, the reader sees that if the meaning of the journey is known, then the movement ever toward it is the richest of all possible human goals.

Landscapes

As a writer of fiction, Ursula Le Guin creates backgrounds against which voyagers travel. But it is dangerous to divorce the backgrounds from the voyager's interaction with his world or worlds. The danger lies in whether Le Guin maneuvers the settings and situations to make it artificially easy for the travelers to reach their destinations, both physically and mentally. Obviously she manipulates the backgrounds. But it doesn't necessarily follow that this violates the integrity of what she is saying about the travelers, nor does it reduce the dramatic impact of the journeys. In Genly Ai's observation at the beginning of his tale, "Truth is a Matter of the Imagination," and in the author's causing her voyagers to cross landscapes suited to their particular quests, Le Guin is exercising her right to create in the light of that higher truth.

The background of *Rocannon's World* is drawn from the fabric of fantasy, in keeping with the mythic tone of the story. It is peopled with trolls, princesses, men riding Gryphons, and evil, mindless, bat-like enemies. It is a place in which Rocannon has a series of adventures on his way to the two final confrontations with the Ancient One and the Faradayans. The mythic locale and events are set against Rocannon's statement that it is a frozen feudal-heroic world he is dealing with. Although he is trained as an ethnologist, Rocannon is slow to perceive that all the races on Fomalhaut II are interconnected. Here Le Guin has done some careful homework in the study of evolution, which results in an ambivalent relationship between the mythic dimension and the realism of the novel. There is a profusion of means in *Rocannon's World,* however; there is invention almost solely for the pleasure of inventing. The mindless bats and the tribal groups of the novel serve only to enrich the general setting of place.

What is considerably more interesting about the background here is the way Rocannon's subjectivity figures in the description and evaluation of his world. In the prologue, Rocannon considers that he would have supported the Liuar rather than the Gdemiar as the species to help on Fomalhaut II. Thus the reader is made aware of the subjectivity implicit in the eye of the observer. Later, this subjectivity causes Rocannon to become unsure of Kyo's mind-speech, since the mindspeech is outside his experience. It leads to the tragic error of assuming that the Winged Ones are a higher life form merely because they live in classical buildings and look like angels. Rocannon's error—which is repeated, with variations, by Genly and Shevek—is his failure to accept the world he is in for what it is. Instead he uses his own preconceptions to shape it. Because he feels above the feudal world on which he is trapped, Rocannon fails to read the signs contained in myth and legend, which would have connected all the races of the planet and revealed to him the existence of the mindspeakers as the basis of the civilization, with each mutated race representing a way of dealing with mindspeech. If this analysis is applied in retrospect, the frozen feudal-heroic culture of the Liuar becomes a compromise in which the represented telepathic powers are controlled by strict cultural patterning, while the Gdemiar and Fiia illustrate different ways of blocking off parts of the total gift. Despite his brief speculation to the contrary, Rocannon does not penetrate this pattern. He accepts the premise that technological advancement is the mark of an advanced civilization. An extreme position, merely hinted at during the moments when Rocannon is summoned to the cave, is that the telepathic powers of the Ancient One have drawn Rocannon over the planet, and will use him to destroy the invaders. The meaning of Rocannon's journey is only presented obliquely by a background which concentrates on generating a sense of mythic mystery. Driven as he is by the desire for revenge and by loyalty to the League of All Worlds, Rocannon doesn't pause to grasp the meaning of his surroundings. This is in keeping with the classic pattern of the mythic traveler; it is the *reader* who grasps the meaning of the fictional dream, not the dreamer.

As Le Guin moves toward a realistic mode of presentation, however, one in which normal human curiosity is accentuated by the strangeness of the place the voyagers find themselves in, the implications of the landscapes must be verbalized more clearly by the travelers. In *The Left Hand of Darkness*, Genly has time to contemplate the implications of the climate, the political structure, and, above all, the changes in sexual behavior which are the main stumbling block in establishing the real contact that he seeks. When his time for contemplation is over, Genly is cruelly exposed to the reality of what he has considered, until he breaks through the barriers and becomes a part of Gethen. Le Guin's technique here and in the Anarres portion of *The Dispossessed* is to reduce the options that are available in the surroundings, to strip away all excess complexity so the essential human problem will be brought into sharp relief.

The ice world of Gethen begins with fewer biological citizens than Earth or Rocannon's World. Genly speculates on the loneliness of the situation, on the brutal simplicity of having to fight the climate for mere survival, and sees in them a possible reason for the failure of the Gethenians to develop militarily. In this, and the way the Gethenians refuse to make themselves too comfortable by excessive use of their advanced technology, Le Guin is undoubtedly commenting on the situation in the Western industrial world of the twentieth century, where the combination of technology and luxury seems to foster aggression.

Much more important to the overall description of Gethen are its sexual and social structures. At first these elements only seem to complicate the picture, but eventually we see that they help us focus on the problem of the relationship with the Other that Le Guin is concerned with in her writing. As the Investigator points out in the report which Genly quotes, a world where sexual role-playing is nonexistent lays bare the demand for a true human contact: "One is respected and judged only as a human being. It is an appalling experience" (*LHD,* VII). It is on the ice—where together, Genly and Estraven fight against the planet, as Gethenians must always fight against it—that Genly finally makes his contact. The background of *The Left Hand of Darkness* is far more consistent and monolithic than that of *Rocannon's World.* Therefore, the sexual characteristics of the Gethenians are seen as adaptation for the sake of survival, as are the Gethenians' narrow nasal passages and their characteristic layer of fat. The Handdara also fit this scheme. It stresses minor variations within the brutal fixed limits of life, in addition to *drothe* discipline which concentrates the individual's power so he can survive in a crisis. All the other minor facets of Gethenian life—from the rules of hospitality and the hearth system, to the style of eating—integrate with the sexual and climatic factors. Although much is "explained" in *The Left Hand of Darkness,* everything points to the situation on the ice. It is essentially a subtractive environment, if we take Earth as a starting point. The course of the novel is the further subtraction of the social and political contexts, until only Genly and Estraven remain.

In making the Gethenians so like the Terrans, except for the sexual difference, Le Guin presents the problem of human relationships much more realistically. She has removed the fantastic creatures of *Rocannon's World*; that way, she can focus on important, but in some ways minor, differences. Thus, in the journey across the ice, Estraven speaks for himself, which allows us to watch as two minds gradually come to understand one another. Estraven's essential humaneness, his ability to care for the Other, is the key to ending Genly's isolation, and therefore to the resolution of his quest. During the journey, Estraven comes to represent all aspects of Gethen, and it is in the narrow focus of Estraven's contact with Genly that the solution lies. When it comes, it's total, for Le Guin implies, within the structure of the concluding portion of the novel, that Genly has solved the problem of making contact. Such an approach to a fully integrated, realistic, and detailed background allows the reader to see the human problem as it is brought into focus. All of the elements of the background form a coherent whole which Le Guin then represents in the person of Estraven. The simplicity of the novel's conclusion is both its strength and a possible flaw. It is a strength because it allows the fictional form its completion, but it may leave the reader with a sense that the personal aspect has too great an immediate effect on the social and political whole. In any event, it's clear that the background of Gethen and its people are what Genly observes and absorbs while coming to terms with the Gethenians in the person of Estraven.

In terms of setting, *The Dispossessed* provides the closest parallel to the reader's world. Urras is a clear parallel to twentieth-century Earth, while Anarres resembles any isolated nation being built under difficult conditions, such as Israel. The only difference (but an all-embracing one) is Odo's anarchial philosophy, which has not only led to the settlement of Anarres but has left a permanent mark on the minds of the Urrasti. Thus, although there are great social and political differences between the Cetian situation and that of present-day Earth, the novel does deal with a human problem in an essentially realistic context.

In the sense that it has already happened before the main narrative line begins, the section of the novel concerning Anarres is background. The complex description of Shevek's youth and the formation of his personality in Odonian society is an impressive achievement for Le Guin as a novelist. As is also true of *The Left Hand of Darkness,* the barrenness of the Anarresti environment enhances the importance of each human act on the planet, thus drawing the community of man closer together and emphasizing the conflict between a political system designed to provide maximum personal freedom, and the necessity of cooperating in order to survive. In the rarefied air of Anarres, the moral and political dilemma stands out, just as it does on the cold Gobrin Ice, except that in the case of Anarres, the human dimension has been added. It can be debated whether the Odonian system has worked because there is little to possess and time for the kind of contemplation required to maintain a high moral standard, or whether only Odo's system could make survival possible on Anarres; in either case, the system and the ecology are inexorably entwined.

Anarres prompts constant comparison with modern Western society on Earth. In Shevek's youth he is exposed to an educational system in which priorities are known. It is this system that brings into being individuals who are capable of responsible anarchy. The talents which later make Shevek such an astute traveler are the result of a combination of a strong individual and the particular cultivation Anarres provides. Similarly, every facet of the social pattern of Anarres contributes to the formation of Shevek's nature. The organization of work, for example, combines the individual's freedom to seek his own way of contributing, with the problem of society's needs. Partnering is a non-possessive family structure, and sexual practice is a logical result of freedom of choice. Every Anarresti practice comes under scrutiny by Shevek, Bedap, Takver, and other Odonians. In this way, the workings of Shevek's mind are explained by his upbringing. Although Shevek is conditioned by the structure of Anarres, the goals of Anarresti society make him—or any subject—aware of the conditioning. Le Guin makes sure the reader sees Shevek's mind act within the limits of this environment.

> Sacrifice might be demanded of the individual, but never compromise: for though only the society could give security and stability, only the individual, the person, had the power of moral choice—the power of change, the essential function of life. The Odonian society was conceived as a permanent revolution, and revolution begins in the thinking mind.
>
> All this Shevek had thought out, in these terms, for his conscience was a completely Odonian one. (*TD,* X)

Shevek, then, is the only traveler in the three novels who is properly equipped for his voyage, who is capable of analyzing the world he goes into and choosing his behavior once he is there. When he encounters Urras, with all its richness and flaws, his mental acumen *must* be brought into play, for he has no means of living the lie or refusing to examine and evaluate experience. The energy of Le Guin's critique of modern society that is embodied in the propertarian states of Urras benefits enormously from Shevek's moral magnitude. At first the planet's richness stuns him. In the novel his mental journey is one of sorting out a profusion of sense data and applying his intellect to a society more complex and less open than his own. When his strength of character and his method finally triumph, he has achieved the *return* of the Odonian paradox—an understanding that the Urrasti way of life has a place in the mind of the anarchist that does not disturb the still center of personal strength.

It was a brilliant stroke to set the crisis of *The Dispossessed* against a background of confusion in a rich, complex society and thus illustrate the strength and value of the strict search for truth and the concomitant denial of excessive materialism. Although Genly Ai's and Estraven's isolation is structurally powerful, it is alien to the confusion of modern life on the planet Earth. Anarres provides a model of nakedness from which mental strength can grow, but it is only on Urras that the reader recognizes (in Shevek's trial) the challenge of carrying an educated moral perception into a rich propertarian society such as that of Western civilization in the last quarter of the twentieth century.

Equally important to the accomplishment of Le Guin's model of a man acting with moral strength to clarify the confusion that is thrust on him is that, at the close of the novel, Shevek does not succeed in engineering some kind of radical change. Change is beginning to come on both Anarres and Urras as a result of his actions, and, of course, he achieves the physics theory he sought. But for Shevek, the experience is essentially a private one which answers the dictates of an aware, educated conscience. The existentialist concept of "being authentically" is perfectly realized in Shevek. He won't submit to the pressures of the moment; instead, he must answer the imperatives of his inner self. He would not be believable as a character if he had arrived on his voyage out of the void. It is the Anarresti background that gives him the fictional right to exist as a character and judge others. *The Dispossessed* is the story of a man who temporarily loses his way in a jungle but who plainly knows where his "true north" lies, who knows he has only to stand still briefly in order to see the right direction. From the background of Anarres, we learn where this traveler gets his sense of direction, and from the Urrasti experience comes proof that he can find his way even if the confusion is as great as that of our own world.

A distinguishing characteristic of the Cetian novel is that it is populated by living humans with whom Shevek has a rich relationship. Except for Estraven, no character in the other two novels attains great depth or goes far beyond fulfilling a function which demonstrates some aspect of his world—or, like Mogien, some type of person. In *The Dispossessed,* Takver, Bedap, Atro, Oiie, and even Sabul lead lives of their own, and this forces Shevek to test his theoretical assumptions against human reality. A fundamental proposition of Odo's anarchy is that it will better the positions of all men through the individual efforts of each, something which Shevek finally acts out on several levels—in the political sphere, with his effect on Anarres and Urras; in the private sphere, with his attempt to save the dying man on Urras; and in the largest human sphere, by giving his discovery to all mankind.

The journeys in the three novels do not exhibit linear progress; rather, they suggest variations on a mythic theme. At first, *Rocannon's World* seems to be a simple playing out of the journey myth. But upon consideration, it is revealed that the implications of Rocannon's single-minded pursuit broaden the classic quest. The dangers that can result from goals set too far in advance, as well as a partial failure to examine the journey itself, are demonstrated. Against a landscape of the rugged outlines of fantasy, Rocannon is both driven by destiny and helped by a force he never fully understands. In achieving his physical goal, however, he does not fully come to terms with Fomalhaut II or with his enemies (who remain the ciphers of mythic evil that he destroys). He suffers partial exile on the planet he has saved, having rejected the opportunity to unite with its inhabitants.

In *The Left Hand of Darkness* the simplicity of myth is offset by the introduction of a more logically integrated background, a more perceptive traveler, and a resolution that is couched in terms of the basic contact that forges the bond between two strains of humanity. The mystery which Genly probes is much more complex than

Rocannon's. Genly is prepared for this probing, in addition to being more aware of how the problem is actually working out. But his inflexibility, due partly to undigested professional training and partly to an unconscious bias, leaves him with no way to solve the problem he is confronted with. The dramatic journey over the Gobrin Ice is an accidental solution. He is open to it, however, as his training is finally translated into experience. The problem of understanding the Other is resolved in *The Left Hand of Darkness* when the Other—Estraven—is able to step away from the background of his race and extend a helping hand. Here, Le Guin has articulated the problem of the journey more explicitly than she does in *Rocannon's World* and thus has domesticated the myth while keeping the structure.

The Dispossessed offers the most extensive examination of the journey. Here, the probing traveler sees the pattern and must follow it. Shevek is driven by an imperative usually thought of as being contradictory to myth or which is, at best, symbolized only in myth—the imperative of free, aware human will. The traveler's exceptional powers of perception are justified; then he sets to work on the idea of a journey within the context of his research, his own private life, and the political life he is a part of. As Shevek moves through the complexity of Urras, we not only understand his actions, but are made aware of how the Odonian experience on Anarres has prepared him, in terms of strength of will and sharpness of perception. Actually, Shevek achieves his goal several times: in his love for Takver, in leaving the mill at Elbow, in founding the Syndicate of Initiative, and in journeying to Urras. As a true Odonian, he recognizes that the only movement forward is the constant return to the conscious personal moral imperative of a mature humanity.

With *The Dispossessed*, Ursula Le Guin has reached the goal of explaining and contemplating the journey as it happens. In the process of putting myth in the realistic clothing of human experience, she has made potent the fact that the human journey is important for the way in which the experience happens and is understood, not for some abstract grail at its end. Shevek's life realizes his own suggestion that brotherhood begins in the sharing of pain and confirms the importance of remaining committed to that sharing at every step in the journey that is man's life.

3. Ursula K. Le Guin: Damsel with a Dulcimer

PETER S. ALTERMAN

SCIENCE FICTION and English Romanticism are both children of the Industrial Revolution. The eighteenth century that saw the rise of the factory also saw the retreat of Christianity in the face of the onslaught by scientific rationalism; among the casualties of this "war" was a complacent definition of man. A product of the philosophical-scientific developments of the time, science fiction grew out of attempts to create a secular Man. The bombardment included Locke's definition of the mind as a *tabula rasa* and continued with studies by Rousseau, Berkeley, Hume, Hartley, and others.

The Romantic poets joined the colloquy, especially with Wordsworth's *Prelude*, Coleridge's theories of imagination, and Blake's mythic theories of mental creation. While the poets focused on the psychology of man, Mary Shelley wrote the first novel to define physical man in light of the new scientific theories and then-popular philosophical-psychological theories. It is not unusual, then, that science fiction, which traces its origins to *Frankenstein,* shares traditional ways of defining the nature of man with Romantic rhetoric and dialectic.

Le Guin's vegetable-world stories, *The Word for World Is Forest* and "Vaster than Empires and More Slow," are good examples of the similarity between Romantic and science-fiction visions of the mind of man. The essence of these stories is Romantic. In saying this, I am not attempting to classify her as a Romantic writer, just to suggest that *Word* and "Vaster" indicate the extent to which Romantic conventions and assumptions infuse science fiction. The vegetable-world stories, both of which are concerned with man in the wilderness, evidence Romantic conventions of the relationship between the natural landscape and the landscape of the mind.

Ian Watson has discussed the metaphoric relationship between the unconscious mind and the forest of Athshe.[1] The natural world has always served as a symbol of human life, with the terms of the symbol shifting as aesthetic, social, and theological beliefs shift. Once as a manifestation of God's divine plan, with mankind as its crown, and once more as a snare of the devil to seduce man from God's Law, nature has served as a foil for man's self-image many times in many different guises.

When the new spirit of scientific rationalism swept England, it undermined traditional concepts of the mind and brought with it speculations about the nature of the mind. In the absence of an omnipresent divinity, Christian and Cartesian definitions of reality and of man gave way to myriad experimental and theoretical models, ranging from Hobbesian materialism to Hume's solipsism. William Blake ridiculed both poles of this argument in his poetry. The synthesis he voiced soon became a standard for the Romantics who followed, who affirmed the creative relationship between perceiving mind and perceived object.

As definitions of man's nature changed, the way nature was used to describe the internal workings and structure of the mind changed. From being a wholly political metaphor, the landscape became an inscape within one generation—the Romantic revolution. Rather than remaining an indication of the power and wealth of English society, description of the English countryside in the 1780s and 90s became a metaphor for the landscape of consciousness. These Romantic metaphors have continued to be applied in science fiction.

In *Word for World,* for instance, there are two distinct perceptions of the forest. For the colonists from Earth, "the alien forest became wood, wood to make products on Earth, 'sawn planks' " (*WW,* 1). The alien forest is transformed into products for human consumption. Trees are seen not as themselves but as raw material for products, in the same way that Windsor Forest's stately oaks symbolize Britain's men-of-war, the heart of its world power. Captain Davidson makes this connection: "There was something about this damn planet, its gold sunlight and hazy sky, its mild winds smelling of leafmound and pollen, something that made you daydream. You mooched along thinking about conquistadors and destiny and stuff..." (*WW,* 1). To perceive the forest as lumber for Earth is to see only its economic and political usefulness, however. In such a view, nature is subservient to and representative of human political power. It is also a social concern. This viewpoint doesn't require unique awareness of the forest as an econolgy of discrete parts. Reducing "forest" to "wood" merely changes it into an object to be manipulated—not a subject worthy of contemplation.

The humans' belief in the object-nature of the Athshean forest is evident in their disregard for it, from creating "Dump Island" to indiscriminately killing red deer. Finally, there is their lack of concern for the humanity of the Athsheans who are enslaved, reduced to "creechies" (green monkeys).

Although the human invaders can see only one side of the forest—its commercial and political potential—for the Athsheans, reality and self are one and the same with the forest: "Athshean man was branch and root" (*WW,* 5). The Athsheans think of themselves metaphorically, as extensions of the forest. Their memories are roots, their minds run like the individual elements of tree, branch, root, vine, river. To themselves, they *are* the forest; the destruction of the forest is their own destruction.

There is a clear-cut shift of perspective. The Athsheans perceive their essential inner life as being mirrored in the forest—each grove, orchard, and clearing; they see it as life, not as object. That is, they internalize the landscape, turning it into a metaphor for mind. It is of paramount importance to them that they see each element of the forest as unique.

In *Word for World* the language used to describe mental states is taken from that of trees. In such lines as "Little paths ran under the branches, around the boles, over the roots; they did not go straight, but yielded to every obstacle, devious as nerves" (*WW*, 2), relationship of mind and forest is clear. There are continual references to roots: "He had feared that he was cut off from his roots," and "They have left their roots behind them, perhaps, in this other forest from which they came, this forest with no trees" (*WW,* 2). What is impressed upon us is the connection between forest and mind, between external and internal life. In contrast to the trees of Windsor Forest, Wordsworth's lines from "Tintern Abbey"—"this dark sycamore...these orchard-tufts..." and "These hedge-rows, hardly hedge-rows, little lines/of sportive wood run wild"—are concrete presences, phenomenological experiences.[2] The descriptions of Romantic nature are one with "roots, boles, branches, twigs, leaves, leaves overhead and underfoot and in your face and in your eyes, endless leaves on endless trees" (*WW,* 1). This emphasizes a common nature—concrete, immediate, teeming with undiscovered spirit, a universe of strange and secret life.

Just as Romantic poetry literalizes traditional metaphors, so does science fiction: "At times, romantic thought and romantic poetry seem to come so close to giving in completely to the nostalgia for the object that it becomes difficult to distinguish between object and image, between imagination and perception, between an expressive or constitutive and a mimetic or literal language."[3]

The natural landscapes of "Tintern Abbey" and *Word for World* are organic; they mirror the complexity of the human mind. Man is viewed as part of the natural landscape, while nature is seen as a metaphor for his intellectual processes. In "Tintern Abbey" the Wye Valley becomes an internal landscape, the thread of remembered youth, as well as the synthesizing agent of psychological growth. Old Athshean men compare themselves to old trees with only their roots alive in much the same way that Wordsworth uses the Wye Valley to exemplify the flow of an individual's memory.

In a well-known correlation, Samuel Taylor Coleridge associates the narrator's state of mind with the external world:

> Sea, and hill, and wood,
> With all the numberless goings-on of life,
> Inaudible as dreams! the thin blue flame
> Lies on my low-burnt fire and quivers not;
> Only that film, which fluttered on the grate,
> Still flutters there, the sole unquiet thing.[4]

The film in the grate—the "stranger"—mirrors the nebulous perception of reality that the narrator experiences.

In the same way, the forest mirrors the experience of the people in *Word for World:* "The air was black and full of moisture, and you couldn't tell where to put your feet, it was all roots and bushes and tangles. There were noises all around, water dripping, rustling, tiny noises, little things sneaking around in the darkness" (*WW,* 7). Davidson has just crashed in a hopper, following an Athshean attack and is lost, alone in the forest. The description above is a metaphor of his terror and paranoia. It serves to define, through natural landscape, his state of mind—lost, twisted, dank, unable to see—as well as the *nature* of his mind, which is a squalid pit of paranoia.

There is a more active relationship between the mind and the natural landscape in "Vaster than Empires and More Slow." Throughout the story, Osden, an empath, receives emotional emanations from his crewmates, emanations of hatred, fear, pity, and so on. Osden amplifies these feelings and returns them, which drives most of his mates to the brink of madness: Eskwana retreats into an almost constant sleep, while the others gobble tranquilizers or undergo frequent therapy sessions. Osden's ability is finally turned outward to the baffling vegetable life of World 4470. He receives a message: "I felt the fear. It kept growing. As if they'd finally known I was there, lying on them there... I couldn't stop sending the fear back, and it kept growing..."

Through Osden, the metaphor linking man's mind with nature becomes an active relationship. Osden's awareness joins that of the vegetable life. For a time he becomes part of it and shares its experiences. When his shipmates leave the planet, Osden stays behind to join the world-vegetable. He blends his mind with the planet's mind in an ultimate synthesis of the nature-mind metaphor.

If we compare the following passages from Coleridge's "The Eolian Harp" with the state Osden achieves in the vegetable world, we can readily see how Romantic the idea is:

> O! the one Life within us and abroad,
> Which meets all motion, and becomes its soul,
> . . . . .
> And what if all animated nature
> Be but organic Harps diversely fram'd,
> That tremble into thought, as o'er them sweeps
> Plastic and vast, one intellectual breeze,
> At once the Soul of each, and God of all?[5]

The metaphoric connection between nature and mind has become active identity. The self is seen as part of nature, in total psychic communion with it. One spirit, one common being, operates to nullify the distinction between self and other.

Both Coleridge and Osden redefine the self-other duality. Rather than insisting that no separation exists, each one blends with nature and thus, through an act of will, creates a common spirit. For Osden, this one "Life" is "awareness of being, without object or subject.'' It fits well into his unique personality and autistic past, in which the only safe form of existence must deny the independence of others. Due to his unique, empathic nature, Osden is tortured by the tides of subject-object-ness. It is impossible for him to accept either love or hatred. The form of existence which he *can* survive is precisely the world-vegetable's form of existence: an animate nature infusing everything, denying individual boundaries and passions.

Similarly, in ''The Eolian Harp,'' Coleridge participates in the unity of existence by denying uniqueness, individuality. He cuts himself off from human lives and proceeds to a perception of the cosmic oneness of life through the contemplation of music, then sound, and finally the natural rhythm of the wind. Even after he has retreated from this insight (note the natural-metaphoric use of the word), he continues to assert the mechanism of stripping away human thought for ''Faith that only *feels*''[6] as the way to achieve unity.

The similarity between Coleridge's ''one Life'' and Osden's self-other identity is an excellent example of how the rhetoric of science fiction operates Romantically. Through the device of empathy, ''Vaster than Empires'' makes literal Coleridge's intellectual breeze, thus creating a mechanism for making the metaphor concrete. Whereas, for Coleridge, the vision of the cosmic unity of all life acts as a metaphor that binds self with other, perceiver, and perceived, in Osden's empathic ability we are caught up in the literal experience of joining self to other, of his joining with his world.

This technique of modern science fiction has been remarked on in several essays. Joanna Russ and Stanislaw Lem, two seminal science fiction writer-critics, accept the device of making metaphor concrete as a possible key to an aesthetic of science fiction.[7] In his novel, *Triton,* Samuel R. Delany goes further:

> Such sentences as ''His world exploded,'' or ''She turned on her left side,'' as they subsume the proper technological discourse (of economics and cosmology in one; of switching circuitry and prosthetic surgery in the other), leave the banality of the emotionally muzzy metaphor, abandon the triviality of insomniac tossings, and, through the labyrinth of technical possibility, become possible images of the impossible.[8]

In this brief example, Delany illustrates the operative mechanism which Wordsworth and Le Guin are using: the metaphor of natural action translated into human feeling. Yet such metaphors can also be literal descriptions of natural activity.

These lines from Blake's "London" show how the dialectic works: "And the hapless Soldiers sigh, / Runs in blood down palace walls."[9] The soldier's blood is both literal and metaphorical. It is real in the sense that soldiers shed their blood at royal palaces while defending their king from attack, as they did in revolutionary France. It is metaphorical in the sense that sighs cannot literally run down walls in the form of blood.

In his *Prelude*, Wordsworth speaks of stealing a boat as a young boy and of experiencing the force of nature moving against him for his crime:

> When, from behind that craggy steep till then
> The horizon's bound, a huge peak, black and huge,
> As if with voluntary power instinct
> Upreared its head, I struck and struck again,
> And growing still in stature and the grim shape
> Towered up between me and the stars, and still,
> For so it seemed, with purpose of its own
> And measured motion like a living thing,
> Strode after me.[10]

Here the developing poet is responding to a metaphor of nature as a moral spirit which is judging the boy's theft and moving to thwart him. In it and the lines that follow, we see the poet as he senses the hidden powers in nature, as well as a moral order to which man is bound. But there is also a literal side. The perspective of the boy rowing across the lake shifts. From his point of view, the mountain *is* moving toward him. This movement, which is a physical fact, invades the metaphor, and nature is realized concretely. Thus Wordsworth's union of metaphor and physical reality is quite reasonable.

The forest in *Word for World* serves the dual function of concrete reality and metaphor of the mind. In the forest the inadequate human vision is exposed, while metaphorically the synergistic dreaming-waking state of the Athshean consciousness is explained. In the forest we inhabit two worlds, the physical forest the humans are attacking, and the metaphorical forest of the Athshean mind, the latter being made concrete by the former. The narrative also exists in these two environments, for Selver's revolution is two-pronged. It is both violently physical (the slaughter of humans), and psychic (Selver's godhood from the dream and his act of bringing a new form of human relation).

The dual vision is referred to in *Word for World* with the branding of Selver as god-translator. He bridges the gap between inscape and landscape, between the physical and the psychic revolutions on Athshe. Selver conceives of murder in a dream and then kills humans according to the requirements of the dream. Similarly, Osden's self is both metaphorically and literally transformed into the reality and spirit of the vegetable world's consciousness. Here again, the world is concrete and psychic, and the dramatic action of the stories unfolds in an external landscape *and* within the mind of the protagonist.

Osden's journey toward a unity and wholeness of awareness without subject-object distinction is, at the same time, the progress of the crew of the GUM toward comprehension of the physical reality of World 4470; each is an image of the other. The alienation of Osden and his crewmates from the process of life, their inability to perceive life on World 4470, indicates their self-absorption and inability to touch each other as human beings. Osden's apotheosis forces the surviving humans to confront their failures as individuals.

In "Vaster than Empires," *Word for World,* and Romantic poetry, there is an identical dialetic at work. The humans cannot cast aside the demands of tangible nature; nor can they allow this nature to be the only element of reality. The tension that results from the conflicting demands of nature and their imaginations is resolved by making metaphor literal.

This rhetoric serves to bridge the gap between the subjective and the objective, between the observer and the observed. Philosophically it resolves the conflicting demands of Locke and Berkeley. In *Word for World* the metaphor is made real when the psychic forest of the Athshean mind becomes the forest of the planet. As noted above, it is also made real through Osden's empathic union with World 4470 in "Vaster than Empires."

If some of the techniques of Le Guin's vegetable-world stories are rooted in the Romantic dialectic, we can reasonably expect the resolution of the conflicts raised by the dialectic of her stories to be Romantic. In terms of the overall plot, this can be viewed as human explorers trying to learn the true nature of the new planet and being stymied when normal scientific analysis (rational analysis) fails them. The true nature of these planets is discovered, not by the rational individual but by the visionary who is often, but not necessarily, an artist.

In the 1970s, Stephen Tall's *Stardust* stories may well be the most obvious use of this device. In these stories, human explorers encounter new life systems and come to understand the planetary life they are studying, not through science but through the visionary paintings of Ursula Potts, the ship's psychic.

The dialectic of these and other science fiction stories such as *Word for World* and "Vaster than Empires" is between the rational mind and the intuitive mind, the scientist and the artist. Not surprisingly, this is also the Romantic dialectical model; the solution is the Romantic one. In a test of understanding, the scientific-materialistic mode is pitted against the humanistic-intuitive mode.

This dialectic is evident in Coleridge's "Kubla Khan." The subterranean caverns of ice cannot be explained solely by the existence of the pleasure dome. Although the rational mind can assess the sunny surface with its formal gardens, it can't evaluate the powerful psychic depths of the caves of ice. The materialist sees a nova as a stellar process and measures it, but only the visionary can see the nova as a transcendent experience. In Delany's *Nova,* the materialist is overwhelmed by the experience, whereas the visionary artist absorbs the vision into his art and—more important—survives. The visionary absorbs the contrary visions of the pleasure dome and its hidden caves, as the damsel with the dulcimer creates art from the chaos of experience and thus combines the pleasure dome and the caverns.

The same problem is apparent in *Word for World.* On Athshe, humans can see only the vegetation. Their inadequate grasp of the planet is portrayed in two ways: through Dump Island and their misapprehension of the enslaved Athsheans' true nature. The Athsheans are seen as objects, not subjects, as demanded by Immanuel Kant's categorical imperative.[11]

Lyubov, the most highly aware of the humans, is the only human who understands the Athsheans organically. He begins his own attempt at Athshean dreaming by slipping into Romantic poetry, specifically Wordsworth's sonnet, "The World Is Too Much With Us." This sonnet is particularly appropriate, since it deals with the inadequacy of the rational vision of nature, ending with a plea for mythic vision as the required corrective.

The true nature of life eludes Lyubov, however. Only the Athsheans understand the truth, and they are a race who integrate dream visions into their everyday existence. The Athshean, Selver, is the first to bridge the two worlds, material and visionary. It is he who commands them, he who oversees the change in the material world. His role is reflected in Wordsworth's sonnet, which calls for visions of Proteus or Triton, gods of the sea and change. The Athsheans themselves consider Selver a "god," which, in the story, is defined as a "link: one who could speak aloud the perceptions of the unconscious. To 'speak' that tongue is to act. To do a new thing. To change or to be changed, radically, from the root. For the root is the dream. And the translator is the god" (*WW,* 5). Selver is the visionary whose new dream bridges the two worlds of dream unconsciousness and conscious rationalism. In him, the dream life of the Athsheans and the reality of the humans is combined; in him, both are synthesized into a new mode. He accepts murder and revolution, seeing both the good and the evil for the first time. He understands both the newfound *necessity* of massacring humans in order to save his world, and the old evil of *taking* human life, and balances them. He accepts the materialism of the invaders by adopting their tactics and weapons and fitting their new ways into his old ones.

Similarly, in "Vaster than Empires," Osden bridges the gap between the two worlds of experience, rational and irrational. As Ian Watson points out in his essay,[12] Osden, who exists in the "real" world, bridges the gap between that world and the irrational awareness of the the Other: "He had taken the fear into himself, and, accepting, had transcended it. He had given up his self to the alien, an unreserved surrender, that left no place for evil. He had learned the love of the Other, and thereby had been given his whole self. But this is not the vocabulary of reason." Osden has taken both motifs into himself, and in doing so, transforms and makes acceptable the fear of ignorance of the vegetable mind. This isn't done rationally, though; it is done by exciting the visionary in man, his inner feelings. The result is an absorption of evil as a reductive judgment into a universal blessing: "Listen. I will you well." Osden fulfills the Romantic requirement that for true comprehension, both the pleasure dome and the caves of ice must be recognized, both self and other, mundane and transcendent; such recognition is the province of the visionary, the artist, the translator of the language of dreams.

That both "Vaster than Empires" and *Word for World* can be resolved, from one perspective, into a conflict between the rational and the irrational is evidence, not of a thoroughgoing Romanticism on the part of Le Guin, but of the controlling power which the Romantic experience has had on science fiction. Living in the shadow of Newton and the rational, William Blake formulated a "doctrine of contraries" in active opposition to each other, the elements of which he called "reason" and "energy." Reason is the reductive, the analytic, whereas energy is the passionate, the feeling—everything proscribed by Newton's great calipers. In *Word for World* this conflict occurs between the closed military mind of the humans and the visionary reach of the Athsheans. As the story develops, the ideological conflict is resolved into two characters, Davidson and Selver, who represent repression-negation and experimentation-affirmation, respectively. When Blake wrote in *The Marriage of Heaven and Hell,* "The tygers of wrath are wiser than the horses of instruction," he could well have been comparing Selver and Lyubov[13]—something that could help explain Lyubov's death.

Both Selver and Davidson are gods; both exemplify a mode of being, not a position. If we accept Davidson's basic assumption that it is man's function to make the universe over in his image, we must view him as rigid and icily logical. While he is a violent god, a god of death, the implied opposition of Selver the healer and Davidson the killer fails, in light of Selver's also being a god of death. Selver is a god of revolutionary change, just as he is a god of death, just as he brings something new—the killing of men—to the Athsheans.

It would be a mistake to reduce the conflict to the issue of murder, however. Both Davidson and Selver, as a function of their personalities, kill; both dream of killing. But Selver views killing not as an end but as a means of survival. He is the revolutionary Orc, the god of change, of energy, of freedom, who creates a new mode of existence for the Athsheans. Davidson is Urizen, who never rises above killing for its own sake: the "constant vision." The conflict between new and old ways defines Selver's and Davidson's conflict.

Over and over, Selver refrains from killing Davidson, rejecting the desire for revenge that is a hallmark of Davidson's thinking. At the end of *Word for World* Selver and Davidson remain on Athshe, symbols of Blake's doctrine of contraries in necessary battle.

It is easy to choose sides in the fight between them. Upon analysis, though, the simplistic issues of good and evil break down. Selver isn't just a virtuous hero, he is an efficient, ruthless killer, too, while Davidson's courage, patriotism, and devotion to duty may be considered laudable. The Athsheans, who can comprehend a complex vision of man, accept both Davidson and Selver as necessary contraries in which Selver without Davidson is as unthinkable as Davidson is without Selver. They balance each other, and dynamic balance between contraries is the Romantic way, as well as the Athshean way.

In the contrast between the revolutionary Selver and the repressive Davidson lies a clear-cut rationale for political terrorism and reprisal. Yet in terms of *Word for World,* the conclusion of the battle of the gods may have been summed up by Blake in his credo to *Marriage of Heaven and Hell:* "Empire is no more! and now the lion and the wolf shall cease."[14] (Note that both beasts are wild predators.)

We can find other attributes of these gods, if we wish. Davidson represents a mechanistic society which operates according to laws gleaned from a supreme authority (another Blakean demon), even though the laws are old ones from an Earth light years away. Davidson is concerned with mechanical things—engines, power tools, and spacecraft—while Selver's Athsheans are natural people whose power is mental, psychic. They do not follow Selver, but rather, the new dream that he brings. In the "war" for Athshe, the Athsheans embody nature and not artifice.

All in all, the visionary dreamer is a vessel of growth, of further movement toward perfection. The natural cycle of contraries—life and death, rational and irrational, spring and fall—is the true way.

Word for World and "Vaster than Empires" incorporate a rhetoric in which nature metaphorically becomes a way of describing the mind. Bound to uniquely realized natural worlds, Le Guin's vegetable-world stories contain Romantic concepts of perceiving, knowing, and being that are organic, as opposed to the rationally artifical modes of a materialistic, object-oriented world. That these motifs are common in science fiction attests to the field's genesis in the Romantic movement.

Implied in Romantic rhetoric is a sense of unity among the disparate elements of life. The duality of subject and object is resolved through the metaphoric correspondence of mind-nature made concrete in science fiction. The two stories we have been discussing also follow this pattern.

The synthesis of language and experience in *Word for World* and "Vaster than Empires and More Slow" agrees with Romantic antecedents in resolving a rational-irrational dialectical argument through recourse to the visionary as bridge between the two realities. Selver and Osden assimilate the rational and the irrational in a whole vision of truth which is transferred to the rest of humanity.

They become the damsel with the dulcimer of "Kubla Khan," whose song is the visionary poem that encompasses the rational and irrational, the whole of truth. Ursula K. Le Guin's vegetable-world stories show her to be just such a visionary artist, to be both a receiver and a transmitter of the Romantic tradition.

4. Unbuilding Walls: Human Nature and the Nature of Evolutionary and Political Theory in *The Dispossessed*

PHILIP E. SMITH II

Things fall apart; the centre cannot hold;
Mere anarchy is loosed upon the world. . . .

W. B. Yeats, *The Second Coming*

"The principle of legal authority must be upheld, or we'll degenerate into mere anarchy!" thundered a fat, frowning man. Shevek said, "Yes, yes, degenerate! We have enjoyed it for one hundred and fifty years now."

Ursula K. Le Guin (*The Dispossessed,* VII)

APPALLED AND frightened by the Russian and Irish revolutionary upheavals of Europe after World War I, Yeats saw "mere anarchy" as destructive, violent, and perhaps degenerate. Fifty years later, Ursula K. Le Guin has written a novel containing a thoroughly different, more optimistic, and corrective view of anarchism as a social philosophy. In *The Dispossessed* she imagines a society based on the theories of her fictional revolutionary sage, Odo. As Le Guin explains: "Odonianism is anarchism. Not the bomb-in-the-pocket stuff, which is terrorism, whatever name it tries to dignify itself with; not the social-Darwinist economic 'libertarianism' of the far right; but anarchism, as prefigured in early Taoist thought, and expounded by Shelley and Kropotkin, Goldman and Goodman. Anarchism's principal target is the authoritarian State (capitalist or socialist); its principal moral-political theme is cooperation (solidarity, mutual aid). It is the most idealistic, and to me the most interesting, of all political theories" (*WTQ,* "Day").[1]

One of my purposes in this chapter is to show the influence of Prince Peter Alekseevich Kropotkin (1842-1921) on Le Guin. Despite the emphasis on this most important anarchist theorist, however, the other writers she mentions should not be overlooked, in case readers of Le Guin might wish to investigate their influence on her work. She has used Taoism mainly in works written before *The Dispossessed.*[2] The Taoist roots of anarchism are found especially in the writings of Chuang Tzu, a disciple of Lao Tzu. While Percy Bysshe Shelley understood anarchy as destructive disorder (see his poem "The Mask of Anarchy"), he believed in the creative and liberating force of the individual's imagination and espoused the principles of the perfectibility of human nature and institutions in poems and tracts such as *Queen Mab* and *The Declaration of Rights.* He opposed authoritarian government and while living in Nantgwillt, Sussex, tried to found an egalitarian commune. Emma Goldman, a Kropotkinian anarchist and Russian immigrant to the United States, was imprisoned and finally deported in 1919 because of her anarchist activities.[3] Paul Goodman, the novelist, poet, teacher, dramatist, literary and social critic, who is perhaps most widely known for *Growing Up Absurd* (1960), also wrote on anarchism in the tradition of Kropotkin, stressing the need to accommodate political systems and social environments to human nature.[4]

An optimistic view of human nature characterizes anarchist theory; basically it sees humans as capable of achieving the good socially and morally only if they arrange to live cooperatively, uncorrupted by the authority of government. Le Guin shares this view and incorporates it as an important factor in the structure of ideas, characterization, metaphor, and theme in *The Dispossessed.* She has discussed the relationship of human nature and anarchism in the novel during an interview with Jonathan Ward:

> *Ward:* It's a nice thing if you believe that people, once their basic needs are taken care of, will find all sorts of things to do.
>
> *Le Guin:* That's the act of faith you have to make. If people have what they really need, then they won't be quite as driven and as grabby. That's the act of faith that all leftists make: that human nature has capacity for being relatively good.
>
> *Ward:* You make that leap of faith for the purposes of this novel [*The Dispossessed*]?
>
> *Le Guin:* Yes. And I do make it; I can't help but make it. I'm obviously a true believer in the sense that give us a chance and we won't be quite as bad as we are.[5]

Le Guin does not sentimentalize or trivialize human nature by choosing this optimistic view. Rather, in *The Dispossessed* she tempers her optimism by clearly showing that in human nature the will to mutual aid is a force co-equal with the will to dominance. One of the central ambiguities of this "ambiguous utopia" is that on the planet Urras there are several political systems based on authoritarianism and the will to dominance, while on the planet Anarres there is no central government—only an anti-authoritarian anarchy, tending somewhat toward bureaucracy but soundly based on the will to mutual aid. The political systems on each planet correspond to the cultural acceptance of one of these two aspects of human nature. Le Guin's thesis is that the anarchism on Anarres, despite its imperfections, represents the best hope for human political, moral, and evolutionary progress.

The idea of linking human nature, evolutionary theory, politics, and ultimately ethics in an anarchistic system comes from the thought of Kropotkin. In several places Le Guin has stated her reliance on Kropotkin's anarchistic ideas. She has explicitly drawn attention to his book on evolutionary and social theory, *Mutual Aid: A Factor of Evolution* (1902; rev. ed., 1914), as a formative influence on *The Dispossessed.* In an interview published in 1974, Le Guin responded to the questions about anarchist theory in her novel:

> I called it "an ambiguous utopia." I think it's a perfectly natural step to go from Taoism to anarchism. That's what I found myself doing. They are definitely related, they appeal to the same type of person, the same bent of mind.
>
> . . . . .
>
> Kropotkin is sort of the central anarchist thinker, the greatest philosopher of anarchism. . . . *Mutual Aid* . . . was written deliberately as an antidote to social Darwinism, which was absolutely top dog in 1910. He says that cooperation is *at least* as important as aggression, and perhaps is the more basic survival mechanism. From that, of course, you can deduce the anarchism, social anarchism. It's a very interesting book, I recommend *Mutual Aid.*
>
> . . . . .
>
> This is what I mean. I want to go on like Kropotkin, and inject a gentle antidote to all this kind of crap [modern social Darwinism as portrayed in the film *2001* and in the works of Robert Ardrey] for this generation.[6]

Le Guin's wish to imitate Kropotkin manifests itself in *The Dispossessed.* This chapter offers a twofold approach to the novel and its ideas. First, it shows the considerable extent of Le Guin's use of Kropotkin's anarchist theories, and second, it traces through the novel the extended metaphor of the wall, which is drawn from Kropotkin and which is linked to the development of both Shevek's character and the novel's theme.

There is space here for only the briefest summary of Kropotkin's life and works.[7] Born in 1842 into an aristocractic family descended from medieval princes, Kropotkin was educated in the Corps of Pages, a military school for the elite, where he repeatedly stood first in his class, an honor which made him, during his final year, personal page to Tsar Alexander II. Immersion in the life of the court convinced Kropotkin that he must escape from it at all costs, and he therefore took a military post in Siberia. His four years (1862-66) on the Russian frontier brought much of the rest of his life into focus. There he first learned about the Russian anarchist, Michael Bakunin, about the perfidy of governments and the inhumanity of the prison system. There he did the field research that resulted in his being recognized as a first-rate geographer, geologist, and naturalist. In his introduction to *Mutual Aid,* Kropotkin described the observations of animal life which were the foundations of the book:

> Two aspects of animal life impressed me most during the journeys which I made in my youth in Eastern Siberia and Northern Manchuria. One of them was the extreme severity of the struggle for existence which most species of animals have to carry on against an inclement Nature; the enormous destruction of life which periodically results from natural agencies; and the consequent paucity of life over the vast territory which fell under my observation. And the other was, that even in those few spots where animal life teemed in abundance, I failed to find—although I was eagerly looking for it—that bitter struggle for the means of existence, *among animals belonging to the same species,* which was considered by most Darwinists (though not always by Darwin himself) as the dominant characteristic of struggle for life, and the main factor of evolution.[8]

Returning to St. Petersburg, Kropotkin continued his scientific work. He journeyed to Finland, visited anarchists in Switzerland, and became active in radical politics. Arrested for revolutionary agitation and imprisoned in 1874, he escaped in 1876 to Western Europe where he lived in exile. Kropotkin was imprisoned again for two years in France. After the Russian revolution, he returned to his homeland where he died in 1921. From the late 1880s until the revolution, Kropotkin lived mostly in England, developing and publishing his theories about anarchism and science. The essays which later became *Mutual Aid* first appeared as a response to T. H. Huxley's social Darwinistic tract, "The Struggle for Existence: A Programme," published in *The Nineteenth Century* in February 1888.[9]

In *Mutual Aid* Kropotkin responded to the ruthless Hobbesian interpretation of Darwinism which Huxley preached. According to Huxley, in the human as in the animal world, "the weakest and stupidest went to the wall, while the toughest and shrewdest, those who were best fitted to cope with their circumstances, but not the best in another way, survived. Life was a continuous free fight, and beyond the limited and temporary relations of the family, the Hobbesian war of each against all was the normal state of existence" (quoted in *Mutual Aid,* 29). In opposition, Kropotkin argued from his studies of animals, anthropology, and history that sociability, mutual aid, and mutual defense were just as important, if not more important, than struggle to achieve human survival and progressive evolution. He contended that sociability provided the greater evolutionary advantage because it favored the development of intelligence and a sense of justice (*Mutual Aid,* 69). Further, he concluded that human cooperation and free association have, since the beginning of the species, instilled in all people an instinct toward solidarity which is the foundation of ethics: "In the practice of mutual aid, which we can retrace to the earliest beginnings of evolution, we thus find the positive and undoubted origin of our ethical conceptions; and we can affirm that in the ethical progress of man, mutual support—not mutual struggle—has had the leading part. In its wide extension, even at the present time, we also see the best guarantee of a still loftier evolution of our race" (*Mutual Aid,* 251). Kropotkin elaborated the idea of ethics based on instincts for the preservation of self and species in his treatise, *Ethics, Origin and Development:*

> *Mutual Aid—Justice—Morality* are thus the consecutive steps of an ascending series, revealed to us by the study of the animal world and man. They constitute an *organic necessity* which carries in itself its own justification, confirmed by the whole of the evolution of the animal kingdom, beginning with its earliest stages (in the form of colonies of the most primitive organisms), and gradually rising to our civilized human communities. Figuratively speaking, it is a *universal law of organic evolution,* and this is why the sense of Mutual Aid, Justice, and Morality

> are rooted in man's mind with all the force of an inborn instinct—the first instinct, that of Mutual Aid, being evidently the strongest, while the third, developed later than the others, is an unstable feeling and the least imperative of the three.[10]

With Kropotkin's evolutionary and ethical theories in mind, his antiauthoritarian, anarchistic, sociopolitical system can be understood as an analogical development founded on those first principles. Further, the similarity of Le Guin's Odonianism to his anarchism may also be appreciated. Both Kropotkin and Le Guin base their communal, cooperative systems on the analogy of a unified natural organism. Kropotkin's *Mutual Aid* may be viewed as a lengthy statement of the analogy: just as mutual aid operates throughout nature, so it has operated and ought to be free to operate in human social and political life. The titles of Odo's books, the *Analogy* and *The Social Organism,* indicate how Le Guin has transferred Kropotkin's basic notion into her fictional anarchist system. She also makes frequent and consistent references to Kropotkin's ideas, for example, stating that her protagonist, Shevek, has been "brought up in a culture that relied deliberately and constantly on human solidarity, mutual aid" (*TD,* VII). Shevek becomes angry when he realizes that his relationship with the Anarresti physicist Sabul is "not a relationship of mutual aid and solidarity, but an exploitative relationship; not organic, but mechanical" (*TD,* IV). In his address to the strikers in Nio Esseia, Shevek describes Anarresti society as follows: "We have no law but the single principle of mutual aid between individuals. We have no government but the single principle of free association" (*TD,* IX).

Just as Kropotkin set out to refute Huxley's social Darwinism, Le Guin has her characters debate the difference between the social Darwinistic ideas of the Urrasti and Shevek's Anarresti anarchism. For example, while Shevek respects Atro's achievements in physics, he finds repellent the older man's aristocratic militarism and ethic of struggle: "The law of existence is struggle—competition—elimination of the weak—a ruthless war for survival. And I want to see the best survive" (*TD,* V). Shevek's clearest rejection of this kind of thinking comes when he argues for the Kropotkinian-Odonian theory of evolution, sociability, and ethics against Vea Oiie, who contends:

> "Life is a fight, and the strongest wins. All civilization does is hide the blood and cover up the hate with pretty words!"

"Your civilization, perhaps. Ours hides nothing. It is all plain. . . . We follow one law, only one, the law of human evolution."

"The law of evolution is that the strongest survives!"

"Yes, and the strongest, in the existence of any social species, are those who are most social. In human terms, most ethical. You see, we have neither prey nor enemy, on Anarres. We have only one another. There is no strength to be gained from hurting one another. Only weakness." (*TD,* VII).

Shevek opposes not only the oligarchic and capitalistic version of social Darwinism which is basic to the political system of A-Io (an analog of U.S. and West European democracies), but also the authoritarian state socialist interpretation found in Thu (an analog of Marxist states such as the Soviet Union and China, which is articulated by the physicist Chifoilisk. To the Thuvian scientist, the idea of an anarchist society built on mutual aid contradicts the familiar social Darwinistic idea of a ruthless struggle for existence: " 'No need to pretend that all you Odonian brothers are full of brotherly love,' he said. 'Human nature is human nature' " (*TD,* III). The Thuvian state is more authoritarian, more centralized, and more repressive of freedom than A-Io; knowing this, Shevek has chosen to visit A-Io rather than Thu. He tells Chifoilisk: "You fear we might bring back the revolution, the old one, the real one, the revolution for justice which you began and then stopped halfway" (*TD,* V). Shevek's rejection of Thuvian state socialism recalls the disputes between authoritarian Marxists and libertarian anarchists (including Kropotkin) that split the international socialist movement in the late nineteenth century, as well as making it clear that Le Guin agrees with Kropotkin in her opinion of state socialism.[11]

Not only has Le Guin relied on Kropotkin for the evolutionary, social, and ethical theory of anarchism in *The Dispossessed,* she has also adopted many of his ideas about the practical problems of organizing an anarchist civilization. Kropotkin's definition of anarchism, originally written for the eleventh edition of the *Encyclopaedia Britannica,* suggests his sensitivity to the totality of human endeavor his system would encompass:

> ANARCHISM (from the Gr. ἀν, and ἀρχη, contrary to authority), is the name given to a principle or theory of life and conduct under which society is conceived without government—harmony in such a society being obtained, not by submission to law, or by obedience to any authority, but by free agreements concluded between the various groups, territorial and professional, freely constituted for the sake of production and

> consumption, as also for the satisfaction of the infinite variety of needs and aspirations of a civilized being.[12]

This definition and the explanatory passages which follow serve equally well as a description of the social system on Anarres. Shevek's address to the strikers (*TD,* IX) recalls Kropotkin's principle of free association, and the several pages of narrative recounting the history and structure of Anarresti society (*TD,* IV) offer many parallels to the society which Kropotkin outlined:

> In a society developed on these lines, the voluntary associations . . . would represent an interwoven network, composed of an infinite variety of groups and federations of all sizes and degrees, local, regional, national and international—temporary or more or less permanent—for all possible purposes: production, consumption and exchange, communications, sanitary arrangements, education, mutual protection, defense of the territory, and so on; and, on the other side, for the satisfaction of an ever-increasing number of scientific, artistic, literary and sociable needs. (*Revolutionary Pamphlets,* 284).

Kropotkin's breadth of knowledge and interest was vast, and he considered in great detail and in several publications (such as in his books, *The Conquest of Bread* and *Fields, Factories and Workshops)* how an anarchist society might provide for the necessities of food, clothing, and shelter, as well as for the functions of artisans, craftsmen, and professionals, the roles of education, agriculture, manufacturing, and transportation.

As a corollary to this proposal for the means of organization, both Kropotkin and Le Guin agree that their societies must never become static, that according to the analogy of a natural organism, they must preserve a dynamic of continual social change. Kropotkin says that "such a society would represent nothing immutable. On the contrary—as it is seen in organic life at large—harmony would (it is contended) result from an ever-changing adjustment and readjustment of equilibrium between the multitudes of forces and influences..." (*Revolutionary Pamphlets,* 284; see also, 157). Similarly, Le Guin has Shevek realize, after hearing Bedap's criticisms, that "he could not rebel against his society, because his society, properly conceived, was a revolution, an ongoing process" (*TD,* VI). This idea is located in its Odonian source when the delegate from a Southwest miners' syndicate quotes from Odo's *Prison Letters:* "Revolution is our obligation: our hope of evolution. 'The Revolution is in the individual spirit, or it is nowhere. It is for all, or it is nothing. If it is seen as having any end, it will never truly begin' " (*TD,* XII).

Le Guin has modified Kropotkin's plan for an anarchist society in one important respect. Kropotkin wanted to undo the economic and social stratification caused by the division of labor into specialized activities. Therefore, he advocated the decentralization of industries and the integration of labor, in order to achieve "a society where each individual is a producer of both manual and intellectual work."[13] In *The Dispossessed,* Le Guin imagines a similar theory: "Decentralization had been an essential element in Odo's plans for the society she did not live to see founded. . . . There was to be no controlling center, no capital, no establishment for the self-perpetuating machinery of bureaucracy and the dominance drive of individuals seeking to become captains, bosses, chiefs of state" (*TD,* IV). But, as Le Guin narrates, the anarchist Settlers of Anarres had to adapt to the harsh conditions of their planet, and they refused to sacrifice their diversified culture and technology by regressing into a "pre-urban, pre-technological tribalism" (*TD,* IV). Therefore, reasoning analogically from "the ideal of a complex organicism," they concluded that "you can't have a nervous system without at least a ganglion, and preferably a brain. There had to be a center" (*TD,* IV). They located in the community of Abbenay (which was the word for *mind)* the "computers that coordinated the administration of things, the division of labor, and the distribution of goods, and the central federatives of most of the work syndicates. . . . And from the start the Settlers were aware that the unavoidable was a lasting threat, to be countered by lasting vigilance" (*TD,* IV).

The reality of this threat, nearly two centuries after the founding of the Odonian society on Anarres, provides the social and economic basis for a central concern of the novel: the struggle of Shevek and his colleagues in the Syndicate of Initiative to combat the power of the centralized bureaucracy which has come to dominate life on Anarres, not only because of custom and its efficiency but also because of the society's need for coordination and central direction in order to survive during the four-year drought called the Dust. The institutionalization of mutual aid has come to threaten the initiative and inventiveness of Shevek and others who find their freedom and creativity stifled or compromised by their own supposedly libertarian anarchist society.

Here Le Guin goes beyond her indebtedness to Kropotkin in imagining the individual, social, and environmental tension that could provoke either stratification and decay or discontent and fragmentation in an anarchist society. Here also is the ideological and practical conflict at the center of her ambiguous utopia—it is the sickness of society and self which Shevek, as true culture hero, strives to diagnose and heal. His physical, mental, and moral journey and return constitute the central action of the novel, as well as embodying and endorsing the Kropotkin principle of anarchist individual/social symbiosis, that free individuals can exist in a truly free society only by a constant dynamic process of testing, adapting, and changing, which will contribute to the preservation and evolution of individual freedom and societal health.

Several critics have called attention to Shevek's role as quester, culture hero, critic, and healer of his society. They have related his journey and his General Temporal Theory to the narrative structure and to the themes of ambiguity, communication, de-alienation, and spiritual evolution in *The Dispossessed.*[14] Although one critic has noticed that, in imagining Anarresti society, "Le Guin takes things to their roots in human nature itself," he has not followed her idea of human nature back to its sources in the theory of anarchism.[15] In creating the worlds of *The Dispossessed,* Le Guin has accepted and adapted Kropotkin's idea of human nature, which Paul Goodman has described as "mutual-aiding, knightly, and craftsmanlike."[16] She also sees that this idea must be combined with another, that of human nature as being aggressive and authoritarian. Kropotkin did not deny the existence of this aspect of human or animal nature. Because he believed, as Le Guin does, that the will to mutual aid is a more important factor in evolution, he proposed that societies be organized so as to encourage mutual aid rather than dominance.

Although Le Guin's Odonian philosophy has the same goal, the Anarresti have forgotten the dichotomy in human nature. Their organization and culture lead them to emphasize and inculcate mutual aid to such a degree that they fail to guard against the possibilities of social subversion arising out of the natural will to dominance. As Bedap explains to Shevek, solidarity and cooperation have become obedience to the authority of an institutionalized, bureaucratized social conscience that encourages stability rather than change: "But that stability gives scope to the authoritarian impulse. In the early years of the Settlement we were aware of that, on the lookout for it. People discriminated very carefully then between administering things and governing people. They did it so well that we forgot that the will to dominance is as central in human beings as the impulse to mutual aid is, and has to be trained in each individual, in each new generation. Nobody's born an Odonian any more than he's born civilized'' (*TD,* VI).

If eternal vigilance is the price of liberty, Wendell Phillips' aphorism would have new meaning on Anarres. There it would signify that anarchist culture must never lose sight of the instinctive and dangerous drive towards authoritarianism that exists in human nature. Le Guin and Kropotkin do not envision a simplistic utopian society which, returned to a state of nature, would simply allow biology to determine a ''natural'' mode of behavior; rather, the strength and hope of Odonian and Kropotkinian anarchism lie in its elevation of a rational, ethical, and dynamic culture to a position of prime importance. To cleanse and heal his society, Shevek must awaken it to its cultural responsibility, cause it to acknowledge and reject the stultifying authority of stability and government and, instead, affirm a truly evolutionary anarchism.

Skeptical of Bedap's criticism, Shevek must face his own personal trials before he can achieve the knowledge and ability to work for the salvation and renewal of Anarresti society. This task can be accomplished only after Shevek has broken out of the prison walls of his own cultural conditioning. If, in ''The Struggle for Existence,'' T. H. Huxley believed that ''the weakest and stupidest went to the wall'' (quoted in *Mutual Aid,* 29), Kropotkin preferred to think that anarchist society would ''overthrow walls and frontiers.''[17] Perhaps finding her inspiration in these sources, Le Guin has woven the imagery and metaphor of walls throughout *The Dispossessed* to suggest the personal and social barriers Shevek and the Anarresti must overcome.[18]

The Dispossessed begins and ends with Shevek's confronting the wall around the spaceport on Anarres, the only boundary wall on the entire planet. Shevek's decision to cross it, to journey outward to Urras, as well as his decision to bring a Hainishman, Ketho, back to Anarres, are the actions which frame the narrative. This particular wall of rocks and mortar ''did not look important. . . . But the idea was real. It was important. For seven generations there had been nothing in the world more important than that wall. Like all walls it was ambiguous, two-faced. What was inside it and what was outside it depended upon which side of it you were on'' (*TD,* I). The structure of the novel compels the reader to look on both sides of the wall, to experience the ambiguity chapter by chapter as the setting changes from Anarres to Urras and back. Similarly, the organization of time in the novel is ambiguous. Beginning truly in medias res, the reader follows two narrative lines, one on Anarres in the even-numbered chapters, and one on Urras in the odd-numbered chapters. Chapters 1 and 13 describe the journey from Anarres to Urras, and the return. In its narrative framework, the structure of the novel unites the same elements of time that Shevek includes in his General Temporal Theory, which allows the reader to experience the simultaneity and sequency of two time schemes. This arrangement of time and setting enhances the ambiguity (in the sense of having two or more possible meanings) of the central action, Shevek's journey and return.

The rich ambiguities suggested by the wall imagery in the novel add complexity and depth to the central action. Walls appear literally or figuratively in every chapter; they are associated with Shevek's experience in his everyday environment and in his thoughts, both waking and dreaming, during childhood and adulthood. A reading of the novel following the temporal sequence of Shevek's life (that is, first reading the even-numbered chapters and then the odd-numbered chapters) offers an approach to understanding the several ways in which wall imagery enriches the characterization of Shevek and the structure of ideas in *The Dispossessed.*

In Chapter 2 are three important instances of wall imagery. Le Guin introduces Shevek as a baby gazing at the sun through "a square window in a white wall" (*TD,* II). Even at two years of age his fascination with looking beyond the walls that surround him prefigures his attempts to see a way through to solving the individual, social, and scientific problems he will face later in life. Shevek's fascination with the sun also foreshadows future scenes in which he seeks solace or inspiration by gazing at the "moon" (either Anarres or Urras, depending on his location). Similarly, Shevek's first dream, at age eight, about a wall which blocks his way ("He had to go on or he could never come home again," *TD,* II), is the precursor of other such dreams in which walls prevent his progress. The solution he dreams here, of finding a primal number which embodies unity and plurality, suggests how he will discover the solution to his General Temporal Theory in an almost mystical vision (*TD,* IX). Finally, the idea of walls as prisons is introduced in this chapter when Shevek, age twelve, and his friends, having read of Odo's imprisonment in the fort at Drio (perhaps inspired by Kropotkin's imprisonment in Russia and France and by Goldman's imprisonment in the United States), construct their own prison and confine one of their number. As a result of this game, Shevek becomes physically ill and vomits. This sickness of body and spirit occurs at other key points, when Shevek is confronted with the inhumanity and brutality associated with physical or mental prisons and walls. For example, when he visits the palace museum in Nio Esseia with Vea and sees the cloak made of human skins worn by Queen Teaea, he becomes nauseous and asks to leave: "Once outside in the garden his face became less white, but he looked back at the palace walls with hatred. 'Why do you people cling to your shame?' he said" (*TD,* VII).

In Chapter 4 Le Guin has Shevek notice both the "great walled field" of the spaceport (*TD,* IV) and the "unwalled workyards," which reveal all the vitality and activity of the city (*TD,* IV). These scenes suggest how the Anarresti, in walling out Urras, have created that civilization of manual work combined with brain work which Kropotkin imagined would need no walls to separate workers from one another. When Shevek undertakes his own solitary work on the theory of simultaneity, however, he feels mentally imprisoned in a locked room until a dream brings him the mathematical formula he requires, and leaves him, forebodingly, with the vision of space shrinking "in upon him like the walls of a collapsing sphere..." (*TD,* IV). The isolation and emptiness Shevek finds in his own work, together with his naiveté about the drive for dominance in others, leave him vulnerable to the manipulation of Sabul; he acquiesces in Sabul's power, allows himself to be exploited, and afterward, in reaction, becomes ill and must be hospitalized. When he is reunited with his mother, who has come to nurse him, Shevek finds that she also has accepted as a normal part of life the "dominance games" played by men like Sabul (*TD,* IV). Rejecting his mother, he also rejects a part of himself and is left at the end of the chapter crying, feeling himself "in the dark at the foot of the wall" (*TD,* IV).

In chapters 6 and 8 Le Guin builds on the foundations of her wall metaphor by bringing Shevek up against the mental and physical barriers of his work and environment and by causing him to acknowledge Bedap's criticism of Anarresti society. Despite Shevek's attempts to overcome his personal isolation by engaging in a more active social life, he feels almost suicidal, because, after three years in Abbenay, "he had come up against the wall for good" (*TD,* VI). Bedap confirms the diagnosis but insists that Shevek understand its causes: "In your case, the wall seems to be Sabul, and his supporters in the science syndicates and the PDC" (*TD,* IV). Bedap wants Shevek to see that he has introjected the sickness of his own society: "Change is freedom, change is life—is anything more basic to Odonian thought than that? But nothing changes any more! Our society is sick. You know it. You're suffering its sickness. Its suicidal sickness!" (*TD,* VI). Despite Bedap's example of how Tirin's literary creativity had been stifled and turned into insanity because the cultural criticism in his play was misunderstood and rejected, Shevek persists in blaming the rigorous planetary environment, and not Anarresti society, for frustrating individual creativity.

Two important changes in Shevek's life begin to draw him away from this point of view. In an affair with Bedap, he overcomes some of his isolation and loneliness; but more significant is the lasting bond of love in partnership with Takver. During this process of personal expansion, Shevek finds "that the walls of his hard puritanical conscience were widening out immensely. . ." (*TD,* VI). The second change involves Shevek directly with the environment and its effect on society and personal relationships. Separated from Takver and their child, Sadik, for four years, Shevek has ample opportunity to observe the functioning of mutual aid and solidarity under the terrible stresses of a worldwide drought. One aspect of the social response to suffering fills him with hope: he sees evidence of joy in spite of the communal sharing of hardship, increased work, and reduced means.

Here, Le Guin's Odonian anarchy reflects the ideal of joy in doing necessary work that Kropotkin imagined:

> Have the factory and the workshop at the gates of your fields and gardens and work in them. . . . factories and workshops into which men, women and children will not be driven by hunger, but will be attracted by the desire of finding an activity suited to their tastes, and where, aided by the motor and the machine, they will choose the branch of activity which best suits their inclinations.
>
> . . . . .
>
> (Technics and science) surely cannot guarantee happiness, because happiness depends as much, or even more, upon the individual himself as upon his surroundings. But they can guarantee, at least, the happiness that can be found in the full and varied exercise of the different capacities of the human being, in work that need not be overwork, and in the consciousness that one is not is not endeavouring to base his own happiness upon the misery of others.[19]

Similarly, Odo writes: "A child free from the guilt of ownership and the burden of economic competition will grow up with the will to do what needs doing and the capacity for joy in doing it. It is useless work that darkens the heart. The delight of the nursing mother, of the scholar, of the successful hunter, of the good cook, of the skillful maker, of anyone doing needed work and doing it well—this durable joy is perhaps the deepest source of human affection and sociality as a whole" (*TD,* VIII).

Both Kropotkin and Odo, however, wrote without taking into account the hostile environment of a planet such as Anarres. In his experience with drought and famine, Shevek learns early that the harsh necessities of survival create a severe test for the principles of anarchism, as when, in a food shortage, instead of sharing with workers stranded on a stalled train, the inhabitants of a nearby village "hid behind 'their' walls with 'their' property..." (*TD,* VIII). Angry and disappointed after returning to Abbenay from his post at Red Springs to find Takver transferred and his job at the Institute canceled, Shevek feels a storm inside himself which "had come up against the wall" (*TD,* VIII). Finally, in confronting the hypocrisy of Desar and Sabul, in recognizing and rejecting their dominance games, Shevek implicitly accepts Bedap's analysis of society: "The devious ways of possessiveness, the labyrinths of love/hate, were meaningless to him. Arrogant, intolerant, he walked right through their walls" (*TD,* VIII). This impulsive act, plus Shevek's final choice in the chapter, the acceptance of a famine-prevention post in the worst area of the Dust, indicate the beginnings of his new understanding of what he must do to retain his own integrity while walking through social and personal walls. However, Shevek acknowledges that the first priority is survival of the society. Only when that is assured can he begin to work for change.

Chapter 10, in which Shevek and Takver are reunited after four years' separation, describes the calm following the crisis, the reaffirmation of love and trust, the reasoning out and acceptance of social criticism, as well as a plan for "unbuilding" the walls of Anarresti society. Bedap's story of Tirin and his play has persuaded Shevek, because he meets Tirin during the Dust and realizes that the increased bureaucratic control of Anarresti society and the institutionalization of the social conscience have made Tirin a criminal:

> "We have created crime, just as the propertarians did. We force a man outside the sphere of our approval, and then condemn him for it. We've made laws, laws of conventional behavior, built walls all around ourselves, and we can't see them, because they're part of our thinking. Tir never did that. I knew him since we were ten years old. He never did it, he never could build walls. He was a natural rebel. He was a natural Odonian—a real

one! He was a free man, and the rest of us, his brothers, drove him insane in punishment for his first free act (*TD,* X).

Shevek resolves that he will never again respond to "our own, internalized Sabul—convention, moralism, fear of social ostracism, fear of being different, fear of being free!" (*TD,* X). Instead, he and Takver plan to return to Abbenay where they work with Bedap and others in resisting these wall-building tendencies in Anarresti society: "Those who build walls are their own prisoners. I'm going to go fulfill my proper function in the social organism. I'm going to unbuild walls" (*TD,* X). The chapter concludes with Shevek's meditation on the place of the creative individual in a free society and on the personal fulfillment that comes with accepting both one's own creative will and one's engagement with society. Having "come home" mentally and physically, Shevek has found the metaphorical opposite of wall-building: the landscape of free creation. "Outside the locked room is the landscape of time, in which the spirit may, with luck and courage, construct the fragile, makeshift, improbable roads and cities of fidelity: a landscape inhabitable by human beings" (*TD,* X). For a moment here, Shevek realizes the promise inscribed on Odo's tombstone: "To be whole is to be part;/true voyage is return" (*TD,* III).

The constructive convictions with which Chapter 10 ends have, by Chapter 12, been applied for five years by the Syndicate of Initiative, but with a mixture of success and disappointment. As much as Takver believes that—because the full text of Shevek's *Principles* has been printed, "the walls are down" (*TD,* XII), and the Syndicate has won—Bedap's judgment about social resistance to their ideas is more realistic: "There are walls behind the walls" (*TD,* XII). Thus, at the conclusion of the chapter and the half of the novel that is set on Anarres, Shevek must admit: "Here I'm walled in" (*TD,* XII). Although he is still reluctant to leave home and family, Shevek must recognize (as Takver urges and Chapter 1 relates) that the demands of personal creativity and social responsibility force him to journey outward, to "unbuild walls" (*TD,* I) on another planet.

In chapters 1, 3, and 5, Shevek finds ample proof of the function of walls in Urrasti society—from the technological surprises hidden in the walls of his cabin in the spaceship *Mindful* to the walling off of free thought in Dr. Kimoe (*TD,* I). At the university Shevek encounters a more sinister wall in the studied "charm, courtesy, indifference" of the Ioti physicist and secret police spy, Saio Pae

(*TD,* III). Noting the contrast to the openness of life on Anarres, Shevek despises the way in which the factories and people who make consumer goods are hidden "behind walls" (*TD,* V) because of the dominance of possessions and the money system over Urrasti social and economic life. But despite the temptations of the opulence and the comforts of existence in A-Io, Shevek remains true to his goal: "I want the walls down. I want solidarity, human solidarity. I want free exchange between Urras and Anarres" (*TD,* V).

In the same way that Shevek had become lonely and isolated as a young man while at the Institute in Abbenay, in Chapter 7 on Urras he discovers another kind of isolation. Chifoilisk, the Thuvian physicist, has rightly warned him: "He had let a wall be built around him and had never noticed" (*TD,* VII). That is, he accepts without question the view of A-Io presented by his hosts; he has made no effort to contact poor people or anarchist sympathizers. On a trip to Nio Esseia alone, however, his yearning for friendly human contact overcomes him, and he spends a day with Vea Oiie, the fascinating sister of a colleague at the university. In her company he visits the palace museum and is sickened by Queen Teaea's human-skin cloak. But he remains with Vea to attend a cocktail party she has planned for the evening. There, intoxicated by alcoholic beverages and Vea's sexuality, Shevek effusively explains his society and theory of time; finally, in an impassioned peroration comparing Anarres and A-Io, he condemns propertarian values: "Here you see the jewels, there you see the eyes. And in the eyes you see the splendor, the splendor of the human spirit. Because our men and women are free—possessing nothing, they are free. And you the possessors are possessed. You are all in jail. Each alone, solitary, with a heap of what he owns. You live in prison, die in prison. It is all I can see in your eyes—the wall, the wall!" (*TD,* VII).

Shevek himself is also possessed—most immediately by intoxication and lust but more profoundly by loneliness, frustration, and alienation. When Vea leads him away to the bedroom to calm him, he attempts to copulate with her. Rebuffed, he ejaculates on her dress and then returns to the party where he vomits on a plate of hors d'oeuvres. The nausea caused by immersion in a fundamentally dominative and often inhumane social system finally erupts in a physical sickness similar to the illness Shevek suffered as a child when he played at being a jailer. In both cases the confrontation with walls, and his collaboration with them, have caused his very human nature to revolt.

In Chapter 9, the aftermath of sickness brings shame and new resolution on the part of Shevek to break through the intellectual walls that have kept him from completing his General Temporal Theory. He determines to escape from the prison of the university and make contact with the underground revolutionary movement in Nio Esseia. To accomplish this, however, he needs help—first, from the relativity theory of the Terran physicist Ainsetain [Einstein], and second, from his valet, Efor. Despite his opinion that Terran physicists are "intellectual imperialists, jealous wall builders" (*TD,* XI), Shevek finds sufficient inspiration in the intellectual method of Ainsetain's relativity theory to allow him to complete his own work. "He saw all that was to come in this first seemingly casual glimpse of the method, given him by his understanding of a failure in the distant past. The wall was down. . . . It was revelation. It was the way clear, the way home, the light" (*TD*, IX). Theoretical fulfillment brings also a sense of the individual and social fulfillment inherent in a holistic view of time and the universe. Analogically, Shevek sees the rightness of his life, his work, and his society: "at this instant the difference between this planet and that one, between Urras and Anarres, was no more significant to him than the difference between two grains of sand on the shore of the sea. There were no more abysses, no more walls. There was no more exile. He had seen the foundations of the universe, and they were solid" (*TD,* IX).

With the help of Efor, Shevek can now walk through the walls of his "jail" (*TD,* IX), the University of A-Io, and help the Socialist Workers Union with his pamphleteering and his address to the rally on the day of the general strike in Nio Esseia. The power of his speech is such that, as he finds in Chapter 11, it has moved the Terran ambassador, Keng, to have respect for the Odonian system on Anarres. In conversation with Keng, Shevek comes to a new realization about his experience on Urras. Finally and fully, he understands the promise Anarres offers to the people of the universe. If he had once thought that "it would be better not to hold apart behind a wall, but to be a society among the others, a world among the others, giving and taking" (*TD,* XI), he now sees that he was wrong. The promise and significance of Anarres as a vision of the future for all humanity is clear: "My people were right, and I was wrong, in this: We cannot come to you. You will not let us. You do not believe in change, in chance, in evolution. You would destroy us rather than admit our reality, rather than admit that there is hope! We cannot come to you. We can only wait for you to come to us" (*TD,* XI). Shevek's testimony to this belief is his determination to broadcast his General Temporal Theory, to prevent its exclusive use by any one nation or world, and to make possible instantaneous interstellar communication by means of its application with the ansible.

While this gift and Shevek's return to Anarres in Chapter 13 constitute the conclusive action of the novel, they do not signify an end to the evolutionary process of social development. Le Guin carefully refrains from the pat conclusion of a happy welcome to Abbenay and the reunification of Takver and Shevek. Instead, she insists on the need for constantly testing and changing Anarres' anarchism. Shevek has another wall to walk through, the stone wall around the spaceport at Abbenay; he agrees to do this in the company of Ketho, the Hainish first mate of the *Davenant.* Ketho, who will be the first non-Anarresti to enter Odonian society, plans to do so, not as a settler but as one who has expressed the wish to return to his own world, perhaps as the prophet of Odonian ideas. Even though the Hainish have tried anarchism in the past, the promise of its success is not negated. If Shevek's theory of time and the Odonian ideas of human nature and social evolution are correct, there is always room in Le Guin's Hainish universe (and perhaps in our own) for progress, change, and a truly free society.

By giving imaginative realization to Kropotkin's evolutionary, social, and ethical theory of anarchism in *The Dispossessed,* Le Guin achieves her goal of providing an antidote to social Darwinism. Odonianism, which stresses the analogy of society to a natural organism and depends on impulses to mutual aid and solidarity in human nature, provides a free and humane alternative to the capitalistic or socialistic states based on the impulse to dominance. Nor does Le Guin overlook the practical problems of the Odonian system on Anarres. Here, serious problems have been created by the modification of Kropotkin's and Odo's ideas of decentralization to allow centralized computer-facilitated coordination, together with the unthinking inculcation of Odonian maxims and the gradual effects of customary behavior. Especially for creative and uncompromising libertarians like Tirin, Bedap, and Shevek, the growing stultification of Anarresti society takes on the metaphorical aspect of encircling walls which prevent free thought and action.

Shevek learns that he must recognize and accept, as related aspects of life, his own personal creativity and responsibility for social action. Only when he has done so can he walk through or unbuild walls that hinder his temporal theory or his relationship with others. At the novel's conclusion, having given away his theory and invited a Hainishman to return to Anarres with him, Shevek acts with the assurance and integrity of one who understands ethically his role as physicist and anarchist.[20] His unbuilding of walls implies that Anarresti culture can be liberated, to allow the creativity of freely adapting individuals to flourish. His action also suggests that this culture can develop by encouraging impulses to mutual aid and solidarity while discouraging the tendency toward centralized authority or bureaucratic domination.

Oscar Wilde, who admired Kropotkin as "a man with the soul of that beautiful white Christ,"[21] discusses utopias and the idea of constant personal and social evolution in his essay, "The Soul of Man Under Socialism": "A map of the world that does not include Utopia is not even worth glancing at, for it leaves out the one country at which Humanity is always landing. And when Humanity lands there, it looks out, and seeing a better country, sets sail. Progress is the realisation of Utopias."[22] Ursula Le Guin's ambiguous utopia, *The Dispossessed,* inspired by the Kropotkinian ideas which Wilde also knew and used, provides the modern reader with an admirable map of a humane utopia which charts not only Shevek's landscape of time but our own. Le Guin deserves special recognition, not only for her artistry in using metaphor, construction, and characterization, but for her imaginative Odonian embodiment and application of Kropotkin's anarchist theory. Her Anarres offers an achieved, dynamic example of the kind of libertarian anarchy Peter Kropotkin proposed as the best hope for the humane evolution of man and culture.

5. Androgyny, Ambivalence, and Assimilation in *The Left Hand of Darkness*

N. B. HAYLES

IF THE amount of scholarly attention a book receives is any indication of its quality, *The Left Hand of Darkness* is in a fair way to becoming a science fiction classic.[1] Despite the breadth and remarkably good quality of recent criticism, however, two aspects of *Left Hand* have received less attention than they deserve. The first is the author's attempt to realize the full implications of androgyny, to imagine how ambisexuality would affect the culture, political institutions, and personal relationships of a people. Le Guin seems to have a gift for arriving at insights (apparently through pure intuition) that are the crux of other people's life work. She says, for example, that she had not read Jung before writing *Left Hand*, yet the way that she uses androgyny is consistent with much that Jung had to say.[2] In fact, the insights into androgyny in *Left Hand* are confirmed by a long tradition of androgyny in myth and literature. In the first part of this chapter, therefore, we will review the tradition of androgyny and the parallels between it and *Left Hand.* Such parallels, although perhaps interesting in themselves to aficionadoes on the subject, are important mainly because they point to a crucial fact about the way androgyny is used in *Left Hand.* Here androgyny has a double valence: it represents both a promise and a threat, an intrusion and a consumation.

The second aspect concerns the book's remarkable unity. Partly because of its unusual narrative structure—with its mixture of myths, legends, first-person narratives, and scientific field notes—*Left Hand* has occasionally been attacked on the grounds that it is mechanical and dogmatic.[3] In my opinion, this view is quite wrong. It results from a misapprehension of the source of the unity. The unity of *Left Hand* emerges from a dialectic among its parts; and an important part of this dialectic is the ambivalence of androgyny. By looking at the role which ambisexuality plays in Gethenian culture and in the central relationship between Genly Ai and Estraven, a strong case can be made for the assimilation of the various narrative fragments into a unified structure.

Now let us turn briefly to the tradition of androgyny. Such a compressed account as this necessarily does some violence to the complexities of the subject, and the reader is invited to consult various other sources for a fuller treatment.[4] Androgyny first appears as a characteristic of ancient cosmogonies, both Eastern and Western. These myths commonly imagine the great entities that existed before the world began as sexually undifferentiated; the division into male and female marks the end of mythic time and the beginning of everyday reality. A late, sophisticated example of this mythic tradition is the fable Aristophanes relates in Plato's *Symposium,* in which spherical, eight-limbed creatures are cut in half because they are powerful enough to threaten the gods. The severed halves become the human race, and each fragment spends his life pathetically searching for his severed half. In pity the gods rearrange the genitals so that the two halves, when they meet, can join sexually in an attempt to regain their original unity. This sense of androgyny as a condition of a lost primordial unity entered Christianity through a mystical tradition in which Adam was imagined as an androgynous being, made in the image of an androgynous God. The division of this first androgynous human being into male and female—Adam and Eve—was associated with the Fall and subsequent expulsion from Eden.

Such interpretations of Christian myth augmented the hermetical tradition, with its roots in Eastern mysticism, and resulted in the discipline of alchemy. In one sense, alchemy can be seen as an attempt to restore, through a combined material and spiritual refinement, the lost androgyny of the incarnate Spirit. Deeply influenced by his study of hermetical and alchemical texts, Carl Jung tried to reconcile this mythic and mystical tradition with everyday reality by suggesting that the alchemists—in their endless search for the Philosopher's Stone, the Rebis, that which would be both matter and spirit, both male and female—were actually pursuing the projection of their own unconscious mind. Thus Jung was led to the conclusion that the unconscious was the opposite gender from the conscious mind: the unconscious for a man is his *anima* (from the feminine form of the Greek word for spirit); for a woman, it is her *animus* (the corresponding masculine form).[5]

From Plato to Jung, these interpretations of myth share a common feature: the implication that androgyny is associated with a state of wholeness, of completion, and that fallen man yearns after that lost wholeness, spending his life, as Plato says, in the desire and pursuit of the whole. But running counter to this interpretation of androgyny is another tradition, most evident when androgyny left the realm of myth and entered the everyday world. For example, Livy, in commenting of the birth of a child of uncertain sex, records that such children were regarded as ill omens and were cast out and left to die.[6] Also in this view are occasional myths describing a metamorphosis from man to androgyne, such as Ovid's account of the transformation of Hermaphroditus into a bisexual being, neither man nor woman, but both.[7] Apparently it is one thing to imagine androgyny as a lost primordial state of being, but another to imagine the transformation as occurring in the opposite direction, as something that might actually happen in the flesh to men or women as we know them. This kind of transformation is much more likely to arouse uneasiness, because it threatens the security of our selfhood. It proposes to change the nature of our being; the addition (or recognition) of the other-sex element that would make us androgynes can be seen as the intrusion of the alien into the self. Even Jung, though he regards recognition of the unconscious as supremely important and ultimately enriching, warns that the conscious mind, when it becomes aware that it is not the totality of the psyche, might be driven into permanent insanity or death by this realization.

Thus, androgyny, as it is found in myth, legend, and history, is basically ambivalent; it can be seen either as the augmentation and completion of the self or as a form of self-annihilation, the intrusion of the alien into the self. Whether she was aware of these specific traditions or not, Le Guin uses the ambisexuality of the Gethenians in a remarkably similar way. On one hand, the peculiar Gethenian sexuality can be threatening, a representation of that which is disturbingly alien, while on the other hand, it can stand as a symbol of the wholeness to which man can aspire but only metaphorically attain—a lost state of perfection. As the title, *The Left Hand of Darkness,* implies, each "hand" evokes the presence and suggests the image of the other.

Since Douglas Barbour's seminal article on the influence of Taoist thought on Le Guin's early works, including *Left Hand,* the importance of the Tao to Le Guin's world-view has been widely recognized.[8] The Taoist vision that informs all of Le Guin's Hainish novels is especially relevant to the problems and potential inherent in androgyny, because the Taoist belief that wholeness derives from a creative tension between dualities provides a way for the ambivalence inherent in androgyny to itself become the basis of a new synthesis, a more nearly encompassing whole. The ambiguous reaction that a sexually bifurcated race (like Genly or us) has toward androgyny, the yearning towards it and the repulsion from it, become, in the context of the holistic vision of the Tao, another set of dualities which are encompassed and transcended by an emergent whole. This new wholeness does not imply either the incorporation or the obliteration of alienness. In this respect it is different from that positive nostalgic aspect of androgyny which views the other as a lost part of the self and yearns for the incorporation of the other within the self. It is also different from the negative aspect of androgyny that views with alarm the approach of the other to the self. The point is not to deny the alien, either by admitting it as part of the self or by divorcing it from the self. Although the alien remains the other, once its otherness is admitted and understood, it can come into creative tension with the self, and from this tension a new wholeness can emerge.

The Taoist vision of wholeness that is embodied in *Left Hand* thus offers a way to admit the ambivalence of androgyny and, at the same time, transcend it. Due to the inclusive nature of this vision, the dualities being explored are not limited to maleness and femaleness; they also include light and shadow, myth and reality, progress and stasis. Perhaps most important for our purposes, in the central relationship between Estraven and Genly Ai, the fundamental duality emerges of I and Thou, the self and the alien. In a sense, the holistic vision that results from this extraordinary concatenation of dualities can be seen as an intense wide-ranging rendering of how the world might appear to an androgynous race. In another sense, the particular theme of androgyny has been included in—and transcended by—a more general theme, the theme of what it means to see the world whole. To understand how this theme takes shape, we will consider first the macrocosm, the tensions and dualities present in Gethenian culture, and then turn to the microcosm, the impingement of these forces on two men, Genly Ai and Estraven.

Of all the Gethenian institutions, the Handdara cult perhaps comes closest to embodying the holistic vision of the Tao. Central to the Handdara way of thinking is the concept of dualities in a creative tension (V).[9] The Handdara prayer, "Praise then darkness and Creation unfinished," is one expression of the Handdara belief that to see requires not only light but shadow; to exist requires not only the ordering of creation but the potentiality of chaos. With an anthropologist's fine sense for how the process of naming reflects cultural assumptions, Le Guin has the Handdarata name objects by negating their opposites. For example, the Handdarata call their ritual state of intense sensory perception and physical immobility the "untrance." Estraven, who is of the Handdarata, characteristically called Orgoreyn his "uncountry." This way of naming implies that a thing can be known only through its opposite. The conjunction of opposites that lies behind Handdarata naming appears in their philosophy as paradox. The highest state of knowledge to which the Handdarata can aspire is ignorance, and the goal of their learning is to "unlearn." Such paradoxes imply that to define something as an abstraction, in and of itself, is to falsify it. To the Handdarata, essence is something that emerges from a creative tension between dualities, not something that exists in isolation.

Opposed to the philosophy of the Karhidish Handdarata are the beliefs of the Yomeshta. Yomesh, the official religion of Orgoreyn, came into being when the Foreteller Meshe was forced to answer the question, "What is the meaning of life?" One member of this Foretelling group killed himself; another committed murder. But Meshe, the Weaver of the group, was said to have lived the rest of his life in that state of intense illumination which characterizes the moment when the answer to the Foretelling is given. The excerpt from the Canon of Yomesh relates several incidents illustrating Meshe's all-encompassing sights and concludes: "In the Sight of Meshe there is no darkness" (XII). The Yomesh Canon therefore renounces the sense of creative duality that underlies Handdarata philosophy. The Yomeshta do not accept the uses of darkness, of the negative aspects of creation; "those that call upon the darkness are made fools of and spat out from mouth of Meshe," the Canon tells us (XII).

In setting up this opposition between Handdara and Yomesh cults, Le Guin, with her emphasis on dualistic wholeness, could be presenting us with a simple contrast between right and wrong ways of thinking. As we shall see, however, no one position, no one philosophy or perspective, is allowed to stand unqualified in *Left Hand.* While there is considerable evidence for the Handdarata being more nearly right than the Yomeshta, the difference is a comparative, not absolute, one.

One indication that the Handdarata are to be preferred over the Yomeshta is the association of the Handdarata with Karhide and the Yomeshta with Orgoreyn. With Genly Ai's fall from favor, we learn that Orgoreyn is, for those out of favor, a much less pleasant place to be than Karhide. Even before he is arrested, Genly senses the dark underside of Orgota life. The grand public buildings, even the corpulent Shusgis, seem to him somehow vague and insubstantial. Genly summarizes his intuitive uneasiness with a significant metaphor: "It was, I thought, as if they did not cast shadows" (X). Lest we dismiss this intuition as mere metaphor, Le Guin has Genly give us a scientific explanation of his feeling:

> This kind of rather highflown speculation is an essential part of my job. Without some capacity for it I could not have qualified as a Mobile, and I received formal training in it on Hain, where they dignify it with the title of Farfetching. What one is after when farfetching might be described as the intuitive perception of a moral entirety; and thus it tends to find expression not in rational symbols, but in metaphor. (X)

Thus, through metaphor, Genly's intuition provides a moral contrast between the Handdarata, who praise darkness and know the uses of shadow, and the Orgota state whose official religion insists that truth comes only from light. While the Orgota may not cast shadows, Orgoreyn does have its dark places, such as the blackness of the cellar where Genly is first imprisoned and the pitch-black interior of the prison truck. The unacknowledged darkness of Orgoreyn is linked with the treachery of its politicians, its secret police, its extensive and inhuman system of prison camps. It is as if the Orgota, lacking the holistic vision of the Handdarata, have perverted the potential of darkness. In Orgoreyn, darkness is a source not of strength but horror.

Le Guin's bias towards the Handdarata becomes even more evident when the Yomesh cult is associated with the increasing probability that Gethen may soon have its first war. As Genly and Estraven lie in their tent one night, Genly comments on how alone the Gethenians are on their planet, with no other large mammals on Gethen, and how alone they are in the universe with their unique ambisexuality.

Estraven replies, "The Yomeshta would say that man's singularity is his divinity," and Genly immediately answers, "Lords of the Earth, yes. Other cults on other worlds have come to the same conclusion. They tend to be the cults of dynamic, aggressive, ecology-breaking cultures" (XVI). To celebrate singularity as the Yomesh do, is to deny that man is part of a complex network of interlocking relationships. On a global scale this leads to a breakdown of ecological balance, while on a national scale it leads to war.

Le Guin has one of the Ekumen Investigators introduce the possibility that there is a causal relationship between Gethenian ambisexuality and the fact the Gethen has never had a war. Noting that the peculiar Gethenian sexuality is probably the result of a Hainish experiment in human biology, the Investigator speculates on the reason for the experiment:

> Did the Ancient Hainish postulate that continuous sexual capacity and organized social aggression, neither of which are attributes of any mammal but man, are cause and effect? Or . . . did they consider war to be a purely masculine displacement-activity, a vast Rape, and therefore in their experiment eliminate the masculinity that rapes and the feminity that is raped? (VII)

If, by virtue of their sexuality, the Gethenians have been given a built-in resistance to war, the immunity seems to be wearing off. All the necessary antidotes are coming together in Orgoreyn: the Orgota have a religion that renounces duality and praises singularity; the Orgoreyn state is efficient and bureaucratic, renouncing that "old darkness, passive, anarchic, silent, the fecund darkness of the Handdara" which, Genly senses, runs like a shadow through Karhide politics (V); and in urban Orgoreyn, as in Orgota prison camps, they control their native ambisexuality artificially through the use of drugs.

Instead of practicing war, with its mobilization of people into interchangeable units, the Gethenians have traditionally expressed their competitiveness through the practice of *shifgrethor*. Estraven tells Genly that *shifgrethor* comes "from an old word for shadow." Like a shadow, the word implies an attachment to a specific person or object. Unlike war, it cannot easily be separated from the personal and translated into an impersonal abstraction. Hence, Tibe, when he wants to convert Karhide into a nation capable of war, stops talking about *shifgrethor* and starts talking about honor. When Genly senses that the Orgota do not cast shadows, his metaphor hints not only at the perversion of darkness in Orgoreyn but also at the Orgota practice of considering its citizens as "units," interchangeable parts without individuality or a unique identity from which they might cast a shadow. Slowly a pattern emerges. On one side are shadows, *shifgrethor,* the absence of war on Gethen, and the Handdarata with their appreciation of dualities. All of these are related in some way to Gethenian ambisexuality; perhaps they are even natural outgrowths of the implications of androgyny. On the other side are perversions of darkness, honor, war, and the bureaucratic government of Orgoreyn, all of which deny in some way the implications of androgyny.

Genly's mission coincides, then, with a turning point in Gethenian history. Up to now, Gethenian androgyny has created a cultural matrix which precludes the possibility of war. But now Orgoreyn has begun to deny the old ways and create a new cultural matrix, one in which war is not only possible but, sooner or later, inevitable. Estraven shrewdly guesses that once the potential which Orgoreyn represents comes into being, it cannot be stopped simply by opposing it:

> They say here "all roads lead to Mishnory" [the capital of Orgoreyn]. To be sure, if you turn your back on Mishnory and walk away from it, you are still on the Mishnory road. To oppose vulgarity is inevitably to be vulgar. You must go somewhere else; you must have another goal; then you walk a different road. (XI)

This is what Genly's mission represents to Estraven: a way to avoid war, a turning that offers an entirely new direction.

At the end of this new road is the Ekumen. The Ekumen has much in common with the Handdara: a philosophy that is comfortable with paradox, a vision that finds complexity more rewarding than consistency, and above all, a delight in the sense of life's diversity. The two are different because the Handdarata characteristically express truth as a conjunction of opposing dualities, while Ekumen philosophy is couched more in terms of multiples than dualities. This difference is appropriate, however, since the Handdara developed from an ambisexual race, whereas the Ekumen developed from multiple races. In a sense, the Ekumen is the Handdara expanded to a cosmic scale. It is the general statement of that which, in the Handdara, finds a specific manifestation. Thus, in his first audience with King Argaven, Genly's explanation of why the Ekumen wants an alliance with the planet Winter is a multiple one: "Material profit.

Increase of knowledge. The augmentation of the complexity and intensity of the field of intelligent life. The enrichment of harmony and the greater glory of God. Curiosity. Adventure. Delight'' (III).

The thrust of the book is toward inclusion, specifically, the inclusion of dualities into a greater whole, and more generally, through the Ekumen, the inclusion of all complexity into a mystical unity. But Le Guin's expression of this is characteristic and personal. Arthur C. Clarke, for example, tends to express the drive toward inclusion by expanding the scale of the action to an ever-increasing size. Le Guin does just the opposite. She achieves closure not by expanding the scale but by *contracting* it. The fate of Gethen and the success of Genly's mission as Envoy for the Ekumen ultimately is made to depend on the relationship of two men—Genly Ai and Therem Harth rem ir Estraven. It may be that the emphasis on personal relationships is one way in which science fiction written by female writers differs from that written by their male colleagues. Le Guin seems to imply as much when she has Genly Ai suggest that the concentration on the personal and concrete at the expense of the abstract is a feminine characteristic. Genly asks Estraven if he hates Orgoreyn, and Estraven replies: ''No, how should I? How does one hate a country, or love one. . . . Insofar as I love life, I love the hills of the Domain of Estre, but that sort of love does not have a boundary line of hate. And beyond that, I am ignorant, I hope.'' About this philosophy, Genly thinks: ''Ignorant, in the Handdara sense: to ignore the abstraction, to hold fast to the thing. There was in this attitude something feminine, a refusal of the abstract, the ideal, a submissiveness to the given, which rather displeased me'' (XV). The Ekumen also shares some of this refusal to sacrifice the personal to the abstract; here, too, Genly resists at first such an ordering of priorities. When Ashe comes to ask Genly to carry money to Estraven, Genly justifies his caution by saying that his mission for the Ekumen has precedence over any merely personal debts, such as that he owes to Estraven.

> ''If so,'' said the stranger [Ashe] with fierce certainty, ''it is an immoral mission.''
>
> That stopped me. He sounded like an Advocate of the Ekumen, and I had no answer. ''I don't think it is,'' I said finally; ''the shortcomings are in the messenger, not the message'' (VIII).

Genly's initial resistance to these manifestations of the feminine principle is linked to his uneasiness about Gethenian ambisexuality. Because the Gethenians are androgynous, and because they are alien to Genly, the fear of the alien that lies behind the negative implications of androgyny merges with a general distrust of the alien. Of all the Gethenians, Estraven is the most threatening to Genly because Estraven is the only one who relates to Genly as a person and who therefore forces Genly to consider him as a person. For Genly, Estraven is an odd combination of the alien and the familiar, the other who contains within himself both maleness and femaleness, the same sex as Genly and the opposite sex; he is also both a member of an alien race and a human being. Genly can thus find within Estraven a reflection of himself and the undeniable presence of an alien element—in two senses. A general xenophobia is thus being focused and directed by a specific reaction to sexual ambiguity.

That the antipathy Genly instinctively feels toward Estraven has its source in Estraven's ambiguous sexuality finally becomes clear when the two men are forced into intimate contact during their journey across the Gobrin Ice. From the beginning, though, Le Guin skillfully associates Genly's sense of unease, distrust, even disgust, with Estraven's latent femininity. When Tibe engages Estraven in verbal parries at the keystone ceremony, Genly is annoyed at the "sense of effeminate intrigue" which the exchange gives him. That evening, as he dines with Estraven at his home, Genly finds that Estraven's performance at dinner "had been womanly, all charm and tact and lack of substance, specious and adroit." Genly goes on to speculate about the effect of Estraven's sexual ambiguity:

> Was it in fact perhaps this soft supple femininity that I disliked and distrusted in him? For it was impossible to think of him as a woman, that dark, ironic, powerful presence near me in the firelit darkness, and yet whenever I thought of him as a man I felt a sense of falseness, of imposture: in him, or in my own attitude towards him? (I)

Just as on a large scale androgyny, with all the complex implications it would have for an ambisexual race, is central to understanding what is happening in Gethenian society, on a small scale androgyny, with all the ambivalence traditionally associated with it, is central to understanding the evolving relationship between Genly Ai and Estraven. In the microcosm, however, emotional nuance, narrative technique, and the very rhythms of the prose are not just the vehicles of the story but part of the story itself. To separate the strands and discuss them in a linear fashion, as I did in discussing Gethenian society, would, therefore, falsify the complexity of the relationship, because such a discussion would inevitably be reductive. To be sure, there is a strong linear development in the relationship. Genly moves from an initial distrust and dislike of Estraven to a grudging admiration, and ends by accepting him completely. Thus, in a sense, *Left Hand* is a *bildungsroman,* a book about the education of Genly Ai.

But this linear movement, while clearly present and important, is complicated by Le Guin's narrative technique. It is Genly Ai who has arranged the fragments that make up the manuscript; hence, he is both a character in the narrative and the presence in whose consciousness the fragments coalesce to make, as he tells us at the beginning, all one story. His role is twofold. As a character, his perceptions are fragmentary, often wrong, continually changing and evolving. As the structuring consciousness, he insures the unity of the story and implicitly provides a unified perspective from which to view the various parts of the novel. That Genly can see the underlying unity of the parts is both a result and a proof of what he learns. The Genly Ai who, at the beginning of the book, can say, "Truth is a matter of the imagination" (I), is not the same Genly Ai Le Guin has described as a "conventional, indeed rather stuffy, young man." [10] Genly Ai is therefore, as the puns on his name suggest, both an "I" and the eye of the story.[11]

Estraven's first-person accounts are subsumed within the structure Genly's eye provides. As the two lie in the tent Genly sees Estraven writing notes in a journal. After Estraven dies, Genly takes the journal to Estraven's Hearth where it will be incorporated in the records of the Domain of Estre. It is this journal, of course, that also comprises Estraven's first-person narrative. When the two comrades are on the Ice, the shifts between Genly's first-person account and Estraven's journal give us two different perspectives on the same events and thus a richer, more complex appreciation of the events than either account alone could. The two accounts serve another purpose, too, one that is perhaps even more important thematically. The interconnections between them, the way they reflect on one another to give us the sense of a greater whole, means that the form of the narrative embodies the creative tension between dualities that is a central theme of the novel.

Keeping in mind the complexity that arises from the interconnections among the accounts, let us return for a moment to Genly's evolving perspective. When Genly awakens after his escape from Pulefen Farm, Estraven's recapitulation of past events finally makes Estraven's loyalty clear to him. But although he now knows the extent of Estraven's commitment to him, Genly still cannot completely come to grips with what Estraven is. As the two companions get into harness for the first time to pull the sledge, Genly thinks of himself as a "stallion in harness with a mule" (XV). It isn't until Estraven comes into kemmer—and comes into kemmer as a woman—that Genly is finally forced to confront and emotionally accept that Estraven is not merely neutral, like a mule, but feminine as well as masculine. The two accounts of this evening—one from Estraven's journal, the other from the retrospective account of Genly—emphasize opposite-sex traits in the other, which have gone unnoticed before. Estraven comments that Genly "spoke with a gentleness that I did not know was in him" (XVI). For Genly, Estraven's emerging female sexuality precipitates a crisis of recognition:

> Until then I had rejected him, refused him his own reality. He had been quite right to say that he, the only person on Gethen who trusted me, was the only Gethenian I distrusted. For he was the only one who had entirely accepted me as a human being: who had liked me personally and given me entire personal loyalty: and who therefore demanded of me an equal degree of recognition, of acceptance. I had not been willing to give it. I had been afraid to give it. I had not wanted to give my trust, my friendship to a man who was a woman, a woman who was a man. (XVIII)

With this recognition comes another: Genly's admission of the sexual tension that exists between them and of the feeling between them that "might as well be called, now as later, love" (XVIII). Perhaps because in Le Guin's world view, wholeness comes not from the *union* of opposites but from dualities in tension with one another, the two friends do not have sex. Genly tries to explain their decision not to consummate their relationship in a sexual union: "it was from the difference between us, not from the affinities and likenesses, but from the difference, that the love came: and it was itself the bridge, the only bridge, across what divided us. For us to meet sexually would be for us to meet once more as alien" (XVIII).

The androgyny of Estraven has therefore begun by arousing antipathy in Genly. When the otherness—the femaleness—of Estraven becomes explicit and can no longer be ignored, it is the catalyst that allows the relationship to move to a new level. The sexual tension between Genly and Estraven means that their relationship can no longer be understood completely in terms of male camaraderie. But neither can it be wholly understood as taking place in the more passionate realm of erotic love. Although both are components of the relationship, neither is allowed to be the defining factor. Thus it is the sense of a tension between dualities that provides a means of recognizing as well as transcending the ambivalence inherent in androgyny. Because the choice is not between admitting the other as part of the self or excluding the other from the self, but an entirely different one (recognition of the other, *as other,* and recognition of the self in a creative tension with the other), androgyny is at once crucial to the relationship and is transcended by it.

In terms of the relationship between Estraven and Genly, the night when Estraven comes into kemmer represents a kind of breakthrough. That the breakthrough is achieved by incorporating in a personal relationship the holistic vision that informs the entire book is remarkable. Truly extraordinary, however, is the way Le Guin then uses this personal breakthrough to extend the implications of that holistic vision so that it provides a means assimilating the book's two different narrative modes.

In collecting the documents that comprise the book, Genly provides us not only with the first-person accounts of Estraven and himself but also with a collage of other documents which portray distinctive aspects of Gethenian mindset and culture. Two distinct modes emerge from this collage. One mode, which includes the central narrative and those sections written by earlier Investigators, takes place in a context we can identify as, if not always objective, at least consistent with everyday reality. The other mode, which includes the myths and legends, takes place in a context we recognize as happening outside present time, belonging to what the Gethenians would call the very-long-ago. Yet as the story proceeds, the two modes seem to blend into one another. Le Guin (I use Le Guin as the artificer now and not Genly, because it is Le Guin who is responsible for the content of the mythic material, though Genly may be dictating its arrangement) achieves this effect partly from the similarity between the names and events in the mythic mode and those in the everyday mode. The material of the mythic mode, mirrored in the first-person narratives of Genly and Estraven, creates a feeling of déjà vu and allows Le Guin to suggest connections without making them explicit.

Feeling that the boundaries are down between him and Estraven, Genly tries to cement their union by bespeaking Estraven. When Estraven hears Genly mindspeak in the voice of his dead brother, Arek, we, like Genly, don't actually know what lay between Estraven and his dead brother, other than love and death. But we have already read a legend ("The Place Inside the Blizzard," Chapter 2) about two brothers who vow kemmering, have a child and then are separated as one commits suicide and the other, held accountable for the suicide by his Hearth, is driven into exile. We know that Arek and Estraven had had a child; we know that they had, in defiance of Gethenian custom, vowed kemmering to each other; we *feel* that Arek, like the brother in the legend, had committed suicide and so been responsible for Estraven's exile from his Domain. Estraven hears Genly bespeak him in Arek's voice presumably because Estraven's relationship with Genly is like his relationship with Arek: it is a bond to which he is totally committed, one for which he has sacrificed his position and been driven into exile (this time not just from his Domain, but from his country as well). In the same way that the narrative structure implies interconnections among seemingly disparate modes, Estraven's unconscious mind (or whatever faculty of mind is responsible for activating the speech centers of the brain in mindspeech) overlays onto Estraven's relationship with Genly the emotional trauma, the sense of pain and passion, that characterize Estraven's memories of Arek. The mindspeech Genly hopes will be an unambiguous bond of intimacy thus becomes, he thinks, "a bond, indeed, but an obscure and austere one, not so much admitting further light (as I had expected it to) as showing the extent of the darkness" (XVIII). Once again we are reminded that wholeness comes not from denying duality, but from encompassing it. Just as the narrative is fragmented into different modes which, nevertheless, reflect on one another, so Genly Ai and Estraven remain separated though together. Joy and pain, light and shadow, history and myth, past and present, self and other, all come to be seen as inextricable parts of a greater whole—not in spite of their differences, but because of them.

During the crossing of the Gobrin Ice the scope of the dualities coming into creative tension with one another constantly increases. Genly comes to see Estraven's androgyny as itself one kind of completeness, and thus draws for Estraven the yin-yang symbol as an emblem of himself. The relationship between Genly and Estraven, with its tension between Thou and I, self and other, becomes another embodiment of the holistic vision. The intensity of this vision is such that at this point it seems to permeate almost every aspect of the narrative. From small descriptive details—as when Genly sees Estraven's careful measuring of their next day's food ration "as either housewifely or scientific" (XVIII)—to the major narrative developments, there is a pervasive sense of the necessity to see things whole.

That this is the essence of what Genly learns during the trek across the Ice becomes clear when Estraven and Genly encounter that peculiar weather found only in Artic regions, in which the equal diffusion of light over every surface causes ice, sky, and horizon to blend together in one unvarying whiteness. This is the legendary "Place Within the Blizzard," the place where in the legend one brother confronts his dead kemmering and chooses life over death. Characteristically, Estraven calls it the "Unshadow," and it proves to be extremely treacherous, because the crevasses in the rotten ice, casting no shadows, can't be seen until one falls into them. When Estraven falls into a crevass and is saved only because Genly does not let go of the sledge, Genly takes the lead, feeling each step with a probe. After several hours he becomes paralyzed with fear and cannot force himself to take another step.

> "What's up, Genly?"
> I stood there in the middle of nothing. Tears came out and froze my eyelids together. I said, "I'm afraid of falling." (XIX)

Genly's admission of fear indicates that he has stopped insisting on what he earlier calls "the more competitive elements of my masculine self-respect" (XV). Metaphor and plot come together as Estraven tells Genly: "Fear's very useful. Like darkness; like shadow" (XIX). This episode is probably the finest example of how Le Guin embodies theme in form, and it indicates that Genly has sensed his own emotional androgyny, the presence within him of hitherto suppressed "feminine" qualities in addition to the traditional masculine ones.

Yet throughout, Le Guin has been careful to distinguish between opposites held in creative tension with one another, and the complete fusion of them into an indistinguishable oneness. When Estraven and Genly finally come off the Ice and enter the village, they have become so much one being that Genly, hearing someone say, "Will you look to my friend?" thinks he has said it, though it is Estraven speaking. But the oneness of Estraven and Genly is still composed of two parts. When Estraven is killed, this oneness dissolves as Genly is forced to face the primal duality of life and death. Once again, descriptive details stress the interplay between shadow and light, this time as a foreshadowing of Estraven's approaching death: "We skied through small frosty woods and over the hillocks and fields of the disputed valley. There was no hiding, no sulking. A sunlit sky, a white world, and we two strokes of shadow on it, fleeing" (XIX).

With Estraven's death the narrative takes shape around the attempt to define the significance of that death. Thus we return to the first question King Argaven asked of the Ekumen stabiles: what makes a man a traitor? As the comment returned via the ansible suggests, the perspective from which an answer is given will influence the answer. The question therefore has not one answer, but several; in fact, it will have as many answers as there are perspectives from which to give an answer. These multiple answers, however, finally are all subsumed into one holistic vision. All are true, but each is only part of the final truth.

In his grief Genly thinks that Estraven, by allowing himself to be killed, has betrayed him. As the acuteness of his grief subsides, Genly comes to see Estraven's death as a final sacrifice to insure the success of Genly's mission. So Genly decides to break his vow not to bring the ship down until Estraven's name is cleared, since to delay would betray the meaning of Estraven's death. Genly views the completion of his mission as putting "the keystone in the arch" (XX), thus coming full circle from that day when he watched the keystone ceremony, the making of one span out of two halves, with Estraven standing sinister at Genly's left side. "Without the bloodbond the arch would fall" (I), Estraven tells Genly then. Later, Estraven seals the bond between Karhide and the Ekumen with his own blood. Estraven's death thus serves as a focal point for the convergence of the different levels of meaning. When Argaven refuses to clear Estraven's name immediately, Genly tries once again to define the senses in which Estraven was and was not a traitor. He tells Argaven:

> "He served the master I served."
> "The Ekumen?" said Argaven, startled.
> "No. Mankind."
> As I spoke I did not know if what I said was true. True in part; an aspect of the truth. It would be no less true to say that Estraven's acts had risen out of pure personal loyalty, a sense of responsibility and friendship towards one single human being, myself. Nor would that be the whole truth. (XX)

Another part of the whole truth is contained in the legend about Therem of Stok and Arek of Estre ("Estraven the Traitor"). The mirroring between this legend and the central narrative is extensive, and the interplay between the mythic and everyday mode again provides us with a sense of an emerging whole. In the legend it is easy to see that Estraven the Traitor is a traitor only from the narrow perspective of the land rights of the Domain of Estre. From a larger perspective, he is not a traitor but a hero, since he stops the blood feud between the two domains and achieves a lasting peace—an accomplishment implicitly recognized by the fact that his name, *Therem,* is thereafter used as a hearth name for the children of Estre, though until then it had been a name used only in Stok. Therem Harth rem ir Estraven thus takes his name from that first Estraven the Traitor, and like him, is a traitor only from a narrow perspective, that of the *shifgrethor* of King Argaven. From a larger perspective, Estraven is a hero because he is instrumental in bringing the Ekumen to Winter. In both legend and history, larger considerations reverse the definitions of treason. Yet Estraven is no more a traitor on the intimately personal level with Genly than he is on the most abstract level with the Ekumen, or mankind. The interplay of the two modes brings into a suggestive tension the duality of macrocosm and microcosm. Truth is found both in the intimacy of personal relationships and in the generally abstract, in archetypal psychomyth as well as the dense detail of a realistic fiction.

The significance of the parrallelism of the modes is not exhausted at Estraven's death, however. Just as the child of Arek of Estre and Therem of Stok held the key to the future as time in the legend came full circle, so Therem Harth rem ir Estraven, namesake of Estraven the Traitor, has a child by his brother, Arek, a child whose name (Sovre) is the same as that of the Lord of Estre in the time of the legend. If the myth reflects reality, reality also reflects the myth.

Like the mythic time of the legend, narrative time seems to be both circular and linear. Circularity is suggested when Genly makes his pilgrimage to Estre and sees the flash of Estraven's spirit in the child Estraven left behind. When the child, Sovre, asks to be told about his parent's death and about "the other worlds out among the stars—the other kind of men, the other lives" (XIX), his eagerness implies a hope for the future, a linearity that contrasts with and complements the circular patterns created by the similarities between ancient legend and immediate history. Thus everything is still the same on Gethen, yet everything is changing as the end of the book is finely balanced between progress and stasis.

Surely one sign of the serious artist is the willingness to subordinate the part to the whole. Somehow, through her faithfulness to the controlling conception of the work, the artist hopes to create a whole that transcends the sum of its parts. I think Le Guin has done this in *The Left Hand of Darkness,* but that is not all of her accomplishment. The artist's desire for coherence can lead to dogmatism; in this case, unity can easily become sterility. Freud observed that life resists order, that perfect order is synonomous with death. This observation is germane to *Left Hand,* not only because the dualism it implies is thematically relevant to Le Guin's holistic vision but because the book offers us both the satisfaction of artisitic unity and the richness of a complex diversity. For almost every statement she gives us, Le Guin supplies a counterstatement. No truth is allowed to stand as the entire truth; every insight is presented as partial, subject to revision and another perspective. For example, the Ekumen Investigator's report, which hypothesizes a causal relation between Gethenian ambisexuality and the absence of war on Gethen, goes on to suggest that perhaps an even more important consideration is the harsh winter climate of Gethen (VII). The second suggestion does not negate the first. We are still encouraged, I think, to make the connection between aggression and unvarying sexual roles: but it forces us to see the first insight as provisional, subject to correction. So, too, Genly insists that joining in sex could bring him and Estraven no closer, since it was from their differences that their bond grew. But he ends by adding: "We left it at that. I do not know if we were right" (XVIII). The contrast that Le Guin draws between the Handdara and Yomesh cults provides yet another example. Though it is clear that Le Guin favors the Handdara philosophy, she nevertheless has Genly say, in a moment of impatience: "Your Handdara fascinates me, Harth, but now and then I wonder if it isn't simply paradox developed into a way of life. . ." (XVIII). In terms of narrative structure, the alternation of Genly's account and Estraven's journal serves a similar purpose by constantly providing us with diverse perspectives on the same events. When the two friends come to the place where the volcanoes pit their fire against the Ice, Genly sees the blackened surface as "DEATH" written across a continent (XV), while Estraven sees it as "the dirty chaos of a world in the process of making itself (XVI).

Such subtle but pervasive insistence that every truth is a partial truth is, of course, wholly consistent with Le Guin's controlling vision for this book, since if she allowed any truth to stand as *the* truth, the sense that wholeness emerges from a tension between dualities would be lost. The delicate balance of conflicting possibilities that Le Guin posits means, for one thing, that the book is rarely in danger of becoming dogma. It also means that, for a complete expression of

Le Guin's holistic vision, nothing less than the entire structure of the book will suffice. The final whole that emerges is the book itself. And this kind of unity, which encompasses within itself all manner of diversity, makes *The Left Hand of Darkness* itself an example of the creative fecundity that is possible when differences are not suppressed but used to create a new whole. For all these reasons, *The Left Hand of Darkness* is one of Le Guin's finest books, and an enduring literary achievement.

6. Anarchism and Utopian Tradition in *The Dispossessed*

JOHN P. BRENNAN and MICHAEL C. DOWNS

THE IDEA of an "anarchist utopia" would, on the face of it, seem to be a contradiction in terms. After all, anarchism is the antipolitical theory of politics, the one that rejects all authority, law, and government as being unnecessary and oppressive. On the other hand, in its search for order and justice in human affairs, the utopian tradition has, for the most part, looked to the state—hateful to the anarchist— as the key to reforming society. While the anarchist tends to regard the state as either the source of all social misery or the tool with which the rich and powerful legitimize their theft of mankind's common material heritage, the utopian theorist hopes to eradicate injustice by using the state to embody a "more perfect union." Thus Peter Kropotkin, the leading theorist of anarchism, characteristically used the term "utopian" to refer to a kind of preconceived social theorizing which, unlike anarchism, is based on a priori conceptions of man rather than a knowledge of what actually goes on in society. In his famous article, "Anarchism," for the eleventh edition (1910) of the *Encyclopaedia Britannica,* Kropotkin cites as the first major anarchist thinker Zeno of Cyprus, "who distinctly opposed the conception of a free community without government to the state-Utopia of Plato."[1]

Another important philosophical anarchist, however, has questioned the mutual exclusivity of anarchy and utopia. In a carefully reasoned reply to Karl Popper's attack on Plato's *Republic,* Herbert Read finds utopianism acceptable to the libertarian, even though it has been rejected by the liberal.[2] In Read's view, the utopian vision entails the concrete and vital embodiment of an ideal, enabling the ideal to give direction to human striving and making it subject to rational scrutiny. What Popper fails to appreciate is Plato's method, which is to pretend with such conviction and logic that political ideals become concrete images, which are the only possible objects of rational political criticism. In fact, utopian vision is necessary to *society,* for it projects ideals by which society attempts to transcend itself, by which man actually creates and thus rises above "mere existence." Far from being a totalitarian trap, then, utopianism is "the principle of all progress." The tendency toward authoritarian systems in envisioning the ideal society is due to a rage for order, for "excessive tidiness," which is as much a human trait as the desire for freedom. Therefore, utopias which respect the "organic freedom of life" are consonant with libertarian ideals.[3]

Kropotkin's strictures on utopianism, as well as the friendlier viewpoint of Read, must be taken into account in any examination of Ursula K. Le Guin's *The Dispossessed,* for the novel has both implicit and explicit connections with anarchism and utopian tradition. Its very title recalls the English title of Dostoevsky's controversial satire *(The Possessed)* on Nechayev and his nihilist gangsterism, a movement related to anarchism through its influence on Bakunin. In its more obvious sense, though, "dispossessed" refers to the freedom from property that is central to anarchism and which is actualized in Odonian society. Indeed, elsewhere Le Guin has indicated her partiality for anarchism as a political ideal, stating that the thematic motivation of *The Dispossessed* was to accomplish for the first time the embodiment of that ideal in a novel.[4] Similarly, the novel's subtitle ("An Ambiguous Utopia") indicates that it is to be read as a contribution to the utopian tradition, while its structure, which alternates chapters narrating Shevek's experiences on Urras with episodes from his life on Anarres, conveys the dialectic of old world and new world that is central to utopian satire and vision.

No matter how clear the relationship of the novel to utopian tradition and the philosophy of anarchism, *The Dipossessed* is not a shallow roman à clef or simpleminded celebration of an outdated revolutionary theory. We regard Le Guin's novel—like all the author's work, so comfortably at home in its remotely futuristic setting and yet so deceptively simple in characterization, incident, dialogue, and sentiment—as a penetrating critique of all utopian experience, even that of anarchism, a critique which raises questions that are fundamental to political theory. No apology is made for treating the novel as a serious inquiry into political ideals and experience, for we agree with Herbert Read that an aesthetic activity such as writing fiction has as one of its goals the "concretization and vitalization of ideals." In this sense—though it is neither dialogue nor treatise, but rather a "mere" novel of science fiction—*The Dispossessed* is just as philosophical as, say, the *Republic* or Locke's *Two Treatises of Government.*

We begin by asking in what sense *The Dispossessed* portrays an "ambiguous utopia." Surely Le Guin doesn't mean her subtitle merely to underline the novel's contrasting of societies on two worlds. After all, some such contrast is the *sine qua non* of utopian fiction. Ambiguity, it turns out, is a feature of practically every detail of setting and action: "Where it crossed the roadway, instead of having a gate it degenerated into mere geometry, a line, an idea of boundary. But the idea was real. It was important. For seven generations there had been nothing in the world more important than that wall. Like all walls it was ambiguous, two-faced. What was inside it and what was outside it depended upon which side of it you were on" (*TD,* I). The novel is concerned with ambiguity of different kinds and on different levels. It is itself "two-faced" (as perhaps all fiction is), in that it presents the reader with two sociopolitical systems (Anarres and A-Io), two sets of values (anarchist and propertarian), two systems of physics (sequentialist and simultaneist), and two demanding loyalties (self and society). But at its conclusion the novel is still ambiguous; it refuses to resolve the tensions brought on by all these dualities, asking instead that the essential dualism which arises from the individual's existence in a universe of objects and other human subjects be viewed from outside, as the condition under which all search takes place, rather than from the inside, as a series of walls which impede or even prevent this searching. To the imagination hungering for certainty, it is an unsatisfactory conclusion, not least because it accepts ambiguity heroically rather than retreating from it or ignoring it. Le Guin hasn't presented us with a utopian vision in which all opposites are united, all contradictions overcome, "all wish ... tobogganed into know." Her utopia is ambiguous because it is, in the usual sense, "real."

The basic source of ambiguity in the Western philosophical tradition is the character of our knowledge of the world, with its opposing modes of subjectivity and objectivity. In *The Dispossessed* these opposing modes, which are often the theme of an *éducation sentimentale,* generate experiences that shape Shevek's later attitudes about the purpose of human existence. An early incident, the attempt of the young Shevek and his pals to discover the meaning of the concrete experience of imprisonment, is an important part of Le Guin's development of her theme by using the "idea of boundary" (symbolized by walls) throughout.

All Anarresti children are told the legend of the imprisonment of Odo, the "founding mother" of Odonian anarchism. In a prisonless society this story has gradually acquired the proportions and function of myth. It substitutes for the direct experience of the lack of freedom, a nightmare vision of this most fearful and undesirable condition.[5] Once questioned, as by the children in Shevek's peer group, the factual or objective horror of imprisonment may be minimized and even ridiculed. When Shevek and his friends test the myth, however, they find the lack of freedom as unthinkable as they have been taught. What this incident illustrates is how the secondhand, objective experience of a socializing legend can be confronted with direct, subjective, firsthand experience. In the union that results from such confrontation, the bloodless, alienated truth must be personalized; it may also be obliterated. In either case, the myth is destroyed, because it has either been placed on a scientific footing or disproved.

Shevek himself is profoundly moved, even shaken, by the experience. Subsequently he makes the removing of walls his mission in life. Immediately after the experience with the primitive prison cell, the narrator presents a discussion that occurs three or four years later, in which Shevek's group examines another myth of their socializing, about life on Urras. (Note here that their orientation toward myth criticism has become more humanistic than scientific; instead of laying plans for an experiment, they form a discussion group!) The degrading quality of Urrasti life is a major part of Anarresti education. But with demythologizing experiences such as the prison episode in mind, new questions are raised:

> "You're saying that PDC and the educational supplies syndicate are lying to us about Urras."
>
> "No; I said we only know what we're told . . ." (*TD*, II)

Shevek's education includes several examples of the walls which close off truth from personal experience. At the age of eight he raised for discussion one of the paradoxical proofs of the impossibility of motion which we associate with the name of Zeno of Elea.[6] The teacher, a sort of anarchist Thwackum or McChokumchild, rebukes

Shevek for "egoizing" (the Odonian terms for elevating one's personal interest above the welfare of society) and won't let the learning group consider the paradox. Thus cut off from his fellows, Shevek begins the search for a resolution of the problem. He comes to realize that mathematics, the least ambiguous form of communication, holds the key: "If you saw the numbers you could see that, the balance, the pattern. You saw the foundations of the world. And they were solid" (*TD,* II).

Beyond the tension resulting from the conflict between objective and subjective, the young Shevek has experienced another kind of tension, that produced by a society which, wittingly or not, excludes an individual simply by not showing any interest in his work, by attaching to it no value or use. Anarresti society, an anarchism which, in theory, exists precisely to secure the individual's highest potential, shuts off not only the unusual individual (Shevek, Bedap, and Tirin each suffer this, in a different way) but any contact with Urras, which for all practical purposes represents the rest of the universe.[7] "I will go to Abbenay and unbuild walls" (*TD,* I), Shevek had said when he returned to the Anarresti *metropolis*[8] to struggle with those who, even in an anarchist society, had created and usurped places of power. His purpose in traveling to Urras, in contravention to the popular opinion so adroitly manipulated by his opponents, flows from the same source.[9]

Good intentions, of course, do not always avail. Shevek's effort certainly seems unequal to the magnitude of the problems he is trying to resolve, the most serious and irresolvable of which are those involving basic human relationships. Shevek and Takver are able to find consolation of a sort in the bond of their life partnership, and the social need is also partly met by his participation in the Syndicate of Initiative. In these associations we find the kind of mutual aid and support of the individual's needs central to anarchist theory, as well as the teachings of Odo. Much less successful, surprisingly, are Shevek's relationships with his "professional" colleagues, with Sabul at the Institute in Abbenay and later with the Urrasti physicists. Functionalism, the political theory which places much faith in people's ability to find social harmony in common work and shared intellectual experiences, is apparently contravened by these facts. Ambition, the will to power, and relentless "egoizing" tend to weaken such functional associations on Anarres. With nationalism and class bias added to this list of faults on Urras, the functionalist dream is rendered totally unrealizable.[10]

Nor is good will sufficient. Shevek's conversations with various Urrasti are especially interesting in this regard. From the doctor on the freighter carrying him to Urras to the friendly but finally unapproachable Oiie, Shevek encounters walls that can't be "unbuilt": "Kimoe's ideas never seemed to be able to go in a straight line; they had to walk around this and avoid that, and then they ended up smack against a wall. There were walls around all his thoughts, and he seemed utterly unaware of them, though he was perpetually hiding behind them" (*TD,* I). The result is that both Kimoe and Shevek are left unsatisfied with their conversations, as if each of them has been speaking in a language which the other only partly understood. There are, indeed, times when Shevek comes close to "unbuilding" the walls, at least on the simplest level of interpersonal communication, that of common humanity. Occasionally Shevek is able to communicate well; at one point he even seems sympathetic with Sabul. But for the most part, his breakthroughs in communication are limited and temporary: "'My grandfather was a janitor. Scrubbed floors and changed dirty sheets in a hotel for fifty years. Ten hours a day, six days a week. He did it so that he and his family could eat.' Oiie stopped abruptly, and glanced at Shevek with his old secretive, distrustful look, and then, almost with defiance, at his wife," (*TD,* V).

While on Urras, however, Shevek twice is able to at least begin to unbuild walls. His last conversations with his manservant, Efor, indicate that suffering and need can serve as the foundation for knowledge of both self and others, and that while not mathematical, such knowledge is the condition both for communication between human subjects and united action. During the insurrection that results in part from his desire to promote renewal and freedom for the Urrasti masses, Shevek rediscovers pain as an unambiguous, basic, shared experience. When a person speaks out of his suffering (*pathos*), he will be understood as his experience finds a way through or around any walls. That this might become the basis for uniting society in the new world is not as clear, but it does suffice for Shevek and his companions.[11]

Thus the ambiguity that builds walls between individuals can be overcome often enough to allow the growth of happiness and hope, and to create living space for human beings; but never is there a complete or universal triumph over the walls of ambiguity. Shevek continues to have communication problems with his closest friends, despite the disambiguity of their relationships. We are left with the impression that, in spite of his efforts, Shevek's desire to "unite" the propertarian (and state-propertarian) societies of Urras with the "dispossessed" anarchist society of Anarres will never come to pass. The novel ends, however, with a final ambiguity which perhaps negates the apparent final reign of ambiguity. In Shevek's conversation with Keng, the Terran ambassador, we learn that he is confident—finally—that he has created the unified theory of the General Temporal Field, a breakthrough which will permit the technological application of transilience known as the *ansible*—a device that will make possible instantaneous communication throughout the known worlds, thus uniting all the human strains in a truly universal brotherhood.[12]

The novel concludes with Shevek returning to Anarres, his quest to unify Urras and Anarres apparently a failure, so that, at least for the moment, there is no "unbuilding" of walls. But the Hainish officer, Ketho, whom Shevek has encountered by accident, as it were, while returning from his failed quest, seems to have arrived at a state of mind that can unite him with Shevek in a direct and profound manner:

> "We have tried everything. Anarchism, with the rest. But *I* have not tried it. They say there is nothing new under any sun. But if each life is not new, each single life, then why are we born?"
>
> "We are the children of time," Shevek said, in Pravic. The younger man looked at him a moment, and then repeated the words in Iotic: "We are the children of time." (*TD,* XIII)

Perhaps the Hainishman will find a common purpose with the Anarresti, for he seems to have passed beyond the selfish limitations of the Urrasti and become less alien to the principles of Odo. In any event, the expression "we are the children of time" sums up the novel's theme of ambiguity. Perhaps it isn't too much to hope that the communications system which will result from Shevek's mathematical resolution of Zeno's paradox (which is, after all, what the unification of Sequency and Simultaneity theories amounts to) *will* unite the human races in an Ekumen of peace and knowledge. That is the novel's final utopian vision. But perhaps it is too much to expect. To attain the tempered wisdom of mature vision, the children of time must suffer experience, as the Hainish have.

One reason for calling *The Dispossessed* an ambiguous utopia is that the narrative doesn't attempt to dissipate the tensions apparently inherent within experience due to certain dualities of knowing and being. Another reason—one that is relevant to the *kind* of fiction it is (a utopian *novel* rather than a utopian *romance*)—is that, like its characters, the novel is an offspring of time. After all, utopian romances take place in a world remarkly free of the ravages of the Second Law of Thermodynamics and are thus visions of information systems unplagued by entropic degradation. A primary law of romance setting is "it will be ever thus." So we don't expect utopian romances, which are timeless ideals, to deal with the complexities, ambiguities, and tortuousness of ordinary experience. *The Dispossessed* is quite at home in the "light of common day."

Ambiguity, however, should not be viewed as entailing a moral relativism in which we cannot distinguish the better from the worse. Only a biased or inattentive reader of *The Dispossessed* could possibly conclude that the novel presents Ioti society as healthier or more desirable than Anarresti society. Unfortunately, the ideal unbiased reader most likely does not exist. One of us has assigned the novel several times to an introductory class in science fiction, only to find that students tend to favor interpretations which see the narrative either as promoting the advanced corporate state of A-Io at the expense of the hard-scrabble anarchist world of Anarres, or as presenting the idea that "one person's utopian dream is another person's dystopian nightmare." It's likely that ideology enters into such interpretive favoritism. A-Io is in many ways not unlike what the post-industrialist capitalist states of the West might become in an age of scarcity, and as such is a plausible image of the future of the bourgeois state, particularly the United States.

Clearly, though, the author doesn't intend that we read the novel as either an attack on anarchism or a plea for tolerance of diversity in social organization. In her introductory comments to "The Day Before the Revolution,"[13] Le Guin states that anarchism "is the most idealistic, and . . . the most interesting, of political theories." She further indicates that her motivation for writing *The Dispossessed* was to embody anarchism in a novel, "which had not been done before," a task that absorbed all her energies for many months and left her an "exile." In pointing to these comments, we don't think we have succumbed to the intentional fallacy, since the contrast between Anarres and A-Io, the chief utopian dialectic of the novel, must be resolved in favor of Anarres.

Northrop Frye has observed that the imaginative universe depicted in myth and literature may be mapped according to four levels of desirability. Uppermost is *heaven*, the home of the gods and the highest projection of human desire. Next is the *earthly paradise,* which corresponds to the state of primal innocence often thought to antedate the "fall" of human experience. Below the primal garden is the *world of experience,* or the here-and-now of middle-earth. The lowest level is *hell,* the ultimate projection of human fear. Various plot types may then be read as patterns of movement within one level or among the various levels. Only a work that encompasses a complete account of human destiny would make use of all four levels at once.[14] An example of such a work is Dante's *Comedy,* in which the narrator explores first the *Inferno,* where unregenerate sinners suffer endlessly the fruits of their rejection of God. The Dark Wood and the mount of *Purgatory* correspond to the suffering and hope of experience, while the Earthly Paradise at the top of Mount Purgatory is a world of restored innocence. Finally, *Paradise* is the ultimate in organized innocence, the fulfillment of man's desire for God and the stellar community of the elect.

Even if they personally happen to believe in an afterlife, however, writers of utopian fiction do not follow Dante to Paradise—for the main point of his great poem is that neither planning nor reform will ever turn the brutal world of experience into an earthly paradise of restored innocence. What utopian writers of every stripe share is the faith that some principle of justice can, to some extent, transform the world of experience. Thus they follow a secularizing strategy best understood by recalling the words of John Lennon's song, "Imagine," which speaks of a future abolishing the religious reference points of heaven and hell. That is, they collapse Dante's four-level house into a two-level structure. Hell and the world of experience become the bottom floor of the utopian imaginative structure, while heaven and the state of innocence merge into the upper floor.[15]

Such compression of imaginative levels not only demands a secular ideology, it also forces a heightening of the contrast between the world of experience and that of innocence. The world of experience must become more fearsome, frustrating, and destructive; it is, in fact, subject to satirical distortion and caricature. The world of innocence, which now must bear the burden of rational or imaginative norm, becomes the focus of all desire for peace, freedom, and justice. Thus utopian works tend to transcend the historical process: the ideal community is a guide or norm which lies outside history in an inaccessible valley, an alternate universe, or a remote future. This transcendence of history in the utopian tradition is one feature of utopian visions not shared by *The Dispossessed;* such a lack, if it is one, is a source of its "ambiguity."

The strategy of a utopian work usually involves an imaginative attempt to explore the contrast between the two worlds—one desirable, the other undesirable. Often, though not always, there is an attempt to show how the old world can be transformed into the new. This may lead to the imaginative (or sometimes literal) destruction of a *dystopia* (that undesirable world of experience) and the creation of a new society in the ashes of the old. Science fiction—which has grown partly out of a delight in the wonders of modern technology, an expectation of some technological apocalypse, and partly out of a romantic preoccupation with extraordinary voyages in time or space—has usually absorbed the utopian dialectic, though often in a negative, or anti-utopian, manner.[16]

The fundamental narrative design of utopian fiction is *the quest,* in which the hero somehow leaves ordinary time and space to discover a world of restored innocence. Three major subtypes of the quest can be discerned. The first is the dream-vision/time-travel type (which, in honor of Woody Allen, we call the "sleeper" narrative). It is used, for example, in *News from Nowhere* and *Looking Backward.* In this type of quest the hero is awakened in a future that has achieved a reordered society. Another type is the more or less perilous journey to a remote community which is similarly reordered (*Gulliver's Travels, Erewhon, Walden Two*). We might call this the El Dorado narrative. The third type is the dialogue in which the utopian visionary is no longer the narrator or a character narratively "on point," but rather an authority whom the narrator draws out. This type, examples of which are Plato's *Republic* and More's *Utopia,* may be called the utopian dialogue.[17] Again, we are struck with an anomaly in considering *The Dispossessed.* To be sure, its hero, Shevek, undertakes a quest, but not a quest for a new and better world. Rather it is a quest to unite the peoples of the Twin Planets as he would unite Sequency physics with Simultaneity physics. Shevek's journey is indeed perilous, to the extent of catching a bad case of hay fever when he first arrives on Urras, experiencing an alcoholic hangover for the first time in his life, and finally, being forced to seek political asylum in an offworld embassy! But he does not discover a vision of restored innocence in A-Io; far from returning with "news from utopia," he returns home to a doubtful welcome on Anarres with hands that are "empty, as they had always been" (*TD,* XIII).

In a sense, Shevek's circular journey has to be taken as a rediscovery of utopia; Anarres is the closest thing he will ever find to Utopia. Not merely because he "is" an anarchist must he return to Anarres with empty hands. He returns with nothing, not even a picture of a lamb for his child. There is nothing fundamental that A-Io and the rest of Urras can give to Anarresti society, something that becomes clear when we compare Ioti society with that of Anarres in terms of several recurrent, if not universal, features of the ideal society in utopian tradition.

Establishment of a utopian community nearly always seems to result from a revolution, from a fundamental change in human relationships. The typical result is a world which stresses cooperation rather than competition, social integration rather than alienation. In Skinner's *Walden Two* the revolution is brought about through the intervention of Frazier's techniques of behavioral engineering, a vast social experiment.[18] In More's *Utopia,* Hythloday explains how the island commonwealth's original lawgiver, King Utopus. severed the island from the mainland and changed its name.[19] This, of course, is symbolic of the king's desire to establish Utopian customs independently of the corrupting influence of the old world (which had been much like the Europe of Book I). After Old Hammond describes to William Guest the beginnings of the civil war that led to the revolution, in chapters 16 and 17 of *News from Nowhere,* he speaks glowingly of "the men and women who go to make up humanity [as] free, happy, and energetic . . . and most commonly beautiful of body also," evidently a dramatic change from the humanity of Guest's own era.[20]

Because Shevek is so commanding as the hero of his own story, it's perhaps easier to overlook the emphasis of *The Dispossessed* on the revolutionary nature of Anarresti society. Just as Utopus severs Utopia from the mainland, so the Odonian Settlement on Anarres cuts itself off from the mother planet, with the ore freighters that belong to the Urrasti Council of World Governments the only remaining link between the two worlds. Anarresti speech and writing is in Pravic, a language apparently not mutually intelligible with any of the dialects spoken among the nations of Urras. Each Odonian uses only a single name that is generated by computer and assigned to one living person at a time. The revolutionary event, the Settlement, is closer in form to the social-science experiment of *Walden Two* than to the conquest of *Utopia* or the insurrection in *News from Nowhere;* but it is still a revolutionary event, celebrated as the Year One of Odonian history on Anarres. The terms of the Settlement, along with the linguistic innovations, are vital symbols of the far-reaching change in human relations. Moreover, one effect of interweaving the narrative of Shevek's career on Urras with that of his life up to the time of his departure for Urras in the opening chapter, is the constant reminder of the gulf between the ways of Anarresti society and those of Urrasti nations.

Another fairly regular feature of utopian communities, both in and out of fiction, is a striving for equality among the people making up society. Perceptions of what is progressive in these matters must change as the consensus changes, and utopian writers have always been just ahead of their contemporaries in extending personhood and citizenship to the outsider. In general, however, the utopian tradition has tended to confront directly the dismal effect of religious bigotry, racial prejudice, and sexism. In Plato's *Republic,* for instance, Socrates designs by "wish-thought" a commonwealth which, while meritocratic, seems as rigidly class-structured as any polity could be and as potentially tyrannical as some of the diseased states he describes earlier. But Plato departs radically from contemporary opinion in awarding women and men equality of occupation and education among the guardian class.[21] Equality of the sexes, without the unattractive feature of class structure, is also a salient feature of the classic utopias mentioned above. More's *Utopia* is clearly patriarchal; husbands "rule" their wives, and only males may be elected to the principate or lesser public office. It is a modified patriarchy, however. If a prospective wife must offer her naked body for inspection by the suitor, the suitor must reciprocate; and both men and women may serve as priests. While slavery exists in Utopia, it isn't practiced on prisoners of war or ethnic minorities; it is the punishment for infamous crime. Often, then, just when a utopian writer seems conservative in the area of equality, he is proposing modifications in the traditional system which would probably destroy it. The more modern a utopian work, the more likely it is to approach the ideal of absolute equality. With the exception of a special position for grandfathers, *News from Nowhere* advocates the equality and fraternity of all people. This is illustrated, in particular, for women in matters of marriage and divorce. Even *Walden Two,* which fairly exudes a kind of men's club atmosphere, makes it clear that in the new community, a woman is as likely to be an architect as is a man, and that a man may work in the nursery as well as a woman.

As with so many other things Shevek comes to know firsthand on

Urras, the meaning of equality doesn't come to him until he has experienced inequality, rather as if innocence is not to be understood without experience. Shevek first learns about the possibility of domination, oppression, and exploitation in the stunning episode of the prison experiment in which he, Tirin, and two younger boys jail Kadagv for thirty hours.[22] From his experiences with Sabul and Desar at the Institute in Abbenay, Shevek learns that the power relationship is not unheard of on Anarres. But it is only in A-Io that he sees how domination actually works, and thus learns the full meaning of the equality he has breathed like the air on his native planet. In A-Io, Shevek finds a social order built on the very assumption of inequality.

The position of Urrasti women is the most obvious contrast with home. As Shevek is traveling to Urras on the *Mindful,* the ship's doctor, Kimoe, asks him about the rumor that women and men have equal status in Anarresti society, and that there is no distinction there between men's work and women's work. This brief exchange, which is reminiscent of the passage from the *Republic* cited above, ends inconclusively, leaving Shevek to reflect: "This matter of superiority and inferiority must be a central one in Urrasti social life. If to respect himself Kimoe had to consider half the human race as inferior to him, how then did women manage to respect themselves—did they consider men inferior? And how did all that affect their sex lives?" (*TD,* I). Later, while spending a day with the seductive (and married) sister of his Urrasti colleague Oiie, he finds that his speculation isn't far from the mark, at least for the pampered and childless wife of an important businessman. Vea may be ironic and playful when she tells him that although the men run industry, education, and the government, the women run the men; but it is clear that she expects (and usually receives) a certain sexual deference. As for the effect this mutual exploitation has on Urrasti sex lives, Shevek gets a taste of that when, aroused by alcohol and Vea's air of wanton availablity, he attempts to embrace her, an act which ends in his ejaculating on her dress and vomiting in the hors d'oeuvres.

If sexual inequality can turn marriage into a prostitution-like mockery of the "life-bond" exemplified by Shevek's and Takver's partnership, the other distinctions of social class are revealed as a source of even greater damage to the social organism. When Shevek arrives on Urras, he is hustled off to a suite of rooms at the chief university of A-Io, Ieu Eun. While the visitor is recuperating from his allergies, the aristocratic old physicist, Atro, brings him a stack of popular newspapers containing accounts of his arrival. While Shevek glances over the sensationalist stories, he is warned by the younger physicist, Pae, to ignore the papers, as they are "awful trash." Shevek reads them anyway. When he is surprised to find attributed to himself a statement he never made, Pae refers contemptuously to "birdseed" journalism. During the conversation Pae makes it clear that he has little respect for the intellect or character of the "working people" who read such papers. Shevek later discovers that Atro has a different attitude toward the masses. Like a Russian aristocrat of the nineteenth century, Atro holds a romantic view of the common man as the backbone of A-Io, especially in time of war: "you'll find the soul of the people true as steel, when the country's threatened" (*TD,* IX). At one point Shevek reflects that because of Atro's obvious contempt for wealth, power, and the government, he is closer to the old man than to any other of his Urrasti colleagues. But Atro's feudal class division of humanity into warrior leaders and common soldiers who follow is sadly out of date in contemporary A-Io, a bureaucratic modern state uniting industry and government. Further, his ultimate distinction of social classes reduces the entire concept to its well-deserved absurdity. Atro's main interest in Shevek's physical theory, more important than his conviction of its truth, is that it could lead to a victory of "Cetian" science:

> "I don't want those damned aliens getting at you through your notions about brotherhood and mutualism and all that. They'll spout you whole rivers of 'common humanity' and 'leagues of all the worlds' and so on, and I'd hate to see you swallow it. The law of existence is struggle—competition—elimination of the weak—a ruthless war for survival. And I want to see the best survive. The kind of humanity I know. The Cetians. You and I: Urras and Anarres. We're ahead of them now, all those Hainish and Terrans and whatever else they call themselves, and we've got to stay ahead of them." (*TD,* V)

Ultimately, Atro's desire is frustrated when Shevek releases his General Temporal Theory, not to the government of A-Io but to the Terran ambassador, as a gift to the people of the Nine Known Worlds.[23] One of the primary reasons for his decision is the realization that Urrasti society, which is saddled with class barriers, is based on assumptions of natural inequality. Through Efor, the manservant assigned him by the university, he becomes aware that the Ioti masses are indeed oppressed by the "owners," that they *are* underemployed, sneered at, and angry. Thus swept up in a massive protest against the war and social injustice in general, Shevek sets himself against the Ioti government by addressing the demonstrators, and ends up seeking asylum in the Terran embassy in Rodarred. Shevek's speech to the strikers sums up his realization that Urras and A-Io have nothing to offer him, a realization that has come primarily from his experience of Urrasti inequality.

Communal (or at least commensal) living arrangements are the third recurrent feature of utopian visions. The communism of the Guardian class in the *Republic* is too well known to require comment, while the physical layout of the apartments, nurseries, dining halls, and commons rooms in *Walden Two* (though it looks suspiciously like a college campus) is presented as an obvious means of social efficiency. While the household based on the large extended family is the basic social unit in More's *Utopia,* each group of thirty households is assigned a common dining hall in which most meals are taken. And although the private (though not privately owned) house or apartment seems to be the norm in *News from Nowhere,* the dining commons is again the locus of solidarity and mutualism, with guest houses dotting the countryside for the benefit of the footloose. With the exception of the *Republic,* these utopias use the dining hall as a symbol of the common life, while reserving greater or lesser space for the life functions that can't be made public (of course, the realm of the nonpublic differs from one work of fiction to another).

This feature of utopianism is important in understanding the contrast between Anarres and A-Io in *The Dispossessed.* Like the design of the community in *Walden Two,* the design of an Anarresti community is based on the social requirement of efficient design, expressed in the Pravic vernacular as avoiding "excrement" (the excessive and nonfunctional). After infancy, children live apart from the parents, in domiciles which are also where their education takes place. Couples who are paired—whether heterosexually or homosexually, permanently or temporarily—are allowed the use of a private room; but for the most part, Anarresti individuals are assigned dormitory accommodations of two to six per room. Meals are taken in common. Privacy, then, is encouraged only insofar as it is functional. When he is settled in at Ieu Eun, Shevek finds similar living arrangements at the university, except that there are no females and he is given a servant, as well as more space than normal.

As far as he is concerned, the important fact about Ioti social organization is the absence of a symbol of the common life outside the university, unless we count the fine public transportation system, the shopping center on Saemtenovia Prospect, and the public buildings of the Ioti state and the Council of World Governments—all of which work better as symbols of alienation than of integration. It's when Demalre Oiie invites him home to dinner that Shevek becomes aware of the radical discontinuity between Ioti public life—competitive, acquisitive, and centripetal—and the Ioti locus of mutual aid, affection, and solidarity: the private home. Having already observed that much is missing from what may be seen in public life (the world of work), when so much is reserved for private life, Shevek receives an apparently grudging invitation from Oiie to spend a weekend with his family.[24] Shevek is surprised to find Oiie's wife Sewa a normal person with whom he can converse simply and matter-of-factly. He is further surprised to find that Oiie, who has expressed thorough distaste for the idea of women in public, is "a changed man at home," one who treats his wife and family with respect and trust—as equals. At home, Oiie behaves much like an Anarresti, "as a simple, brotherly kind of man, a free man." What is missing from Ioti public life is the family spirit of brotherhood, which, of course, is the raison d'etre of the communal life of the Anarresti, however much it might be argued that these communal arrangements are necessary for efficiency.

Another fairly common feature of utopian visions is eradication of the conventional distinction between work and play, between activity aimed primarily at producing a good beyond itself (such as economic security) and activity undertaken for its own sake. In the vaguely puritanical utopias of the *Republic* and *Walden Two,* the distinction seems to have been abolished, mainly to turn play into work, that is, to direct all activity toward making the community perfect. Even in the spacious humanist *Utopia* of Thomas More, the distinction isn't so much abolished as modified; work is devoted to the general welfare, while recreation is intended for self-improvement, which, in itself, contributes to the general welfare.[25] It is *News from Nowhere*, though, which contains the clearest embodiment of this utopian ideal, perhaps because it is a superabundant utopia in which the economic necessity of human labor has been reduced almost to the vanishing point, due to an unspecified "great change in the use of mechanical force."[26] The concluding festival of the romance, from which the narrator fades out of his vision to return to his (and our) old world, is an Oxfordshire haymaking, to which Londoners travel up the Thames in a holiday mood. Having abolished the old economic order of wage slavery, the inhabitants of this visionary England are able to undertake an economically useful task as if it were a game—in effect, making sport of business. As Dick Hammond says, it is "easy-hard work," work which tires and develops the body but doesn't "harass" the spirit.[27]

While the Odonian society of Anarres is not a superabundant utopia, neither is it a puritanical one, at least in conception. Shevek has grown up as something of a loner, but this is as much the result of his absorption in the work of physics as anything else. He doesn't reject Odonian mutualism; in fact, his views on mutualism are more orthodox than those of his friends. but when he comes to the institute in Abbenay to work with Sabul, his commitment to his work is so total and free as to be imbalanced, Although this intemperance leads to physical and mental exhaustion and is thus dysfunctional, it is, as it were, a fine excess that results from a refusal to distinguish between work and leisure. As the narrator puts it: "He work/played" (*TD,* IV). Even his dreams become part of the work, a sign (since dreams are the mind's way of relaxing) that the functions are integrated. Shevek's plunge into his work at this time, however, is no more total than his plunge into the community's work later in life, when he is given an emergency assignment during a drought and is separated from Takver and physics for four years.

The difference between A-Io and Anarres in the matter of work is not as obvious, if only because the question of work and play doesn't come up in Shevek's conversations with his Urrasti colleagues. But it does linger near the surface when Shevek is considering the educational system of A-Io, in his brush with Urrasti sexuality, and in the matter of alcohol. Upon Shevek's arrival in A-Io, the popular press makes much of the fact that he, like all Odonians, doesn't consume alcohol. In discussing the question, Pae asks Shevek what, since they do not drink, Anarresti workers do at night to forget their troubles. But Shevek cannot deal with the question. What the question reveals about Pae's attitudes is much more interesting than Shevek's rambling comments on fermented holum juice and brainwave training. Apparently Pae can't grasp the idea that Anarresti society makes no distinction between a class of manual laborers and a class to which Shevek, as a physicist, belongs. It is also clear that Pae regards work as something fundamentally different from the activities of leisure time, which are trivial, not serious, and perhaps basically irresponsible. This attitude is partly the basis of the humor displayed when Shevek discusses his theories at Vea's cocktail party. At first reluctant due to the difficulty of discussing physics with laymen, Shevek warms to the subject, until it is clear that he is "doing physics" as seriously as he would be if he were at his desk computer. Unable to adopt the role of impractical professor which he is supposed to be playing to another guest's role of hard-headed businessman, Shevek ends up delivering a lecture and offending the others. It is shortly after this that Shevek tries to take Vea, thus illustrating, among other things, his ignorance of a type of stylized sexual play which isn't supposed to end in copulation.

Although Anarres and A-Io differ in their attitudes toward work and play, they seem to concur on another feature of utopias, even science fiction utopias: technological stability. Perhaps because utopias, especially those of the nineteenth century and later, are often the result of rapid technological innovation, there often seems to be an assumption that, having achieved a certain plateau of technological development, a society will attempt to maintain order by halting or retarding the pace of innovation. Whether or not this is desirable, it is a goal unlikely to be achieved, for technological innovation usually has its own momentum.[28]

Given the interpretive tradition, it would be natural to assume that Plato, interested more in the otherwordly ontology of the ideas, would not readily observe the possibilities inherent in the momentum of technology.[29] Plato lived in an age of technological consolidation and refinement, rather than one of rapid change. [30] But we needn't invoke cultural determinism to explain the absence of change in the classic utopia. It may be true that a guiding principle of Socratic and Platonic thought is the idea that the best and strongest members of a class are the least susceptible to change.[31] It is also true that a fundamental goal of utopian works is to present a vision of justice—the perfect ordering of human society—and that the stability of the ideal city or the model state is not a peculiarity of the *Republic* and the *Laws.* More's Utopians, for example, do not totally resist change and new ideas; they have eagerly reprinted books containing the "arts and sciences of the Greeks" brought them by Hythloday, and they experiment in the useful arts. But having established the basic plan of their social economy 1,760 years earlier, they make only those additions that will improve and refine their life, such as the art of printing learned from examing Hythloday's Aldine editions.[32] However, in order to avoid "future shock'' (in Book I, the situation in Europe, which is ravaged by innovation in military and agricultural technology), they practice the doctrine of ''appropriate technology.''[33] This premium on technological stability is also characteristic of *News from Nowhere.* During the discourse in which he compares his own time with that of the nineteenth century, the history-minded Old Hammond points out that the latter period was wondrous in that it created ingenious and well-made machines which were then used to produce worthless manufactures. He goes on to observe that the momentum of industrial innovation compelled the exploitation of labor and the institution of colonialism, in order to create the ''World-Market.'' Since now only those things are made which are for genuine use, ''immensely improved'' machinery may be reserved for truly irksome tasks. He even leaves open the possibility that new industrial processes may be introduced, provided they produce desirable wares and remain pleasant.[34] Even *Walden Two,* the main point of which is the social stability to be gained from a major innovation in behavioral engineering, stability not attainable through either democratic politics or totalitarianism, is carefully structured to lead into consideration of that topic by first focusing on the traditional, small-scale human engineering of the community's dining halls, work areas, and living space.[35] In Morris's and Skinner's utopias, then, the stability of the new world is based on the avoidance of unplanned change and the nourishing of an appropriate technology.

An interesting fact about this agreement among the four utopian writers considered is that they come to insistence on stability from quite different technological milieus. As pointed out above, whatever Plato's personal opinions on technological innovation, he appears to have lived in a time when it wasn't rapid enough to be frightening. More's *Utopia,* on the other hand, reveals itself clearly to the reader in Book I as being written out of anguish at the social penalties exacted by the technological rationalization of agriculture. *News from Nowhere* shows Morris's concern with the conditions of workers under industrial capitalism during the century that appeared to have overthrown the old order. The casual reader may be forgiven for thinking that he was concerned mainly with the aesthetic effects of ''cockneyfication.'' *Walden Two* is evidently written not only out of the author's conviction of the truth of his psychological theories, but also out of a disillusionment with the social order as a result of World War II. There would seem, then, to be no particular cultural explanation to be invoked for the similarity in attitudes toward technological change. In fact, we are dealing with a demanding archetype of the literary form, an archetype required by the thematic idealism of the utopian tradition.[36]

It would be difficult to show that either Urras or Anarres is a utopian society because of a typical attitude toward technological change. The keynote of their similarity in that respect is sounded by Shevek on the evening at Oiie's when he meets Vea and escorts her to the railroad depot. When she asks him whether he will be in danger when he returns to Anarres (a question that embarrasses him since he knows he will), he changes the subject by observing of the approaching train: "You know, our trains look very much like these? A good design need not change" (*TD,* VII). Both Urras and Anarres, in fact, seem to have rejected the ideology of "change for the sake of change" that seems to be the usual concomitant of high technology, although for different reasons.

This should not be taken to imply, by the way, that either society (and thus, by implication, the author) rejects the machine. Space vehicles kept in orbit by the Anarresti Defense Federative are capable of attacking intruder ships, but their primary function is to provide weather monitoring essential to the planet's drylands agriculture. Since Odonian society is pragmatic as well as romantic, Odo's ideas—and their realization on Anarres—are intended to solve the classic anarchist problem of economic administration in lieu of the state, the market, or an intersecting network of private firms. So transport, communications, and the central computers at Abbenay provide the technical substructure of Anarresti society:

> They cut back very hard indeed, but to a minimum beneath which they would not go; they would not regress to a pre-urban, pre-technological tribalism. They knew that their anarchism was the product of a very high civilization, of a complex diversified culture, of a stable economy and a highly industrialized technology that could maintain high production and rapid transportation of goods. However vast the distances separating settlements, they held to the ideal of complex organicism. (*TD,* IV)

Anarresti concern with the technology of communication is reflected in Shevek's conviction that the ansible will be the first practical result of his General Temporal Theory. Although neither individual autonomy nor the social organism would be served by technological regression, such a view means that no innovation is likely to be made frivolously without being evaluated for its necessity and usefulness. The Odonian attitude toward "excrement" is warrant of that.

If Anarresti technology is appropriate in terms of resources and the goals of the social organism, the technology of Urras, and specifically that of A-Io, is adapted to a postindustrial culture in which resources must be and are husbanded. From the narrator's discussion of the economic relationship between Urras and Anarres we learn that "the self-plundering eras" (*TD,* IV) of Urrasti history have exhausted certain mineral resources and that the need to mine the moon is why there are any people at all on Anarres. Early in his Urrasti sojourn, when Shevek is taken on many tours of the cities and the countryside, he observes that not many other cars are on the road, even though A-Io is a propertarian society that might be expected to support the private auto. This is so because they are kept expensive and heavily taxed. His guides are quite proud of the fact that any ecologically dangerous or resource-squandering consumer goods are strictly controlled in A-Io. Until Shevek discovers the slums of Nio Esseia late in the novel, all he sees of A-Io—the parks, the well-kept public buildings, the carefully tended farms—tends to confirm our perception of the country as a middle-class ecotopia. No rapid technological change will result from competitive behavior of innovators, as in a laizzez-faire economy; none will result from a corporate state's need to maintain industrial growth. The Ioti ecological code, the results of which are so impressive to a Terran ambassador from a wasted planet which has maintained minimum viability only through stringent, even Draconian, controls, is designed to secure class stability and the good life for the Ioti bourgeoisie who are represented by the academic bureaucrats, Pae and Oiie. From different material conditions and with different social goals, therefore, both propertarian A-Io and anarchist Anarres exercise technological restraint: there has to be a compelling reason to alter a good design.

Still another feature of classic Western utopias seems to be their concern with what has come to be known as the "urban problem": undirected growth, blight, the poverty of the industrial reserve army, and so on. It wasn't until the late eighteenth century that these problems (and the attendant dystopian imagery, as in Blake's famous lyric, "London") began to assume their modern form. Since the utopian vision seems to be the urbanized cousin of the pastoral vision, however, even premodern works must come to terms with the "urban scene." In Plato's time philosophy was characteristically an urban enterprise; yet there is no reason in principle why a utopian vision should not have dispensed entirely with the city, especially since it is the source of so much injustice. But in the *Republic,* inasmuch as the healthy city is a model of the healthy individual (and vice versa), the pattern of just governance elicited in the dialogue is the ideal to which the wise man aspires and the only city of which he is truly a citizen.[37] Given the status of the *Republic's* model city, it would perhaps be foolish to see it as a set of concrete proposals for social reform, although there is much in the dialogue's diagnoses of civic illness that was to become a traditional part of the dystopian satire accompanying utopian visions: the corrupting influence of great wealth, the destabilizing effects of extremes of wealth and poverty, and the bestiality of high living.[38] Many of these themes are again touched on in the *Laws.*

If Plato had to deal with the city because it was a fundamental feature of Greek life, as well as a handy metaphor for the condition of the individual's soul, the other writers cited above had to deal with it because it presented itself to them in much the same guise as it did to writers as diverse as Charles Dickens, Upton Sinclair, and Franz Kafka—as a metaphor for hell, whether inner or outer. While More's *Utopia* contains no imagery that can compare with the modern urban hell, we see in Book I an allusion on Hythloday's part to the beginnings of what has become a continuing urban social problem. Hythlody relates that during his discussion with the company at Cardinal Morton's, he brought up the creation of a rural *lumpenproletariat* by the destruction of traditional village and manorial agriculture with sheep grazing and enclosure. In a later step in the evolution of the modern industrial state, this rural dispossessed became the nucleus of capital's industrial reserve army, the underemployed, and thus came to the attention of utopian writers. One of the components of the nightmare "past" of *News from Nowhere* is undoubtedly Morris's disaffection with ugly railway bridges and cockney villas. Far more important to its theme, however, are the social and economic causes of such ugliness. A focal point for the urban image is Chapter 7, in which Guest comes upon Trafalgar Square, site of the Bloody Sunday police riot of 1887 and, we also learn, the site of the 1952 massacre that has led to the revolution. As he and young Dick Hammond enter an open space ornamented with pear and apricot trees, Guest shuts his eyes and sees "a phantasmagoria of another day'': a mob, ugly buildings, and mounted police.[39] Not only here but throughout the text, the narrator continually compares the London scene remembered from his own day with that of his visionary future. Thus he reminds us that the scenes of ugliness are also the scenes of alienation, exploitation, and oppression, giving a cumulative impression of the nineteenth-century, industrial-commercial city as a secular hell to be contrasted with the secular paradise of a deurbanized future. More concentrated is Skinner's image of urban desolation in *Walden Two.* As Burris, at once disturbed by and attracted to the social experiment of Frazier's community, waits with Castle for the train that will return them to their university, he decides to ditch the other man along with his fulminations against Frazier. Leaving the station, he wanders through a poorer section of the town afflicted by blight and social despair. The contrast with the community he has just left is borne swiftly into his mind, especially after he sees that the president of his university has given another trite baccalaureate address on the dignity of man.[40]

There are no large cities on Anarres to serve as images of hell; Abbenay, the largest town of the planet's Odonian Settlement, is structured like any other Anarresti community. Where there is no property, there is no great gulf of power, wealth, and class to be expressed in slums and ghettos. When Shevek arrives on Urras, he sees there no such scenes of woe. He sees rather his suite of rooms at the university, with its apparently contented manservant and its hearth of marble. He looks from his window and sees the contrasting greens of an abundant agricultural valley and is taken on tours of the countryside:

> Traveling by car or train, he saw villages, farms, towns; fortresses from the feudal days; the ruined towers of Ae, ancient capital of an empire, forty-four hundred years old. He saw the farmlands, lakes, and hills of Avan Province, the heartland of A-Io, and on the northern skyline the peaks of the Meitei Range, white, gigantic. The beauty of the land and the well-being of its people remained a perpetual marvel to him. The guides were right: the Urrasti knew how to use their world. (*TD,* III)

Everywhere Shevek is taken he sees what appears to be a superabundant land filled with happy people, the sort of place we might characterize as a utopia. Two false notes, however, are sounded. The visitor, we are told, would have liked to confirm his impression that he should revise his preconceptions about the lot of the poor on Urras, but there never seems to be time, so busy are his guides. As the physicists return from the Space Research Foundation in Drio, Shevek recalls that the Fort in Drio had been the scene of Odo's imprisonment for nine years. The smooth-talking Pae believes the fort has been pulled down:

> But as the car followed a riverside highway toward the turnoff to Ieu Eun it passed a bluff on the curve of the river Seisse, and up on the bluff there was a building, heavy, ruinous, implacable, with broken towers of black stone. Nothing could have been less like the gorgeous lighthearted buildings of the Space Research Foundation, the showy domes, the bright factories, the tidy lawns and paths. Nothing could have made them look so much like bits of colored paper. (*TD,* III)

The contrast between the old dungeon and the more recent architecture is Shevek's first real hint of the continuing reality underneath the smooth exterior of Ioti society, the massed power of the state and the upper classes. As a citadel in a commanding position, as well as a reminder of the prison episode of Shevek's youth, it stands as a symbol—much more blatant than the newer public buildings—of the scene of urban despair Shevek will encounter later in Nio Esseia's underworld.

Little need be said to demonstrate that the old image of the city as a secular hell is subsequently developed when Shevek wanders through the slums looking for the anarchist group that has contacted him, evidently through Efor, his manservant at the university. It is interesting to note, however, that Shevek's reaction to the commercial center of Nio Esseia, Saemtenevia Prospect, associates the more recent *anti-utopian* image of the "air-conditioned nightmare" with the older *dystopian* image of the urban hell; twice the narrator refers to it from Shevek's point of view as "the nightmare street" (*TD,* V, VII). The more traditional urban nightmare is evoked through a conversation with Efor and Shevek's involvement in the abortive demonstration against the war. In a rare moment of confidence while nursing Shevek through the three-day hangover resulting from his great drunk at Vea's party, Efor speaks of the life led by his class, who call themselves "Nioti" rather than Ioti and who speak the "city dialect." The conversation is initiated by Shevek who unthinkingly observes that Efor should have been a physician (an occupation his class is unlikely to enter). There follows Efor's description of the sort of hospital his kind die in (the hospital in which his baby died), with rats crawling over the patients' beds. As the conversation continues, Shevek learns about aspects of Ioti life which neither his upbringing nor his sightseeing have served to acquaint him with directly, and which, with the exception of imprisonment, he has encountered only in Odonian history books: "... a rat, or an army barracks, or an insane asylum, or a poorhouse, or a pawnshop, or an execution, or a thief, or a tenement, or a rent collector, or a man who wanted to find work and could not find work to do, or a dead baby in a ditch" (*TD*, IX). When Efor asks about Anarresti life, Shevek feels constrained to observe that Anarres is not "all milk and honey." But the manservant's bitterness is revealed momentarily when he says: "All the same there's none of *them* [owners] there" (*TD*, IX).

Shevek's personal contact with the urban nightmare hidden by the bourgeois facade of Nio Esseia comes about when he slips away from the university to seek the anarchists who have contacted him. Competently using the subway map, he finds his way to the Old Town station and, when he comes up from the underground platform, confronts a scene that does "not look like Nio Esseia":

> A fine, foggy rain was falling, and it was quite dark; there were no street lights. The lampposts were there, but the lights were not turned on, or were broken. Yellow gleams slitted from around shuttered windows here and there. Down the street, light streamed from an open doorway, around which a group of men were lounging, talking loud. The pavement, greasy with rain, was littered with scraps of paper and refuse. The shopfronts, as well as he could make them out, were low, and were all covered up with heavy metal or wooden shutters, except for one which had been gutted by fire and stood black and blank, shards of glass still sticking in the frames of the broken windows. (*TD,* IX)

The scene, of course, is only too familiar. We are looking at a slumscape on a satellite of Tau Ceti, but we might as well be in any of the metropolitan centers of the "first world" of Sol III. The only curious thing is that the subway is kept so handsome. We may assume that the authorities in A-Io are to maintain it (since it is used by the upper classes) to insulate the bourgeoisie from any perception of the "other A-Io." When Shevek joins the demonstrators after learning of Nio Esseia's "four hundred thousand unemployed" (*TD,* IX), he experiences firsthand the lengths to which the same authorities will go to prevent the expression of social grievances. As he finishes a romantic speech on suffering, mutual aid, the spirit of revolution, he is drowned out by the racket of police helicopters and machine guns. The demonstration turns into a rout, and Shevek, now a fugitive from Ioti "justice," ends up hiding in a basement with a man dying of a gunshot wound. Again, we are viewing a scene on a distant planet, but we may be forgiven if we recall the description of the two Trafalgar Square riots in *News from Nowhere.*

In terms of the image of the urban scene, then, we receive a clear indication that Urras, and specifically A-Io, is the *dystopia* of *The Dispossessed.* Whatever the faults of Anarresti society, it offers us (and Shevek) no nightmare comparable to the slums of Nio Esseia. Similarly, we find a clear sign when we examine the novel's treatment of theories of knowledge and learning, for a seventh (and central) theme of utopian fictions is the reform of education. Such a concern is eminently logical, since any change in values must be accompanied by a change in the system of creating and transmitting values. This is borne out by the classic utopian works to which we have been referring. The *Republic* can be read as a proposal to reform the heroic-aristocratic *paideia* based on epic poetry; when Plato composed the *Laws,* he again made a central theme the right ordering of education.[41] More's *Utopia* isn't just an attack on agricultural policy and the use of mercenaries, it also proposes to reform the Christian education of sixteenth-century Europe by showing that the Utopians eschew sterile dialectical theology in favor of a humanistic study (in Greek, of course!) of classic authors and the New Testament.[42] Skinner's *Walden Two* also has education as a central theme, and rightly so, since Frazier's "behavioral engineering" is the application of a learning theory, that of operant conditioning through positive reinforcement.

It is *News from Nowhere,* however, which confronts the same issue Shevek confronts in *The Dispossessed.* In one of the romance's more amusing passages, Guest idly mentions to Dick Hammond that the children who apparently spend unsupervised summers camping in the woods will be "all the fresher for school." Dick protests that the use of the word *school*—which applies to fish or painters of some such—is peculiar. Embarrassed again at having made a cultural slip, Guest thinks it best not to explain "the boy-farms which I had been used to call schools," saying simply that he uses the term to refer to "a system of education" which Dick professes to have heard used but never understood. When Guest huffily exclaims that education is "a system of teaching young people," Dick jokingly asks why old people should be left out, and goes on to point out that learning does indeed go on in his culture, but it is organized primarily according to the principle that people will learn to do something when they are ready for it and when they need it, whether the subject be reading, writing, languages, or mathematics.[43] This conversation (which, incidentally, relieves Old Hammond of the burden of explaining education in this visionary England) sets apart the educational philosophy of *News from Nowhere* from those of the other utopias we have referred to, including that of *Walden Two,* which, while learner-centered, is manipulated by society. In the other utopias the reformed education agrees in an important respect with the systems it is meant to displace: the needs of society come first, while those of the individual come second. *News from Nowhere,* the proto-anarchist utopia, sets the needs of the individual above those of society for the simplest reason of all: it seems to work better to arrange things thus.[44]

When we look at Anarresti education we are struck by the fact that its problems are the result of an apparent failure to resolve the duality implied above: the initiative and needs of the individual in conflict with the goals of society. This tension is clearly related to the sources of ambiguity we analyzed earlier. It is one of the virtues of the novel that it does not attempt to ignore or pass over the conflict, as does Dick in *News from Nowhere.* We have already mentioned the incident in which Shevek is accused by the director of the learning center of "egoizing" when he volunteers at eight years old his discovery of the paradox that motion is impossible. Although the learning center is a learner-oriented pedagogical setting, and in spite of the fact that he has simply volunteered his discovery while participating in speaking-and-listening (the Anarresti term for show-and-tell), Shevek comes up against the wall of his teacher's inability—one shared with a good many "progressive" pedagogues—to deal with an individual's creativity. Many other details touching upon Anarresti education reveal that its major problem seems to be that the principle of mutual aid and solidarity—one of the anarchism's twin pillars—tends to degenerate into mindless mediocrity and the reign of public opinion, threatening individual initiative, which is anarchism's other pillar. The careers of Sabul and Desar illustrate this phenomenon; but perhaps its most heartbreaking manifestation occurs after Shevek and the Syndicate of Initiative have made enemies by communicating with Urras. His daughter, Pilun, doesn't want to return to her dormitory learning center because the other children are being allowed to abuse her by calling Takver and Shevek "traitors." In a society which recognizes the independence of child from parents, we would expect that, at the very least, such antics would be discouraged; but public opinion can take its toll on even the innocent.

In spite of troubles in the learning centers and institutes of Anarres, the Odonian educational philosophy comes off clearly superior to that of Urras and A-Io. When Shevek begins offering seminars and lectures while working at Ieu Eun (taking a three-course load even though he is expected to do only research), he is pleased that the lecture course comes into being after petition by a delegation of students, for this is the way courses are initiated in Anarresti learning centers. Inevitably, the administration tries to euchre him and the students out of the course, proving that bureaucratic inertia can overwhelm even the desire for high enrollment (the initial enrollment is 2,000). But Shevek, amused by this manifestation of the fundamental "anarchism" of the young, persists, and the lectures are given. Shevek is surprised and pleased that many of the students are "capable of following both the philosophy and the mathematics." He is engaged by their politeness and rather likes them; yet he cannot feel any "great warmth towards any of them." They are all careerists, training for industry or the academic profession, and it seems that to them physics is only a means. What most upsets Shevek, however, is their demand for grades. Initially he sees the demand for tests and grades as a quirk of the administration and accedes out of courtesy to his "hosts." But when he tries the ploy of allowing the students to write a paper on any physics problem that interests them, and giving everyone the same grade, the students are upset and complain. They want Shevek to set the questions so that they won't have to think of questions but only of the right answers; they want competitive distinctions so those who work hard will be rewarded. The point of this becomes clear when the students tell Shevek that the university is clearly a democratic institution, in light of the fact that the scholarship competition grows keener every year. With one of the withering remarks characteristic of Shevek when he can no longer put up with another person spouting garbage, the physicist shows his contempt for "meritocracy": "You put another lock on the door and call it democracy" (*TD,* V).

The complementary defects of Anarresti and Ioti education, in fact, illustrate the opposing worst tendencies of competitive and communitarian societies. In competitive societies, the economic metaphor for which is the market, the danger is that social ties will be destroyed in the race for power, prestige, and place, even in the rare instance of everyone's having an equal opportunity. In communitarian societies, whose economic model is the central plan, the danger is that social goals will override the legitimate desires of the individual for freedom and fulfillment. It's a measure of Le Guin's clearsightedness that she does not attempt to gloss over the defects of Anarresti education. If an anarchist model of education were fully operative on Anarres, it would certainly be preferable to the grotesque records-and-admissions bureaucracy of the meritocratic University of Ieu Eun and the similar institutions of Terra. Unfortunately, the learner-centered trappings of Anarresti education cannot disguise its dangerous tendency to put social harmony above the individual's intellectual freedom. As Bedap puts it in explaining to Shevek how Sabul is able to lord it over him: "Public opinion! That's the power structure he's part of, and knows how to use. The unadmitted, inadmissible government that rules the Odonian society by stifling the individual mind" (*TD,* VI).

A brief review may be in order here. We claim to have established that the primary source of ambiguity in *The Dispossessed,* with respect to its being a utopian work, lies in the fact that it is a novel and not the simple stylized vision of a perfected society usually dealt with by utopian visionaries.[45] As such, it must deal with suffering, conflict, and discovery, with becoming rather than with the essence of perfection. We will return to this point later; what we wish to underline here is that, in spite of the novelistic bent of *The Dispossessed,* it does not use its ambiguities, its temporality, to suggest that the reader should use his wits in choosing from a smorgasbord of conflicting social values. Rather, it clearly displays a lively contrast between the two Cetian societies in terms of certain recurrent features of the utopian tradition. On nearly every point of this contrast, Anarres is clearly the society that most closely resembles what might be called the model utopian society—revolutionary origin, equality, communalism, work as play, concern with the urban scene, and educational reform. Only in the case of technological stability do we find that Urras and Anarres are both "utopian." With respect to this tradition, then, Anarres is unambiguously a utopia.

In listing what we consider the salient features of the utopian tradition as primarily a branch of political theory. However, what initially. Naturally we assumed that a common political theme could be found in classic Western utopias, for we regarded the utopian tradition as primarily a branch of political theory. However, what we found in thinking about the matter and in reconsidering works with which we were familiar, is that the "constitutions" of utopias differ so widely, so widely as to make a search for any common, "utopian" political theory meaningless. In the ordinary sense of the word, politics is abolished, for example, in the different technocracies of *Looking Backward* and *Walden Two*. The utopian anarchism of *News from Nowhere* leads to the shortest chapter in Old Hammond's discourse, XIII ("Concerning Politics"), which is only five sentences long. On the other hand, the Island of Utopia makes extensive use of deliberative councils and magistrates in something approaching a federal system, and discussion of public affairs is encouraged. Plato's model states have been characterized as examples of everything in political systems from the extreme right to the extreme left; it is not a question we wish to discuss, beyond observing that Plato shows more than an average amount of concern with the management of political affairs, something not universally characteristic of utopian writers. And so on.

One thing that might be said about all utopian works is that they usually do not deal with the question of politics ambiguously, as a process and a problem to be worked out in the crucible of experience. Rather they tend—rightly so, as model societies—to present one solution or another to the question of politics, even when the solution is abolition. Perhaps this is the source of the modern liberal intellectual's disaffection with the utopian tradition, for the liberal tradition places great value on pluralism and the clash of values and ideas in the marketplace of politics. But the liberal also holds certain values dear, values that may well be endangered in the political marketplace; thus he often seems to be acting irrationally or inconsistently, as when a Civil Liberties Union attorney defends the First Amendment rights of the Nazi Party, which would like nothing better than to deprive Jews and blacks of the prior rights of liberty and life and then set to work on liberals. Robert Pirsig has stated the dilemma well: "Programs of a political nature are important *end products* of social quality that can be effective only if the underlying structure of social values is right. The social values are right only if the individual values are right. . . . Other people can talk about how to expand the destiny of mankind. I just want to talk about how to fix a motorcycle."[46]

As Pirsig suggests, there are different levels of action which are directed by their own value complexes—political, social, and individual. That these value levels are seldom congruent or even complementary is taken as axiomatic by most contemporary political theorists. This condition is produced by, and in turn produces, the kinds of ambiguities described above. Pirsig believes that whatever is accomplished in the social and political realms originates with the individual. Unfortunately, individuals in our tradition, and apparently those of the Tau Ceti system as well, are caught up in a conflict between two dispositions, one analytic, scientific, and technological, and the other synthetic, imaginative, and poetic. Attempts to overcome this duality usually consist of rejecting one or the other disposition, asserting that the world is simpler than, in fact, it is. Social and political policies developed from such assertions cannot be successful.

Shevek's individual values aren't compatible with the social values of Anarres. His individual fulfillment requires that he study physics, do research in pursuit of discoveries, and seek the "solid foundations of the universe." As a scientist he is not immediately concerned with the practical applications of his research. Meanwhile, plagued with famine and other material scarcities, Anarresti society may be forgiven its lack of interest in Shevek's quest. In this regard, the anarchist instinct is Rousseauian; such investigations are usually supported by societies which exploit the poor to subsidize the scientist or the artist. Urrasti society is willing to subsidize and support Shevek's research out of its relative abundance, for it sees in his work a terrific potential: cosmic dominance.

Clearly, Shevek cannot be completely at home in either society. To be true to himself, he must, in Camus' phrase, be "in revolt" against both. Everyone must live somewhere, however; thus, from what we know of his character, Shevek's final decision is acceptable. It also accords well with the comparison of social and political values in the two societies, which Le Guin has carefully built into the novel's structure. The important difference between the two societies is a matter of possibilities. Every political system operates within constraining limits. With regard to ambiguity, the limits exist in the individuals comprising the system. Plato's anthropomorphism established the link between the individual and the city: the soul of the one corresponds to the soul of the other; the City is Man writ large. Shevek is not a typical Anarresti any more than he is a typical Urrasti. While Anarres has much remaining to encourage—or at least make possible—the unbuilding of walls, Urras, aside from the affluence and leisure of its upper classes, has little potential for overcoming or mitigating the effects of ambiguity. The common enemies of human solidarity and intellectual clarity—fear, suspicion, and misunderstanding—have gained the upper hand on Urras.

But there is hope that Anarres will avoid this condition.

The potential for dealing successfully with ambiguity, for realizing true community on Anarres, depends on two aspects of the Anarresti political culture, the level of political articulation and the reliance on speech for political communication. Odo's anarchism, which is the ideological basis for Anarresti politics, has eliminated the one political role on which the politics of archism depend. In a complex society, a society where a sophisticated technology has developed and which consists of a considerable number of persons, there are usually three distinguishable political roles: ruler, agent, subject. Each has a place in the archist firmament.

Originally the act of acquiring a leader or ruler to represent an entire people must have symbolized the coming of age of a society, as well as being a step toward more efficient organization. Agents, whether appointed by the ruler to carry out his will or by the people to carry out theirs, operated within carefully prescribed limits in performing specific tasks; they had no right to claim plenipotentiality. The people, in depending on the structure of the political system and the content of the political culture, may be either citizens or subjects, the major difference being the degree of political articulation. Having a ruler to represent an entire people implies both trust and control—the less of one, the more of the other—and the arrangement that began as one of trust may end as one of strict control. The divergence between the theoretical justification of a role hierarchy and its usual operation is portrayed excellently in Le Guin's description of Urrasti political culture.

In the tendency to base their view of the state on practice rather than theory, anarchists may be forgiven their tendency to link the concepts of king, priest, and representative with the facts of hierarchy, oppression, and alienation. Odo, unlike Babeuf (who wanted to create freedom by strangling the last priest with the entrails of the last king), has created a society without rulers or representatives. So strongly inculcated is the idea that no one can represent another person or group of persons, that Shevek is at pains to explain that he is not a representative of Anarres or any subdivision of it: "I come," he said carefully, "as a syndic of the Syndicate of Initiative, the group that talks with Urras on the radio these last two years. But I am not, you know, an ambassador from any authority, any institution" (*TD,* III). The physicist Oiie is willing to accept Shevek's formulation. But in his questions lurks a suspicion that what Shevek is saying is only a veil, accepted on Anarres, behind which business and politics are carried out in the usual manner. Shevek acknowledges that contempt, fear, and tribalism are not unknown on Anarres, but says he has come to Urras to change that. "Entirely on your own initiative," Oiie says. Shevek's reply is indicative of the degree to which Anarresti individuals consider themselves rulerless citizens rather than subjects: "'It is the only initiative I acknowledge,' Shevek said, smiling, in dead earnest" (*TD,* III). Not only does Shevek refuse to represent or be represented, he even rejects all titles, making a point about his not being a "doctor." Rigorous equality among the Anarresti complements the distribution of political articulation, and this articulation makes almost every Anarresti a representative, not of other Anarresti but of the idea of Anarres, the empty-handed. Thus there is no function on Anarres for rulers to represent and to bind the people, for each person embodies the essence of the political ideal. It is an experience that admits of no ruler.

What requires some explaining is the place of administration and bureaucracy in the politics of Anarres. The explanation Shevek gives Oiie is important:

> The network of administration and management is called PDC, Production and Distribution Coordination. They are a coordinating system for all syndicates, federatives, and individuals who do productive work. They do not govern persons; they administer production. They have no authority either to support me or prevent me. They can only tell us the public opinion of us. (*TD,* III)

Even on Anarres there is no escape from administrators. Shevek's distinction, however, establishes the difference between agents acting for citizens (administering things) and agents acting for rulers (administering their subjects). This distinction is related to the ends-means dichotomy against which Shevek inveighs in another context. That dichotomy, borrowed from the workshop (as Hannah Arendt has pointed out), enables rulers and their agents to view persons as tools with which to attain political ends—that is, as things. Although Anarresti anarchism has eliminated rulers, it has been less successful in eliminating the tendency to view human relationships as instrumental—for such a perception is clearly practical, contributing, as it does, to dispassionate objectivity and cold-blooded efficiency. The Syndicate of Initiative exists partly to fight such an attitude, which is growing in acceptability as the new class of administrator-agents (epitomized by Sabul) gathers power to itself. We are justified in fearing that these agents will soon graduate into rulers, as Bedap has been warning Shevek since the days of their youth. But if prospects aren't entirely bright, Anarres still has a chance to maintain the balance between solidarity and individual initiative, to overcome the fundamental ambiguity by accepting it and doing something about it.

That political articulation in Anarresti society is fairly widespread is indicated by the fact that its members rely on spoken communication. The value placed on speech by the Anarresti is implied rather than being stated by the narrator or by a character; nonetheless, it is an important component of the theme. Although there are few villains on Anarres, the two we become most familiar with—Sabul, the ambitious but unimaginative scientist, and Desar, the overspecialized, disloyal mathematician—are laconic almost to the point of incomprehensibility. Sabul's cryptic notes produce only annoyance, while Desar's manner of speech is one of calculated esotericism which enables him to use the social organism to his personal advantage: " 'Hell,' he said, 'work? Good post here. Sequency. Simultaneity, shit,' " (*TD,* VI). Both of these intellectual parasites betray Shevek, Sabul as a matter of course and Desar unnecessarily: " 'Put in a word for you, Institute meeting,' Desar said, looking up but not meeting, because he could not meet, Shevek's eyes. As he spoke, though Shevek did not understand what he meant, he knew that Desar was lying. He knew it positively. Desar had not put in a word for him, but a word against him" (*TD,* VIII). Shevek comes to see that in Desar, as in Sabul, there is both malice and love, as well as the will to acquire power over Shevek—certainly a serious character fault in an anarchist.

On Urras, though, even the best people (those of good will) come to distrust speech. The Urrasti are hampered in political communication by the fear that is characteristic—as Tocqueville pointed out—of class- and caste-ridden societies and nourished by an archist political system. Shevek's manservant, Efor, is a case in point. His extremely laconic speech is indicative of what might be called an antipolitical bias, as is that of Sabul of Desar; but a member of the Ioti servant class comes by his distrust of political speech language more honestly than does an Anarresti bureaucrat. Once the bond of common humanity has been established between Shevek and Efor, however, the servant's speech becomes fluent and unguarded, like the conversation of a free Anarresti.

Even apolitical Urrasti discourse is difficult for Shevek to comprehend. The ability of Shevek and Takver to communicate accurately about a wide range of topics convinces us that their relationship, as partners and brethren, is healthy and complete. In general, Anarresti talk much and well; speech is pithy and direct in Pravic, and deeds are meant to match words. But Vea's cocktail party is a dramatic example of how Urrasti language is, on one level, divorced from truth and, on another, divorced from action. Shevek completely misunderstands the messages being sent him by Vea, messages meant to reveal reality, to serve as the counters in an exploitative relationship. The statements of the attending "influentials" during the rambling discussion of Anarresti life, and of Shevek's theories, uncover a corrosive and debilitating disregard for ideas as well as feeling. The Pravic of Anarres has several different modes—existential, analogical, theological, and others—but they are used to clarify thought and feeling, whereas the resources of Iotic are all too often used to obfuscate, poison, and betray.

As a feature of utopian fictions, then, political articulation may be taken in two senses. It refers to the structure of citizenship and the degree of subjection to rulers and agents, while also referring to the form and content of speech in relation to politics. In both senses, although there's a tendency for the unadmitted government of public opinion to threaten the total citizenship of anarchism, Anarresti society represents a much more advanced stage of political articulation than does that of A-Io and the rest of Urras. Thus are we able to identify another respect in which Urras plays the dystopia to the Anarresti utopia.

The ambiguity remains, as surely as the Syndicate of Initiative must remain in conflict with public opinion as Shevek and Keitho head for Anarres and as surely as Subal's administrative grip on the Institute must have tightened in Shevek's absence. The reason for this is as easy to see as recalling that the shortest chapter in *News from Nowhere* is the one "Concerning Politics." As already observed, Le Guin has stated that her reason for writing *The Dispossessed* was to embody anarchism in a novel, since it had not been done before. But what of *News from Nowhere* which—according to a leading historian of modern anarchism, George Woodcock—is the utopian vision closest to the ideas of Kropotkin, as well as the only utopia "that has ever appealed generally to anarchists"?[47] Is *News from Nowhere* not a precedent for the anarchist novel?

The answer lies in Woodcock's remarks on Morris's utopian vision, which apply to most utopian fictions. He observes that *News from Nowhere* induces in the reader a feeling "of having passed into a continuum where ordinary time relationships have ceased," that "the idea of progress as a necessary good has vanished" into the "mellow stillness of a long summer afternoon." The reader is thus "surprised by goodness" for the simple reason that, in terms of literary form, *News from Nowhere* is a romance rather than a novel, and—as we have pointed out—the romance, unlike the novel, dispenses with the law of entropy, with the ordinary experience of time. In fact, *News from Nowhere* owes its medievalistic content as much to its specific form (that of the dream vision) as to Morris's well-known attraction to a nostalgic view of medieval English village life and craftsmanship. The talkiness of *News from Nowhere,* which Robert Elliott regarded as a blemish with which Morris was "clearly" unhappy,[48] owes more to the necessities of visionary form (which demands a therapeutic dialogue of some sort) than to the alleged longwindedness of speakers and pamphleteers for the Socialist League (the longwindedness of political orators being, by a law of nature, in inverse relationship to their amount of political power).

Devotees of science fiction will recall the similar features of Arthur Clarke's recent "novel," *Imperial Earth,* which set a new standard for longwindedness in technological utopias, precisely *because* Clarke apparently wrote in response to what he feels is a dangerous and growing disenchantment with the idea of progress.

The Dispossessed is not a dream vision or romance. Thus it can't help portraying its utopia ambiguously. The Odonian planet is "ambiguous" because it is *not* perfect, because it is a utopia that comes to terms with man as he *is*—mortal, weak, and potentially spiteful—rather than with man as he *would be* were he angelic. Its carefully portrayed syndical anarchism—designed to maximize both solidarity and individual autonomy—is no fail-safe system; it must constantly be purged of the individual's "egoizing" and society's narrow-mindedness, two contrary forms of "excrement." In being ambiguous, Le Guin's anarchist utopia meets a charge that may be leveled against many utopian visions, that they depend on an impossible *metastasis* of human nature. This means simply that the form of *The Dispossessed* is novelistic rather than visionary, for it is with evident passion that the author wishes us to consider whether we may not improve our way of being through a *metanoia,* or change in mind, through a *conversion* rather than a *transversion.* The romance can deal with new transformations and eternal species, but the novel must present us with "the children of time." Or as Bedap puts it, ". . . we forgot that the will to dominance is as central in human beings as the impulse to mutual aid is, and has to be trained in each individual, in each new generation. Nobody's born an Odonian any more than he's born civilized!" (*TD,* VI).

Anarres must remain an ambiguous utopia, an unrealized ideal, a community in danger from itself; its each new generation must contain men and women as yet untransformed by the promise of anarchism. As Shevek tells us, time cannot be abolished by the general theory which unites Simultaneity and Sequency physics. The ansible and transilience will remain illusions, illusions productive of real effects, but still illusions. In a way, we can see that if Shevek were a novelist or literary critic, he would be dealing with the problem of reconciling the eternal idea of Romance (Simultaneity) with the entropic procession of time in the Novel (Sequency). Thus, his quest for the resolution of ambiguity in physics is a metaphor for his creator's search for the resolution of the ambiguity inherent in the dualism of a visionary ideal immersed in "real" time. *The Dispossessed* cannot resolve this ambiguity; it can only leave the Odonians to their uncertain future, which is in the hands of real men and women, some of them mean and some of them noble. But Anarres has the right individual values and a set of admirable social values. Thomas More's King Utopus gave his islanders a blueprint for the future, as permanent and well-founded as human prescience would permit; Ursula Le Guin's founding mother gave her Odonian followers some thoughtful books and a place to begin, and a legacy of hope in every frustration. No more can be left to the children of time.

7. The Other Side of Suffering: Touch as Theme and Metaphor in Le Guin's Science Fiction Novels

THOMAS J. REMINGTON

SEVERAL COMMENTATORS have stressed the "connectedness" of Ursula K. Le Guin's fiction, its themes and methods.[1] This connectedness makes the treatment of any of her works in isolation from the others seem inadequate. What is present in her more recent works is usually there, at least incipiently, in the earlier ones.[2] The themes of the Hainish novels find themselves, with minor sea changes, in the Earthsea trilogy.[3] Even such an apparent isolate as *The Lathe of Heaven* can be pivotal in the development of the canon.[4]

Thus any study which concentrates on a select part of Le Guin's work will be incomplete. Yet, by following the development of a particular theme or image through the six science fiction novels, we gain considerable insight into the development of Le Guin's art. Writing of the Hainish novels, Douglas Barbour noted that

> "These narratives are bound together by a consistent imagery that both extends and informs meaning. Although Le Guin has used particular images which emerge naturally from the cultural and ecological context of her imagined worlds as linking devices within each work, she has also consistently used light/dark imagery as a linking device for the whole series."[5]

In making such a statement, Barbour is clearly aware that Le Guin's light/dark imagery extends beyond being a "linking device for the whole [Hainish] series." As he himself has pointed out, she also uses light and dark as major motifs in the Earthsea trilogy.[6] Light/dark imagery isn't the only pattern that informs Le Guin's works and draws them together, however. At least one other image of equivalent importance is that of touch—particularly a touching of isolated opposites, what I have called "a touch of difference, a touch of love."[7]

As is also true of the light/dark imagery, the imagery of touch extends throughout Le Guin's work. In an earlier study, I discussed its significance in three of the Hainish short stories ("Nine Lives," *The Word for World Is Forest,* and "Vaster than Empires and More Slow").[8] This imagery can also be found in the non-Hainish stories, and especially in the Earthsea trilogy. But, by following its development from *Rocannon's World* and *Planet of Exile* (both 1966), through *City of Illusions* (1967), *The Left Hand of Darkness* (1969), and *The Lathe of Heaven* (1971), to *The Dispossessed* (1974), we see how the pattern of touch imagery is deepened and made richly complex as Le Guin becomes more confident (and perhaps more conscious) of her own artistry.

We should keep in mind Slusser's comment that *Rocannon's World* is "no 'apprentice' piece."[9] In the novel the imagery of touch is both present and relevant, though hardly central. But here the joining of differences is significant, for there are hints of how the union of disparities will be treated through the medium of touch in the later works. Rocannon himself is a product of alien connections. An "ethnologist of the High Intelligence Life Forms," he has a Hainish mother and an adopted Terran father. He is white-skinned, which makes him an anomalous presence among the dark-skinned Angyar, into whose race he eventually marries. Despite his job of maintaining alien contacts, Rocannon at first is unable to accept fully the differences between himself and those he must work with. He corrects his assistant's disparaging use of the word *trogs* in referring to the Gdemiar, but finds himself slipping into the same terminology: "I wish we could talk to her without those tr-- Gdemiar as interpreters" (*RW,* "Prologue"). Thus it is apparently significant that when Rocannon prepares to give the Eye of the Sea jewel to Semley, "she does not raise her hands to take it" (*RW,* "Prologue"), but instead permits him to place it around her neck.

It is only after Rocannon has shared the life of the people of Fomalhaut II and has come to love Mogien "as a friend and somewhat as a son" (*RW,* IV) and has been "hugged. . . like a brother" (*RW*, VI) by him that he is truly in contact with the planetary "natives." As is typical in Le Guin's vision, Rocannon finds that such contact involves sharing both pain and love. Thus he completes his "contact" with the species of intelligent life on

Fomalhaut II through a mental link with the Ancient One, who is "like the Clayfolk...like the Fiia" (*RW*, VIII). The Ancient One gives Rocannon "the gift...of unsealing the telepathic sense" (*RW*, VIII) but demands as payment, "*that which you hold dearest and would least willingly give,*" warning Rocannon: "you will cry aloud its name when it is gone" (*RW*, VIII).

The Ancient One's gift permits Rocannon to reach his enemies with "the uncomprehending touch of mind on mind," but the touch has destruction as its goal: "*I will go south and find my enemy and destroy him*" (*RW*, VIII). Just as in *Word for World*, where Selver's dream of killing his enemies also destroys his friend, Lyubov, here, Rocannon's "touch of mind on mind," which will help him destroy his enemies, results in the loss of Mogien. Mogien's death occurs simultaneously with—and is symbolically connected to—the loss of Rocannon's right hand. Later, Rocannon says: "I would give both my hands to have saved what I lost" (*RW,* IX). But having touched the people of Fomalhaut II, Rocannon is now one of them in spite of his differences with them. The union is formalized by his marriage to Ganye.

The imagery of touch used to show the union of opposites in *Planet* is much more explicit than in *Rocannon's World*. Its significance is portended in the title of the opening chapter, "A Handful of Darkness," as well as the image with which the title is specifically connected. Once again, we have an alien (the Terran, Jakob Agat Alterra) who must relate to the natives of the planet Werel. Further, the differences between alien and native are stressed. One of these differences is skin tone; the Terrans are dark-skinned, while the Werelians are fair.

Neither the Werelians nor the members of the Terran colony led by Jakob are willing to recognize the humanity of the other group, however. A Werelian says the Terrans are "not men" (*PE,* IV) and a Terran asks the Werelians: "Can't you leave men alone?" (*PE,* XIII). Yet the survival of both groups depends on their joining forces to battle the Gaal, a nomadic people who are trying to overrun the shaky civilizations of the Werelians and the Terrans. The union of the two cultures depends on Jakob, of whom the Werelian woman, Rolery, thinks: "He was the only one of them all that spoke of her people and his own and the Gaal all as men" (*PE*, XIII).

Jakob is warned by Alla Pasfal, the "elder states-person" of the Terran colonials, that "*we can make no alliance but among ourselves. We're on our own. Never hold your hand out to any creature that belongs to this world''* (*PE*, VI). Alla's advice echoes the chapter title, "A Handful of Darkness," where Rolery, whose father had once taken a Terran wife, meets Jakob, that woman's nephew. Initially, Jakob telepathically mindspeaks to Rolery, warning her to escape a surging tide. Nearing safety, Rolery "reached up her hand and was half led, half dragged" from danger by Jakob (*PE,* I). Subsequently, on parting, Jakob "put out his hand in the salute of equals so that without thinking she did the same, laying her open palm against his" (*PE*, I). In the chapter's last sentence, from which its title comes, Rolery kneels by the fire in her village. "Closing her right hand, she seemed to hold against her palm a handful of darkness, where his touch had been."

The image of touching hands reappears in the later chapters. In Chapter 2, Wold, Rolery's father and the leader of her tribe, remembers that Jakob, in addition to being the leader of the Terran colony, is (at least technically) his nephew. He offers Jakob the openhanded "greeting of equals," which Jakob returns. At the end of Chapter 3, Jakob's mind returns to his first meeting with Rolery: "He. . . recalled briefly, irrelevant and yet seeming both an explanation and a sign, the light, lithe, frightened figure of the girl. . . reaching up her hand to him from the dark, sea-besieged stones." In Chapter 4, when Jakob proposes at a Werelian meeting that the Werelians and the Terrans join to fight their common foe, the response comes from one of Wold's sons: "Umaksuman was on his feet in a flash, his hand against the farborn's. They stood there for a moment in the firelight like day and night." In Chapter 5, "Twilight in the Woods," Jakob and Rolery meet and recognize their mutual need for each other.[10] At first, Rolery fears Jakob's alienness, what a relationship with him will do to her in the eyes of her people. He asks her to take his hand, but she refuses, telling him not to touch her. Eventually, though, "she put out her hand and he took it" and again she remembers their first meeting: "She had always been quite alone. . . But now. . . she had met him, the dark figure near the tower-rock over the sea, and had heard a voice that spoke in her blood."

As is typical of Le Guin's works, touching involves pain as well as love. When Jakob is attacked by Rolery's kinsfolk, his front teeth are knocked out and he is left drifting into unconsciousness. Rolery reaches him first, takes his head on her knees, and stains her hands with his blood as she tries to soothe him. Alla sees the attack as justifying her warning Jakob not to hold his hand out to any Werelian. But Jakob ignores the warning and asks Rolery to become his wife.

We assume that the marriage between Jakob and Rolery will be sterile, for, despite the fact that both Werel and earth were "seeded" with human life by the Hainish in the distant past, the genetic stock of the two races is slightly different. Still, the mere physical bond represented by the marital relationship of Jakob and Rolery, as well as their peoples' mutual fear of the Gall, is enough to unite the two groups. The fact that the marriage represents a union of differences is stressed:

> She the stranger, the foreigner of alien blood and mind, did not share his power or his conscience or his knowledge or his exile. She shared nothing at all with him, but had met him and joined with him wholly and immediately across the gulf of their great difference: as if it were that difference, the alienness between them, that let them meet, and that in joining them together, freed them. (*PE,* IX)

The fact that Jakob and Rolery are bound together *because* of their differences, and not in spite of them, is important. In Le Guin's vision, differences in human relationships are not to be ignored or minimized; rather, they should be embraced and cherished. This point is emphasized later in *Planet* when evidence is discovered that the original Terran stock has adapted to Werel in a way that might permit such marriages as Jakob's and Rolery's to be fruitful. Huru Pilotson—whose homosexual devotion to Jakob is significant, because it represents the yearning for a "bond of sameness" rather than one "of difference"—is appalled at the suggestion that the Terrans will be able to breed with the Werelians: "Damn your cross-breeding and fertility!" he cries out in fever, "So long as we've bred true we've been Man...Now the drop of our human blood will be lost...Diluted, thinned out to nothing" (*PE*, XIII). What Pilotson doesn't realize is that by "breeding true," by failing to adapt to the planet, the Terran colonials have doomed themselves to extinction. "Little by little...this world was killing them" (*PE*, III). The preservation of the Terran stock is possible only if the colonials "embrace the Other" and mix their blood with that of the Werelians.

It is also significant that the Terrans' adaptation to the planet, which makes interbreeding with the Werelians possible, is discovered through a wound Jakob suffers (like Rocannon) in the right hand. Rolery is concerned that the wound (which is received from a Gaal dartgun) might become infected—but she is told that

Terrans are immune: "We can't interbreed with you; or digest local organic food without help; or react to your viruses" (*PE*, XIII). Rolery recognizes the symptoms of infection in other colonists, however, and insists on cleansing Jakob's wound, thus saving him from the blood poisoning that eventually kills another Terran, a boy "who died in pain, holding onto her hand" (*PE,* XIII). Eventually she forces a skeptical Terran doctor to recognize that the colonists, over many generations, have adapted to Werel.

At the battle's conclusion, Jakob seeks "the alien, the stranger, his wife," and "taking her hands," tells her of the victory of her people and his (*PE*, XIV). The book closes on a scene of reconciled, touching opposites. A young child lights the funeral pyre of the oldest member of Rolery's tribe, and the fire burns in the cold air. The tide recedes, "grinding and thundering" at the land it vacates. The clear sky stretches from East to West, causing Jakob to recognize that "the old man's death and the young man's victory were the same thing" (*PE*, XIV). The planet can now touch all its people with the pain of infection; but by the same token, it has become their homeland.

Metaphors of touching appear less frequently in the third novel, *City of Illusions,* than in *Planet of Exile*, for two reasons. First, the Self and the Other, which must be embraced, are internalized as the two independent personalities of the central character. Falk, the isolated personality developed from the mind-razed hulk of Ramarren, must be reintegrated with Ramarren's original personality for the sake of his own wholeness and completion, as well as for that of mankind's future. Secondly, the major conflict in the novel is not between humans, as is the case in *Rocannon's World* and *Planet of Exile.* In *City,* the enemy are the Shing who "could not get into touch with men" (*CI,* X), "were unable to mate with Terrans. . .were still alien. . .after twelve hundred years; still isolated on Earth" (*CI,* IX). Nevertheless, metaphors of touch do occur frequently in *City*; thematically, touch is central to the novel.[11]

The first contact with humans that the remnant of the mind-razed Ramarren experiences is the touch of Parth's hand on his shoulder. To learn the nature of his empty mind, the blind Kretyan places her hand on his forehead and then lays her hand on his own. Later, after the personality of Falk has been developed on the emptiness that was Ramarren, and just before Falk begins his long pilgrimmage across the American continent, Falk and Parth "held each other and neither would break free'' (*CI,* II).

The alien Shing ''keep themselves a caste apart'' (*CI,* VIII), ''never got physically close to anyone'' (*CI,* X), and subjugate men by keeping them separate. Falk tells Zove: ''We're in hiding—we live apart, so that they'll let us be. If we tried to build any of the great machines, if we gathered in groups or towns or nations to do any great work together, then the Shing would infiltrate and ruin the work and disperse us. I tell you only what you told me and I believed, Master!'' (*CI,* I).

Falk's lesson is correct. He is repeatedly advised to travel alone and to trust no one. Those whom he meets live in isolation or in enclaves and mistrust strangers. Thus, as he leaves the House of Fear, Falk is warned to move quickly or have his hands burned off. The Thurro-dowist who lends Falk a vehicle calls himself ''All-Alonio,'' who lives ''alone here, my lad, alone and all alonio'' (*CI,* III). The Mzurra Society of the Basnasska Nation is ''conformist'' because it is ''defensive''; its members ''warded strangers from their territory with bombirds'' (*CI,* IV). The Beekeepers say: ''Do not put your trust in any but brother and hive-twin, known since infancy'' (*CI,* V). The Enclave of Kansas ''is a great territory, but barren and without people'' (*CI,* V). The people of the prairies, Estrel tells Falk, ''live alone'' and ''are full of fear'' (*CI,* V).

Despite their isolation, those whom Falk meets on his journey to Es Toch demonstrate their humanity by sharing physical contact. Even in the House of Fear the man who beats Falk does so with ''his open hand'' (*CI*, II). ''All-Alonio'' apparently accepts the hand Falk offers when departing. Moreover, All-Alonio is an empath, and, we are told, ''empathy was to telepathy somewhat as touch to sight, a vaguer, more primitive, and more intimate sense'' (*CI,* III). The horrible initiation rites of the Basnasska involve grotesque physical contacts: ''whippings, emetics...tattooing,...sexual abuse of one woman by all the males in turn'' (*CI,* IV). Despite the introversion of their society, the Bee-Keepers live entirely without privacy, believing that ''solitude is soul's death: man is mankind'' (*CI*, V). When Falk is finally taken in by the members of the Kansas Enclave, he is too exhausted to obey their command to move and is forced to obey by ''rough and expeditious hands'' (*CI*, V).

Estrel, the Shing agent who takes Falk to Es Toch, is ambiguous in her physical contact with him. To be sure, she is human; her sexual relationship with Falk is seen by Har Orry as proof of this. When Falk asks Orry if a Shing would not have slept with him, the boy shrugs, and says, "They do not touch common men...they hold themselves apart" (*CI,* VII). As a Shing agent, however, Estrel is under the alien influence, with which she tends to act in accordance. Thus she shows a Shing-like disgust at Falk's having killed a Basnasskan in their escape. Her sexual relationship with Falk is marked by her own "curious passivity" and "want of response," by the "endless promise and unfulfillment of her embrace" (*CI,* IV). Indeed, as they enter Es Toch and Estrel takes Falk's arm, it is "the first time she had ever done so in all the way they had walked together" (*CI*, VI). But this is merely to distract him so she can take his weapon.

There is no ambiguity on the part of the Shing, though; they avoid all physical contact. Falk soon discovers that the Shing hold their meetings via holographic projections, "each in his own room, apart...instead of face to face" (*CI,* VII). Later, when he asks Orry whether a particular Shing had actually been present or was merely an illusion, he is told: "They never come close...In this long time I've been here, six years, I have never touched one of them. They keep very much apart, each one alone" (*CI,* VIII). Falk sees them "only one or two at a time, and very few of them in all" (*CI,* VIII).

As Falk realizes the full duplicity of Es Toch and the Shing who have created it, the realization is phrased in metaphors of connection, of touch:

> This was not a Place of Men. Es Toch gave no sense of history, of reaching back in time and out in space, though it had ruled the world for a millennium...Though there were said to be so many of the Lords, yet on Earth they kept only this one city, held apart, as Earth itself was held apart from the other worlds...Es Toch was self-contained, self-nourished, rootless...It was...timeless, alien. (*CI,* VIII)

When Falk later succeeds momentarily in discomfiting one of the Shing by suggesting that the erasure of personality he is being asked to undergo is a violation of their principle of not killing, he thinks again of his victory in terms of metaphors of touch: "He had made the mask wince, he had touched, for a moment, the very quick of the lie; and in that moment he had sensed that, had he the wits or strength to reach it, the truth lay very close at hand" (*CI,* VIII).

The necessary "wits or strength" belong to the Ramarren personality, however, not to Falk. To recover Remarren, Falk must submit to the Shing, he must become "helpless in their hands" (*CI,* VIII). But in doing so, he recognizes the terrible chance he is taking. In a series of images central to the novel, Falk considers the hope and the faith (or trust) on which his plans depend:

> In a good season one trusts life; in a bad season one only hopes. But they are of the same essence: they are the mind's indispensable relationship, where hands do not touch, emotion atrophies in void and intelligence goes sterile and obsessed. Between men the only link left is that of owner to slave, or murderer to victim. (*CI,* VIII)

Although Ramarren has the wits and strength necessary to combat the Shing, he does not have Falk's knowledge of their alien aloofness; he must discover it for himself in his own way. Ramarren's awareness of Shing duplicity is triggered by the empathy which we are told earlier, is "to telepathy somewhat as touch to sight." The Shing Abundibot, with his ability to mindlie, is detected by Ramarren's reception from him of "vague empathic impressions so much at discrepancy with what the man said as to hint at dementia, or at lying" (*CI,* IX). Whereas Abundibot's "telepathic guard was flawless," Ramarren realizes that the Shing has "very little empathic ability or training" (*CI,* IX). Even on a purely mental level, the Shing do not "touch." This absence of touching arouses Ramarren's suspicion, driving him to pick up the book to which Falk had asked Orry to guide him. Taking the book in his own unfamiliar hand, a "hand. . .darkened and scarred beneath an alien sun" (*CI,* IX), Ramarren recovers Falk's personality and briefly integrates with it: "He touched for the first time. . .the balance-pole, the center, and for a moment was *himself*" (*CI,* IX).

Between them, Falk and Ramarren overcome their Shing captors, who "could not get in touch with men" (*CI,* X). By touching the center of himself, Falk-Ramarren escapes and returns to Werel to bring humanity's disparate fragments back in touch with each other, to begin the process by which men can reach out to men once more.

This outreaching process is far advanced in the next novel, *The Left Hand of Darkness.* Over three thousand nations on eighty-three worlds are joined in the Ekumen, the Human Family that has grown in the two centuries following the "Age of the Enemy" that begins to close in *City.*[12] As Darko Suvin has noted, "all of Le Guin's opposed discords—foreigness and identity, loneliness and togetherness, fragmentation and connection, and a number of others all rooted in the split between I and Thou, Self and Other—emerge" in this novel which, according to Robert Scholes, by "today's critical consensus is still. . .her best single work."[13] Again, the touch of isolated opposites is central to the expression of Le Guin's vision, both thematically and metaphorically.

The Gethenian race that inhabits the wintry world on which the action of the novel takes place "is appallingly alone in its world," the only mammalian species on it (*LHD,* XVI). Because of their ambisexuality, the Gethenians are "isolated, and undivided" (*LHD,* XVI); their physiology is "unique among human beings" (*LHD,* III). Moreover, Genly Ai, the Ekumen's envoy sent to establish contact with Gethen, arrives alone: "Alone, the relationship I finally make, if I make one, is not impersonal and not only political: it is individual, it is personal... Not We and They; not I and It; but I and Thou" (*LHD,* XVIII). His journey through space has relativistically cut him off from his parents, now "seventy years dead" (*LHD,* XVI).

Estraven, the Gethenian with whom Ai eventually establishes the "I-Thou" relationship, is also an isolate, the survivor of the nonrepeatable "vowing of kemmer" he had taken with his brother who is now dead. Estraven has been banished from his homeland as a traitor and is mistrusted in the country of his exile. As Ai says to him, together they share their exile, their isolation, "you for my sake—I for yours" (*LHD,* XVI).

Touch is very important to the Gethenians. It is through touch that the sexual role of a Gethenian is determined at the time of kemmer, or sexual activity. Strong emphasis is placed on the touching of hands in the novel's sexual episodes. And in the legend of "Estraven the Traitor," Therem of Stok warms the frozen body of Arek of Estre with his own; then, heated by kemmer, he

> put out his hand and touched Estraven's hand . . . for a while both held still, their hands touching. "They are the same," said Stovken, and laying his palm against Estraven's showed it was so: their hands were the same in length and form, finger by finger, matching like the two hands of one man laid palm to palm. (*LHD,* IX)[14]

Later in this episode, young Estraven, the son of the union, meets his parent, Therem, who "felt the young man's pulse and hand for fever, and for an instant laid his palm flat to Estraven's palm; and finger by finger their two hands matched, like the two hands of one man" (*LHD,* IX). In another passage, Estraven relates the attempt of the Orgota, Gaum, to seduce him: "He put his hand on mine... and held on to my hands" (*LHD,* XI). The relation of touching hands to kemmer is central to the lines from "Tormer's Lay" which give the novel its title:

Light is the left hand of darkness
and darkness the right hand of light.
Two are one, life and death, lying
together like lovers in kemmer,
like hands joined together,
like the end and the way. (LHD, XVI)

The significance of touch on Gethen goes beyond sexuality. The warmest form of Karhidish salutation is to grasp both hands of the person being greeted, though the gesture has been reduced to mere formality in Orgoreyn. It is also worth noting that the only Karhider who shares this gesture with Ai is Faxe, "a Listener" and, like All-Alonio in *City of Illusions*, "a natural empath" (*LHD,* V). Estraven is at first too distant from Ai and then too close for the gesture to be meaningful between them. "The Place Inside the Blizzard" is a Karhidish "hearth tale" in which the ghost of a man's brother finds him in a storm and, "reaching out his arms to hold him. . . seized him by the left hand" (*LDH,* II). Later the hand is found to have been frozen and is amputated.

The narrative of *The Left Hand of Darkness* covers the efforts of Estraven and Ai to bridge the gap of alienation between themselves and the people they represent. In Le Guin's three earlier novels, there is the suggestion that the joining of fragmented parts into union, like the setting of a broken bone, involves pain and suffering. We see this in Mogian's death in *Rocannon's World*, Wold's in *Planet,* and the parting of Parth and Falk forever (as well as the loss of Ramarren's crewmates) in *City.* That pain is intrinsic to any meeting with the Other is stressed by the author in "Nine Lives," a story published in the same year as *The Left Hand of Darkness:*

> It is hard to meet a stranger. Even the greatest extravert meeting even the meekest stranger knows a certain dread, though he may not know he knows it. Will he make a fool of me and wreck my image of myself invade me destroy me change me? Will he be different from me? Yes, that he will. There's the terrible thing: the strangeness of the stranger. (*WTQ,* "Nine Lives")

The pain of meeting the alien and the sacrifice involved in embracing the Other are integral to *The Left Hand of Darkness,* and is evidenced in the Gethenians' fear of being swallowed up by the Ekumen, in the mutual distrust and animosity that separates Karhide and Orgoreyn, and in the mistrust and misunderstanding that threaten to block Ai from Estraven. The theme is apparent in the symbolism of Chapter 1. The parade celebrates the placing of a keystone uniting "two piers, making them one, one thing, an arch" (*LHD,* I). Ai notices that each keystone he sees in the city of Erhenrang is joined by red cement to the stones it touches, and he is told: "Very-long-ago a keystone was always set in with a mortar of ground bones mixed with blood. Human bones, human blood. Without the bloodbond the arch would fall, you see. We use the blood of animals, these days" (*LHD,* I). Maybe the passage suggests that "these days," arches are weaker than they once were. At the very least, it hints that human bone and blood will be needed to cement a permanent arch joining Gethen to the Ekumen.

It is only through feeling their pain and sharing their suffering that Ai even begins to understand the Gethenians whose physiology and culture are so alien to him. When he is arrested in Orgoreyn, he is placed in the back of a metal prison truck with a group of fellow prisoners. One of the Gethenians, who has been clubbed and kicked in the abdomen, dies with his head on Ai's knees. During the cold night they huddle together for warmth, merging "into one entity occupying one space" (*LHD,* XIII).

Such contact and shared suffering is only terrible kindness, though. "Terrible, because when we are finally naked in the dark and cold, it is all we have. We who are so rich, so full of strength, we end up with that small change. We have nothing else to give" (*LHD,* XIII). Contact among the prisoners in the van isn't voluntary, for Ai or the Gethenians. The true sharing of pain and touch must be willingly given and knowingly received. In the van, Ai tells us,

> I was unable to do anything about any of this suffering, and therefore accepted it, as they did, placidly. . . They formed a whole, I among them; each felt it, and it was a refuge and true comfort in the night, that wholeness of the huddled group each drawing life from the others. But there was no spokesman for the whole, it was headless, passive. (*LHD,* XIII)

No deep human relationships develop from the involuntary contact in the van. When a young Gethenian in kemmer grasps Ai's hand, Ai pulls away from the touch. During the day, when the cold doesn't force them together, the prisoners crouch, "each in his own place, his territory, his Domain" (*LHD,* XIII). The prisoners share only their body heat, not their thoughts, enduring "in silence, always in silence" (*LHD,* XIII). Thus Ai says, despite their shared suffering and contact, they "remained strangers. I never learned the name of any of them in the truck" (*LHD,* XIII).

In Le Guin's works, the touch that transcends difference and truly draws people together must be voluntarily offered and voluntarily accepted, as Estraven and Ai accept the hardship and suffering of the journey across Gobrin ice. Even before the journey begins, we are reminded of the need for the "bloodbond." Estraven calculates the supplies for the trip "with the same obdurate patient thoroughness I had seen in a mad king up on a scaffolding mortaring a joint" (*LHD,* XV). After hunting some small animals, Estraven becomes the first Gethenian whom Ai has seen "with blood on his hands" (*LHD,* XV).

But even as they prepare for the journey, and despite the fact that Estraven physically carried Ai from the Orgota prison farm, it is the distance between them that is emphasized, the gap across which neither will touch the other. Significantly, Ai is unconscious when Estraven takes him from the prison. On the first night of their trip, Ai tells us that Estraven

> was remote, out of reach, two feet from me in a tent eight feet across... What is a friend, in a world where any friend may be a lover?...Not I, locked in my virility: no friend to Therem Harth [Estraven], or any other of his race. Neither man nor woman, neither and both...metamorphosing under the hand's touch, changelings in the human cradle, they were no flesh of mine, no friends; no love between us. (*LHD,* XV)

In the word *love* lies the key to the enduring touch that binds human to human in Le Guin's vision, the reality for which physical contact is only a metephor. In her work there are at least two ways of reaching out to the "not-self," the stranger. One is the "fear of the other." As Estraven says, "its expressions are...hate, rivalry, aggression. It grows in us, that fear" (*LHD,* I). Musing on love of one's country, Estraven asks: "Is it hate of one's uncountry: Then it's not a good thing. Is it simply self-love? That's a good thing, but one musn't make a virtue of it, or a profession." Genuine love of country, like all true love, does not have "a boundary-line of hate" (*LHD,* XV).

The relationship of one's self with the other is a constant in the human condition, as found in Le Guin's work. When Ai suggests that the Gethenians must be concerned less with duality than single-sexed humans are, Estraven points out: "Duality is an essential, isn't it? So long as there is *myself* and *the other*"—which causes Ai to recognize that "it does, after all, go even wider than sex" (*LHD,* XVI).

In Le Guin's earlier novels, touching the Other human with love finds a major symbolic manifestation in sexual contact across the lines of difference—in the relationship between Parth and Falk, in the marriages of Rolery and Jakob and of Ganye and Rocannon. But in *The Left Hand of Darkness* we find made explicit what is present only by implication in the earlier works; sexual contact is merely one manifestation of human love, the touch of which is even more intimate than sex. The point is stressed in the scene in which Estraven enters kemmer. Although sexual intercourse between a Gethenian and a Terran seems possible, Estraven tells Ai: "I must not touch you" (*LHD,* XVIII). Ai agrees that sex between them should be avoided, even though, by this time, their friendship

> might as well be called . . . love. But it was from the difference between us, not from the affinities and likenesses, but from the difference, that the love came: and it was itself the bridge, the only bridge, across what divided us. For us to meet sexually would be for us to meet once more as aliens. *We had touched, in the only way we could touch.* (*LHD,* VIII, my italics)

Robert Scholes and Eric Rabkin have noted that one advantage science fiction has over many other fictional modes is that it can attribute metaphors literally.[15] Thus, as Samuel Delany says, a cliché such as "suddenly her world exploded" can, in a science fiction context, undertake a literal meaning: "the world owned by that woman blew apart without warning."[16] In her introduction to the 1976 Ace edition of *The Left Hand of Darkness,* Le Guin says that "science fiction is metaphor," and she is quite capable of using it in the way Delany describes.

Thus, the touching which Ai notices between himself and Estraven is a touching of minds rather than an actual physical contact, since, due to Estraven's sexual receptiveness, all touching between their bodies must be avoided. "*Touching of minds*" takes on a literal meaning though, following Ai's comments. With "the barriers . . . down" (*LHD,* XVIII), Ai introduces Estraven to paraverbal speech despite the fact that aliens are not ordinarily taught techniques unknown in their culture until they become members of the Ekumen. Significantly, the first connection between the minds of Estraven and Ai comes about through empathy, the force that is to true telepathy what touch is to vision. When Ai's mind speaks within Estraven's, it speaks with the voice of Estraven's long-dead sibling and spouse, Arek. Thus Ai takes on an identity in Estraven's mind that is literally "flesh of his flesh."

Subsequently, the intimacy of the contact when Ai bespeaks Estraven causes the latter to wince, "as if I touched a wound" (*LHD,* XVIII). As Ai tells us: "A profound love between two people involves, after all, the power and chance of doing profound hurt'' (*LHD,* XVIII). Because we must throw down our defenses to reach beyond ourselves with love, love always involves the risk of hurt. In describing the empathic contact between himself and Rolery in *Planet,* Jakob says: ''It happens sometimes between two people: there are no barriers, no defenses.... When that happens... it's necessary that they love each other. Necessary... [ellipses in text] I can't send my fear of hate against the Gaal. They wouldn't hear. But if I turned it on you, I could kill you. And you me'' (*PE*, XIII). Like Jakob and Rolery, Estraven and Ai have removed their defensive barriers of fear; ''*there's nothing to fear between us*'' (*LHD,* XVIII). They have no choice but to entrust themselves with the power to hurt each other. It is the power to hurt which Estraven recognizes must still be feared, even when all other matters of fear have been eliminated.

Structurally, this relationship ''closes'' the novel at the moment of Estraven's death. Just as he had done for the unknown Gethenian in the back of the prison van, Ai holds the dying Estraven's head on his knees. But the boundary of difference has been crossed, and the touch between them transcends the mere contact of their bodies. Estraven, says Ai, ''answered my love for him, crying out through the silent wreck and tumult of his mind as consciousness lapsed, in the unspoken tongue, once, clearly, *Arek*!'' (*LHD,* XIX). Thus, in death, Estraven identifies the stranger, the strangely sexed alien from the stars, with the sibling he had known from birth and the spouse with whom he had begotten his child.

Estraven's identification of Ai with Arek takes on additional meaning when we realize that Ai himself has begun to identify with the alien Gethenians. When the Ekumen's space ship lands he experiences a Gulliver-like revulsion at his emerging single-sexed colleagues: ''They were like a troupe of great, strange animals, of two different species; great apes with intelligent eyes, all of them in rut, in kemmer....[ellipses in text] They took my hand, touched me, held me'' (*LHD,* XX). When he returns to his room, Ai's revulsion at the touch of his own kind makes it necessary for him to be treated by a Gethenian physician, whose ambisexual features ''were a relief to me, familiar, right'' (*LHD,* XX).[17]

Ai recognizes, though, that his dread of touching and being touched by the Other is a lapse in himself, an absence of delight in difference, a lack of courage to throw down defenses, ''the delight, the courage, that is most admirable in the Karhidish spirit—and in the human spirit'' (*LHD,* XX). This willingness to reach out to the unknown other becomes the main emphasis of the book's last sentence, a question asked by Estraven's child, in which the word *other* is spoken three times: ''Will you tell us about the other worlds out among the stars, the other kinds of men, the other lives?'' (*LHD,* XX). As Ai tells the Karhidish king, Estraven had lived for and served mankind. At the novel's conclusion, Estraven, through his son, continues to reach out to touch the myriad Others of the human race.

In *The Lathe of Heaven* Le Guin turns from the universe of the Hainish novels to the surreal Portland of George Orr's dreams; but the imagery of touch remains a constant.

Haber, the unsympathetic psychologist, ''did not like crowds.'' He considers himself ''a lone wolf''; he ''got what he wanted and got clear again, before he or the other person could possibly develop any kind of need for the other'' (*LH,* VIII). He is feared by Orr because ''he isn't in touch. No one else, no thing even, has an existence of its own for him; he sees the world only as a means to his end....He is insane....[ellipses in text] He could take us all with him, out of touch'' (*LH,* X). When Orr's fears are realized, we are told, ''Haber was lost. He had lost touch'' (*LH,* XI).

In contrast, Orr is both empathic and sympathetic. When he feels joy, ''seven or eight'' people ''pressed closest to him felt a slight but definite glow of benevolence or relief. . . . He did not see connections. . . . He *felt* connections—like a plumber'' (*LH,* III). ''He had no defenses'' (*LH,* II).

The relationships between Orr and those who share his world are often signaled by the touching of hands or by its empathic absence. Thus Orr is embarrassed when he almost offers his hand to Haber as the two men meet for the first time, and then has to withdraw it when Haber doesn't extend his own hand. Later, when Orr meets Heather and likes her, as she likes him, he shakes hands with her; great stress is placed on the handshake as a representation of touching opposites:

> She stuck out her brown hand, he met it with a white one, just like that damn button her mother always kept in the bottom of her bead box, SCNN or SNCC or something she'd belonged to way back in the middle of the last century, the Black hand and the White hand joined together. Christ! (*LH,* IV)

Orr and Heather later repeat their handshake in front of Haber who views the exchange between them with the obtuseness characteristic of one who cannot sense the connections between opposites: "The two were shaking hands in the most ridiculously stiff way. Crash clank! went. . . [Heather's] bracelets. The contrast amused Haber: the harsh fierce woman, the meek characterless man. They had nothing in common at all" (*LH,* V).

To be sure, Haber, as a psychologist, pays lip service to people's relationships. In the isolation of his "inner sanctum" he considers the single patient he has retained and thinks: "There is nothing important except people" (*LH,* V). But in a tour de force of carefully chosen prepositions, Le Guin clarifies for us how Haber views his relationship with others: "A person is defined solely by the extent of his influence *over* other people,. . . and morality is an utterly meaningless term unless defined as the good one does *to* others" (*LH,* V, italics mine). Typically, for someone who does good *to* others (whether the "others" agree that the thing done is good or not), Haber's main physical contact with Orr is to touch his neck as a method of inducing hypnotic trance. Heather says of this: "I hate to watch...it looks like a murder" (*LH,* VII). Unable to sense connectedness, Haber "found it terrible to be alone" (*LH,* VIII), but cannot bring himself to overcome his sense of isolation with any relationship that transcends the casual or the mercenary: "He had never wanted marriage nor close friendships,. . . he had avoided entanglements. He kept his sex life almost entirely to one-night stands, semipros" (*LH,* VIII).

In contrast to Haber, the lone wolf, Heather is "a person who believes. . . that things fit: that there is a whole of which one is a part, and that in being a part one is a whole" (*LH,* VII). Within herself she reconciles jarring opposites. "Although she snapped and clicked, Haber suspected that the whole affair was. . . a lot of sound and fury signifying timidity" (*LH,* V). She says to Orr: "My father was a black, a real black—oh, he had some white blood, but he was a *black*—and my mother was a white, and I'm neither one" (*LH,* VII).

As someone who doesn't respect differences, Haber is pleased when Orr's "effective dreams" eliminate the problem of race simply by eliminating race, giving all people an identical gray color. Haber can rejoice at the removal of differences, at a world in which "every soul. . . should have a body the color of a battleship" (*LH,* IX). But Orr, when he sees Heather as a gray person, takes her hands in his and says: "You should be brown" (*LH,* X). Nevertheless, Orr and Heather "hung on to each other, in touch at all available surfaces, absolutely unified'' (*LH,* X).

Finally, the most significant contrast between Haber and Orr is that Orr is ''in the middle of things'' (*LH,* IX), even to the point of becoming a statistical median. He understands ''that we're in the world, not against it,'' that ''it doesn't work to try to stand outside things and run them'' (*LH,* IX), and that ''you have to . . . [ellipsis in text] be in touch'' (*LH*, X). Haber, on the other hand, is ''out of touch'' and seeks to ''take us all with him'' (*LH*, X), remodeling the world and its people to omit all differences from his own mental construct. But the omission of all that is different gives the mind nothing to reach out to, no Other to touch, with the result that Haber becomes locked in his own mind and cannot escape from his catatonic withdrawal.

Orr's triumph is that he is ''expert with tangibles'' (*LH,* XI). In the book's last paragraph we see him shake hands with his Aldebaranian employer, ''his boss, . . . the Alien,'' who gives sanity and relationship to the world (*LH,* XI).

Ian Watson has commented that ''*The Lathe of Heaven* . . . at first sight seems to represent something of an anomaly in Le Guin's development,'' but concludes: ''on the contrary, *Lathe* fits logically into the set of her ideas as a pivotal work.''[18] As Watson views the progress of the Hainish novels, the increasing role of paranormal phenomena in those works leads into an artistic blind alley: ''The particular danger inherent in SF treatment of the paranormal—and particularly in adopting a time scheme for a 'future history' which indicates increasing prominence of paranormal talents as an index of increasing human wisdom—is that this can too easily become a quasi-mystical escape route from real problems: ethical, psychological, epistemological, and practical.''[19]

While it seems strange to view *Lathe* (as Watson apparently does) as a *necessary* ''summation and discharge'' of the paranormal theme of the Hainish novels, there is evidence to suggest that, in having Estraven die while in mental contact with Ai in *The Left Hand of Darkness*, Le Guin comes perilously close to presenting a paranormal ''solution'' to the fundamental problem of the human condition as she sees it. Shevek states this problem in *The Dispossessed,* when he says: ''Suffering is the condition on which we live. . . . We can't prevent suffering. . . . And in the end we'll die'' (*TD,* II); ''you can't do anything for anybody. We can't save each other. Or ourselves'' (*TD,* II). In her earlier works, Le Guin touches on the possibility of telepathic contact overcoming the isolation of death. Although Rocannon is in mindhearing contact with the doomed aircar pilot in *Rocannon's World,* the contact is only one way; the pilot is unaware of Rocannon's presence in his mind. Certainly there was no emotional relationship between Rocannon and the unknown pilot. In *Planet,* however, Rolery wonders "if, when [Jakob] was killed, he would cry out to her mind before he died; and if that cry would kill her" (*PE,* XIII). Thus, the suggestion is made that telepathic contact might cause Jakob involuntarily to share his death with Rolery—though there is still no hint that she might be present telepathically in his mind at the moment of his death. In Ai's mental contact with the dying Estraven in *The Left Hand of Darkness,* he seems literally to share the Gethenian's moment of death. We can't help but assume that, if the dying Estraven is present in Ai's mind, Ai must also be in Estraven's mind. Once posited, such sharing threatens to become a *deus ex machina.* The terrible isolation of death has always been an inescapable part of being human; to suggest a paranormal solution to the problems of this isolation is to offer an answer which, here and now, we cannot accept as being humanly possible.

Le Guin does not use telepathy as a *deus ex machina* in *The Left Hand of Darkness*. It is the dying Estraven whose presence we see in Ai's mind, not vice versa; the idea of "shared death" is not explicitly raised. Still, it is one of the novel's triumphs that it can come so close to this precipice without faltering. Further development of telepathy as a device to solve the thematic problems of shared pain and death's loneliness might force ingenious explanations for not using it regularly to solve these problems. What solutions to this difficulty Le Guin might develop in the future is considerably beyond my powers of speculation. In *The Dispossessed* she avoids the problem by choosing a setting earlier than the time of telepathy's being recognized as a human capability.

Thematically, contact with others is central to *The Dispossessed.* Shevek, by leaving Anarres for Urras, establishes the first true connection between the two planets since the settlement of Anarres by the Odonians. His General Temporal Theory promises, as one of its results, the invention of the ansible, by which the "Worlds of Man" will be able to join together. Upon his return to Anarres, Shevek brings with him the first non-Cetian to set foot on the planet.

Touch is used repeatedly in *The Dispossessed* to illustrate and symbolize the connections between Self and Other which, in this work, cannot be indicated by mental contact. Many of the uses of touch parallel those found in the other novels. For instance, Shevek characterizes himself as "the Beggarman" (*TD*, I) who has nothing to offer but himself. Later he is associated with a Urrasti myth of the "Forerunner," "a stranger, an outcast, an exile, bearing in empty hands the time to come" (*TD*, VII). As he returns to Anarres we are told that "his hands were empty, as they had always been" (*TD*, XIII). Shevek's empty hands seem to emphasize his readiness to reach out, as well as his willingness to give of himself. As he says in his speech to the people in Capitol Square, "All you have is what you are, and what you give" (*TD*, IX). Shevek's views flow naturally from his being a true disciple of Odo, on whose tomb is written "*To be whole is to be part*" (*TD*, III). As we are told in the related short story, "The Day Before the Revolution," touch is one of the central Odonian themes. Regularly in *The Dispossessed*, we see Shevek embracing and touching others in friendship, brotherhood, and love, while the corrupt Urrasti society he despises attempts to keep him from others, to insulate him. The Urrasti hope to isolate him on the trip from Anarres to Urras. While there, he is kept from contact with any nation but A-Io or with any citizens of A-Io other than those chosen to present him with a picture of general splendor. The Urrasti package all their goods in layers of wrappings. "Nothing was to touch anything else," and Shevek begins "to feel that he, too, had been carefully packaged" (*TD*, VII).

Just as Shevek's General Temporal Theory is intended to reconcile the Simultanist and Sequentist views of time, so must he, as an individual, reconcile the wealth and splendor of Urras' rich with the squalor and deprivation of its poor. "To him a thinking man's job was not to deny one reality at the expense of the other, but to include and to connect. It was not an easy job" (*TD*, IX).

On Anarres, sex is open. Even in the description of Shevek's sexual encounter with Beshun, where nothing but sensual pleasure is involved, touch leads beyond the self where "the two bodies striving to join each other annihilate the moment in their striving, and transcend the self, and transcend time" (*TD*, II). But while such sexual episodes offer their own kind of satisfaction, the driver of a truck train later offers an Anarresti view of the significance to be attached to a more permanent sexual relationship. Granting the pleasure of multiple and transient sexual interludes, and viewing sex as a way of reaching the Other, he adds: "But still, what's different isn't the copulating; it's the other person. And eighteen years is just a start, all right, when it comes to figuring out *that* difference" (*TD*, X).

Although sexuality and other forms of physical touch, including the touching of hands, are frequently used in *The Dispossessed* to indicate the importance of connections between individuals, these elements have a symbolic significance which differs little from that found in Le Guin's earlier novels. In the area of shared suffering, however, the theme and metaphor of touch find more profound statement in *The Dispossessed* than in the previous works, a fact that supports Barbour's opinion that this novel is Le Guin's most complex to date.[20]

In Le Guin's science fiction novels fear and suffering are often the starting points from which human relationships must begin. In *Rocannon's World* it is initially fear of the Shing and later, fear of the Faradayan rebels that motivates the League's efforts to form an alliance with the people of Fomalhaut II. In *Planet,* mutual fear of the Gaal promotes contact between the Terran colony and Rolery's people, while in *City,* fear of the Shing prompts Falk to allow the resurrection of Ramarren's personality within himself. In *The Left Hand of Darkness,* Ai's first close contact with the Gethenians occurs as he huddles for warmth with his fellow prisoners in the back of the prison van. It is fear of Haber that drives Orr to see Heather for the first time.

In each case the initial bond of fear is strengthened and becomes a more humane bond of love: the love of Rocannon and Mogien, the fertile wedding between Jakob and Rolery,[21] the union of Falk with Ramarren, the love between Ai and Estraven and that between Orr and Heather. However, in *The Dispossessed,* Le Guin strongly emphasizes the point that love, however admirable it may be as a perfection of the human condition, is not naturally "the true condition of human life" (*TD,* II).

In discussing *Word for World*, Barbour refers to "the Hobbesian vision of man" apparently in the belief that, more than at first seems likely, Le Guin's view of man's "natural condition" agrees with that of Hobbes in *Leviathan.* In Chapter 13 of *Leviathan,* "Of the NATURALL CONDITION *of Mankind, as concerning their Felicity and Misery,"* Hobbes states that in this condition, "the life of man [is] solitary, poore, nasty, brutish, and short."[22] For Hobbes, the only way men can find felicity in spite of this natural condition is to be driven, through fear, to form a social contract that forces them mutually to observe the "laws of nature." He offers nineteen laws of nature but recognizes that most men's minds aren't subtle enough to encompass all of them. "To leave all men unexcusable, they have been contracted into one easie sum, intelligible, even to the meanest capacity; and that is, *Do not that to another, which thou wouldest not have done to thy selfe.*"[23]

Although the comparison between Le Guin and Hobbes may seem farfetched, it seems more than mere coincidence that the first words spoken by Aldebaranian in *Lathe* are directed at the meddling Haber and show an inversion of the golden rule that closely parallels that of Hobbes: "Do not do to others what you wish others not to do to you" (*LH,* VIII). The reasons for forming a society in *The Dispossessed* appear similar to those suggested by Hobbes. For example, in conversation with Takver, Bedap refers casually "to the basic societal bond, the fear of the stranger" (*TD,* XII).

The fear, isolation, and suffering that form men's natural condition serve as a structural link in *The Dispossessed,* binding the early sections to the later ones, binding Anarres to Urras. In one of the novel's early episodes, Shevek states flatly: "suffering is the condition on which we live" (*TD,* II). To make his point he tells them about the crash of an air car, after which, because no anesthetic was available, the terribly burned pilot suffers for two hours before dying.

> He was in terrible pain, mostly from his hands. I don't think he knew the rest of his body was all charred, he felt it mostly in his hands. You couldn't touch him to comfort him, the skin and flesh would come away at your touch, and he'd scream. You couldn't do anything for him. There was no aid to give. . . you can't do anything for anybody. We can't save each other. Or ourselves. (*TD,* II)

When one of his listeners accuses Shevek of "denying brotherhood," he replies that he is only attempting to state what he believes brotherhood to be: "It begins—it begins in shared pain." But when asked where brotherhood ends, Shevek can only say: "I don't know. I don't know yet" (*TD,* II).

This episode is balanced by another one near the novel's conclusion. On Urras, Shevek speaks to the dissidents gathered in Capitol Square, saying:

> It is our suffering that brings us together. It is not love. Love does not obey the mind, and turns to hate when forced. The bond that binds us is beyond choice. We are brothers. We are brothers in what we share. In pain, which each of us must suffer alone, in hunger, in poverty, in hope, we know our brotherhood. We know it, because we have had to learn it. We know that there is no help for us but from one another, that no hand will save us if we do not reach out our hand. And the hand that you reach out is empty, as mine is. (*TD,* IX)

The police break up the demonstration, and Shevek escapes with a companion whose wounded hand is described in gruesome detail. "More than one bullet must have struck it, tearing two fingers off and mangling the palm and wrist. Shards of splintered bone stuck out like toothpicks" (*TD,* IX). Later, as they hide in a cellar, Shevek pleads with the man not to scream from the pain. As Shevek and he huddle together for warmth, the man dies. Still later, Shevek remembers this episode. He thinks of Urras as a beautifully wrapped package: ". . . you open the box, and what is inside it? A black cellar full of dust, and a dead man. A man whose hand was shot off because he held it out to others" (*TD,* XI).

Explicit in both episodes is the understanding that one meets the Other, the not-self, not with love but with fear of making contact, with fear of alienness and of pain. With such fear the only thing one can possibly share is the fear itself and the pain of touching the other; anything else must be pretense and politeness. By offering the fear and pain one feels, by accepting them from the Other as the only possible gifts that can be given, one is, in effect, sharing the only initial human contact that is possible.

However—and in this Le Guin and Hobbes part company—shared suffering is only the *beginning* of brotherhood. Unlike Hobbes, Le Guin shows that something more is possible. Ai finds no permanent human relationship while sharing the misery of his fellow prisoners in the van, only the limited relationship of the mutually exchanged warmth of their bodies. But later, with Estraven, he finds it possible to share much more. Similarly, Shevek discovers that one can transcend the bleak human relationship of shared suffering. When asked where brotherhood ends, he could only say, "I don't know." Shevek's inability to answer the question leads him into a life of isolation. "His efforts to break out of his essential seclusion were. . . a failure. . . He made no close friend." Even sexually, he concludes, "masturbation was. . . the suitable course for a man like himself. Solitude was his fate" (*TD,* VI).

On seeing Bedap again, Shevek is reminded of the earlier conversation; "it was. . . very important. . . to me," Bedap says. When he learns that Shevek has been thinking about suicide, though, he points out that self-destruction is "hardly the way to come out on the other side of suffering" (*TD,* VI). Yet Shevek's isolation leaves no answer other than suicide. Significantly, it is also in Chapter 6 that he sees Takver once more, and the two become partners. It is Takver who says "one person can't make a bond, after all!" (*TD,* VI).

In his relationship with her, Shevek *can* "come out on the other side of suffering." His awareness of this is evident when he says to her at the end of the chapter: "All you have to do to see life whole is to see it as mortal. I'll die, you'll die; how could we love each other otherwise?" (*TD,* VI). In such love lies—not an end to fear, for a few lines later Shevek says, "I am afraid, Takver" (*TD,* VI)—but the knowledge that there is something in life that makes the terrible fear and its concomitant suffering worthwhile. This knowlege becomes clearer later, in Shevek's toast to the birth of his daughter, Sadik: "I'll drink to this hope: that as long as she lives, Sadik will love her sisters and brothers as well, as joyfully, as I do now tonight" (*TD,* VIII).

As one would expect in a vision as rich and complex as Le Guin's, no question as difficult as "How does one 'come out on the other side of suffering'?" can be answered simply with the monosyllable, *love.* The Hobbesian view cannot be so easily dismissed. As Bedap notes in the conversation at the party: "Love's just one of the ways through, and it can go wrong, and miss. Pain never misses. Therefore we don't have much choice about enduring it! We will, whether we want to or not" (*TD,* II). Pain is inevitable, and love must be chosen. Shevek makes the same point in his speech in the Capitol Square: "The bond that binds us is beyond choice" (*TD,* IX).

But Takver responds to Bedap's assertion that humans will endure pain because they have no choice: "But we won't! One in a hundred, one in a thousand, goes all the way, all the way through. The rest of us keep pretending we're happy, or else just go numb. We suffer, but not enough. And so we suffer for nothing" (*TD,* II). For suffering to be sufficient, one must *willingly* share the pain of others. One must hold out one's hand, even if by doing so one risks having the hand shot off. The gift of love shares everything impartially, suffering *and* joy. When Shevek and Takver discuss the fact that their actions have caused Sadik to be tormented by her schoolmates, Shevek says: "If we choose to give the child the intensity of individual love, we can't spare her what comes with that, the risk of pain. Pain from us and through us" (*TD,* XII). And Sadik, in admitting to Shevek the pain she feels, "jerked as if she had been shot" (*TD,* XII). She parallels the victim "whose hand was shot off because he held it out to others." There is a depth in such communion of pain that is almost sacramental, and Bedap senses this. Watching Shevek comfort Sadik and share her pain, he recognizes the "one intimacy which he could not share, the hardest and deepest, the intimacy of pain" (*TD,* XII). Because Bedap is a sympathetic character, Le Guin won't allow us to respond to him as being evil or even shallow. For him there is only the sharing of joy, and of the pains which no human can avoid. Clearly he recognizes that, without more, his life is empty.

In *The Dispossessed,* as elsewhere in Le Guin's work, there are characters who respond to the outstretched hand as do the faceless Ioti soldiers, with fear and hatred and violence. Such a response is a way of searching for the "other side" of suffering, since it transfers one's own pain to the Other. However, with the exception of a few anomalies such as Captain Davidson in *Word for World,* Le Guin spends little time on such portraits. Instead, she shows us, on one hand, the sympathetic but unfortunate characters such as Bedap who refuse to take the chance of sharing the intimacy of another's joy *and* pain, and, on the other, the one in a hundred, one in a thousand, who *does* take the chance, who, like Shevek, goes through life with hands that are always empty. Those who choose Shevek's way know that their hands are in danger, but they are willing, despite their fear, to reach out and touch their fellow sufferers, to share with them, willingly and lovingly, the terrible pain of being human. For these lucky few, life transcends its Hobbesian bleakness; they suffer enough to come out on the "other side of suffering."

8. Mythic Reversals: The Evolution of the Shadow Motif

SNEJA GUNEW

THE SCIENCE FICTION novelist has traditionally been limited, with respect to environment predominating over characterization. In this type of fiction the author can take nothing for granted. He or she may assume no shared or common experience on the mundane level in the reader's mind, since the reader comes to the work with a distinct suspension of belief. In response, the author must devote a disproportionate amount of his energies to making credible the external world of his characters—to the interlocking of red seas with yellow skies and animate rocks, or whatever. At the same time that *place* is stressed to the point where we are inundated with it, we are usually left with wooden characters from whom no subtlety of thought or behavior is expected. Thus we remain outside, viewing a kind of ingenious three-dimensional effect, scarcely involved in one of the basic impulses of serious literature: to render the familiar, marvelous. In most fantasy writing, the emphasis is on the merely exotic.

Ursula K. Le Guin is a serious writer, one of the few who have expanded the genre of science fiction to include characterization that is as subtle and complex as any to be found in mainstream novels. Certainly she creates exotic worlds and alien beings; but she does so in such a way that these worlds and beings enhance and shed light on our familiar prejudices against anything alien. By placing her tales in an obviously unearthly setting, she bypasses the censor in the reader's xenophobic mind. Instead of being content with providing the clichéd exotic escapist, Le Guin is concerned with those wider implications through which good literature expands a reader's world of experience. She is not primarily an allegorist, however. That is, while both myth and symbol strengthen her writing, she is not concerned primarily with the animation of preset conceptualized myth. It would be more accurate to say that, by penetrating to the mythopoeic impulse, she has created a new mythology and that this often involved revolutionizing the symbols of the old mythology. Through myth she endeavors to bridge the gap between her felt, imaginative reality and the reader's automatic alienation, through establishment of the kind of empathy or rapport that the best writers have always aroused in their readers—so that this same felt reality becomes part of the reader's experience. Le Guin has confronted the limitations of the allegorical school and converted the static symbolism of allegory into the dynamic symbols of the waking dream of mythology, thus spanning the gulf between her alien worlds and her reader's skepticism. Whereas she may not assume an area of mundane experience held in common, she can and does assume one of reactions to basic mythic symbols.

What testifies to Le Guin's artistry is that she quite often takes a familiar symbol and reverses the values it traditionally holds. Such is her use of the familiar dualism of light and darkness. By relying on her readers to become engaged with the emotional impact of this symbolism, she creates a clearing of credibility in which she nurtures the growth of sympathetic characterizations. Acceptance of the symbolic construct thus paves the way for our accepting her characterizations. Once Le Guin has penetrated the reader's emotional guard, she takes this familiar symbol and transforms it, for, with this symbol we are not dealing with simplistic good-evil polarization but, interestingly enough, with a play on what could perhaps be called the middle ground of darkness and light, playing on the province of the shadow. Whereas black-white and darkness-light indicate a large-scale, cosmic polarization, the shadow refers specifically to the microcosm, or to that polarization in terms of the individual burden. On the whole, the shadow constitutes the twilight area involving the existential choice that dogs the footsteps of everyman.[1] In Le Guin's work its adjunct is the "name," or area of certainty, with respect to identity.

We expect to find consistency in a serious writer—an imagistic cohesiveness that can be traced from one book to another. We also expect to find that metaphysical complexities have been captured and enhanced by imagistic motifs. What we find in Le Guin's work, though, is a palimpsest of such motifs which recur with accreted richness and density in successive books. Part of this palimpsest is the image of the shadow which, when traced chronologically through her work, is seen to form a spectrum of meanings that translate her Taoist-inspired, holistic metaphysics into the particular. At one end of the spectrum, the shadow is a microcosmic image signifying individual chaos, which forks into two paths, one carrying the negative connotation of chaos, in the sense of loss of identity, deception, and death; while the other sees the shadow and the larger cosmic darkness as chaos which is the matrix of potential life. To this fecund area the individual comes to seek the word (give a shape to contextual, *external* confusion) and the name (a shape to identity, *internal* confusion). Midway in the spectrum is the Jungian-derived confrontation with the shadow as the suppressed self, the other, or—sometimes fixed even more objectively and, apparently, intransigently—in the figure of the alien. At the other end of the spectrum, the shadow represents either a blending of opposites (light and dark), which is often linked with trees or forests, or it throws into relief the necessary separation of light and dark, a separation that engenders the most dynamic interaction. Usually this is linked to the yin-yang symbol. The organic interaction of extremes is related to the Taoist whole, and constitutes the balance or state of dynamic equilibrium which is celebrated, for example, in the Earthsea trilogy and the novella, *The Word for World Is Forest.*[2]

We begin with the negative end of the spectrum: shadow and chaos as antilife and loss of identity. The novel that uses the shadow motif most consistently, in this sense (shadow as the loss of self), is *City of Illusions*. It opens in darkness:

> Imagine darkness. In the darkness that faces outward from the sun a mute spirit woke. Wholly involved in chaos, he knew no pattern. He had no language, and did not know the darkness to be night. . . . Through the dark forest of things he blundered in silence till the night stopped him, a greater force. (*CI,* I)

The protagonist Falk is constantly driven to blindness, which is emblematic of his inability to define and accept the creative polarities, hence, his own identity within it. His confusion is that of a mind that has become unhinged. He partially recovers in the healing environment of the forest, a place of "shadow and complexity." Gradually his psychic blindness is exposed to light, so the fruitful interaction can take place and speed his growth to full consciousness of identity.[3] But periodically in the novel, the seedling is plunged back into exclusive and inimical darkness. At one point Falk is thrown into a totally dark room where his patiently won identity is tested by being returned to blindness and chaos. But by this time he has learned to find the light within the darkness (a recurring paradox in Le Guin's work).[4] When released, he wanders, "a grey shadow slipping westward through the cold wilderness." Ominously, west is the traditional symbolic direction of death, and Falk is indeed literally blinded before reaching the end of his quest. Again, he is rescued, only to stumble back into a greater psychic blindness, the fearful, deceptive labyrinth of the shadow world of the Shing. It is in this part of the novel that the shadow image is most consistently linked with the fragmentation of identity, in the translucent rooms where Falk encounters numerous shadows but never the substance, and where he thus loses sight of his own substance.[5] From these chimerae Falk rescues himself by becoming aware of his own dual identity by means of the holistic word, the canon of the Tao which becomes a shaping force within the chaos.

Written several years later, *The Lathe of Heaven* again utilizes the shadow to indicate a mind disintegrating into madness. Rather than being a quest for identity consciousness, as so many of Le Guin's stories are, here she is concerned more with the individual's responsibility for cosmic equilibrium through his own actions.[6] Here chaos is macrocosmic; it is related only incidentally to the microcosmic, the individual, so that, characteristically, the shadow appears only once. Although subtle, it is, at the same time, a major intrusion, since it is related to the escalation of individual madness into universal madness, where the superpsychiatrist Haber's nightmare is externalized and hardens into environmental reality. In their negative connotation of the fragmented individual, shadows usher in formless chaos, the macrocosmic void, and the destruction of the center, both in the individual and the universal sense.

Although loss of identity is a form of death, the shadow motif, especially in the early novels, is used to prefigure actual death. In this respect, Le Guin's use of the motif corresponds to the more traditional, symbolic meaning. To Haldre in *Rocannon's World*, the necklace, the "Eye of the Sea," is a "burden and a shadow" (*RW,* III), because it is emblematic of her son's imminent death. When the wanderers make camp, the shadow at the edge of their firelight, though it prefigures the wisdom of the "Dweller in the Cave," is also a messenger of death for Mogien. Because he is cast in the Nordic heroic mold, Mogien's fatalism causes him to accept this. The necessary, and not merely fatalistic, acceptance of death is a major theme of the Earthsea trilogy and is discussed more fully below. *Planet of Exile*, the second novel, also uses shadow to suggest death, particularly death by ambush. It is used in this context only once in *City of Illusions*, since, by this time, the shadow is assuming the complexity (undergoing a sea change) it acquires in the later novels. The obverse of the image of shadows, as betokening death, is death occurring when there is the sterility of full light with no shadows (which will be discussed below).

Shadows and chaos and darkness, in the benevolent sense of the matrix of potential life, is consciously used in *The Left Hand of Darkness,* although there are hints of it earlier. Indeed, this treatment of the motif can be seen as an analog of Le Guin's own creative, mythopoeic processes, her worlds before they are shaped by words:

> Angels of the shadowed ancient land
> That lies yet unenvisioned, without myth,
> Return, and silent-winged descend
> On the winds that you have voyaged with... (*Wild Angels,* p. 7)

In *Rocannon's World* the Fiia, for example, weave a curious dance of shadows:

> The dancers broke apart, their shadows running quickly up the walls, the loosened hair of one swinging bright for a moment. The dance that had no music was ended, the dancers that had no more name than light and shadow were still. (*RW,* VII)

Here the shadow indicates their corporate racial identity.

It is in conjunction with the name that the shadow motif is most strongly invested with connotations of the microcosm as opposed to the macrocosm. In *City,* darkness and shadow are the space "between the words," thus giving the impression of a spawning, dynamic tension. Later, words—as shaping agents amidst the chaos, as acts of conscious creation—find their most potent expression in the "name," the secret talisman of the individual entity set against original chaos. The development of names into the keystone of the philosophy of the microcosm, the individual, culminates in the concept of *shifgrethor* in *The Left Hand of Darkness.* Again, the ground work had been laid in earlier books. Just before the dance of the nameless shadows in *Rocannon's World,* Rocannon and Kyo discuss the importance of names. In answer to the siren myth of

Semley's brief but spectacular appearance before Rocannon in a museum which is, by its nature, inimical to myth, Rocannon goes to the alien planet to recover a myth. There he finds his new name and new allegiances waiting for him in the name of Olhor (Wanderer), whose destiny is that very quest. In *City,* Orry's calling Falk by his former name, Ramarren, to some extent recalls that identity, that shadow self. But it is in the Earthsea trilogy that the potency of the name is most consistently explored in conjunction with the shadow.

In the first book of the Earthsea trilogy, *A Wizard of Earthsea,* much is made of the naming process; it establishes the secret, or true, name as a kind of talisman guarding true vocation and thus, the true identity. The protagonist Ged is named by the wizard, his master, in a "rite of passage" which indicates entry into the certainty of identity. The wizard guardians of Earthsea maintain the equilibrium of their world by knowing and safeguarding the true names of all things:

> The Master Hand looked at the jewel that glittered on Ged's palm, bright as the prize of a dragon's hoard. The old Master murmured one word, "Tolk," and there lay the pebble, no jewel but a rough grey bit of rock. The Master took it and held it out in his own hand. "This is a rock; *tolk* in the True Speech," he said, looking mildly up at Ged now. "A bit of the stone of which Roke Isle is made, a little bit of the dry land on which men live. It is itself. It is part of the world. By the Illusion-Change you can make it look like a diamond—or a flower or a fly or an eye or a flame—" The rock flickered from shape to shape as he named them, and returned to rock. "But that is mere seeming. Illusion fools the beholder's senses; it makes him see and hear and feel that the thing is changed. But it does not change the thing. To change this rock into a jewel, you must change its true name. And to do that, my son, even to so small a scrap of the world, is to change the world. It can be done. Indeed it can be done. It is the art of the Master Changer, and you will learn it, when you are ready to learn it. But you must not change one thing, one pebble, one grain of sand, until you know what good and evil will follow on the act. The world is in balance, in Equilibrium. A wizard's power to Changing and of Summoning can shake the balance of the world. It is dangerous, that power. It is most perilous. It must follow knowledge, and serve need. To light a candle is to cast a shadow..." (*WE,* III)

When the equilibrium is upset in *The Farthest Shore,* the third book of the trilogy, it involves the loss of these names, of the True Speech. The blight manifests itself through an inability to speak not only the names of things but, more important, the secret name of the individual concerned. In other words, the boundary of certainty implied by the name has been erased; indeed, the movement is illustrated through the image of light (or certainty) trickling away through a hole in the darkness (or uncertainty). On one occasion, Ged resurrects a stricken woman by giving her a new, secret name to restore the core of her identity. These names are usually associated with totemic plants or animals or with ruling daimons externalized in animal or plant shapes. Possibly this indicates the kinship between the human and the nonhuman, which is further emphasized in Ged's case, since he carries a small rat-like familiar during his apprenticeship. The apparent incongruity of Ged's name signifying the predatory falcon is resolved when the familiar, because of its loyalty and affection, succeeds in calling him back from the dead. In this episode Ged demonstrates his ability to arouse loyalty and devotion, which, in turn, belies the superficial pride and fierce courage Ged displays as a youth (represented by the falcon). Both Ged's true name and his common one, Sparrowhawk, are indicative of the tension between his use of power and his hunger for more. Thus the names covertly point toward the potential of his character.

Until a character acquires integrity, or identification with his true self (a synthesis which represents a confrontation with the shadow self), he is often ill at ease with his common name. Prince Arren, whose common name signifies the sword, cannot wield his ancestral sword until he has learned the responsibility of his guardianship, and that entails coming to terms with his own identity as represented by his secret name, Lebannen (rowan tree). Under the rowan tree by the fountain, in the central court of the House of Roke, he confronts his destiny and begins the quest that leads to his becoming the last king of Earthsea. On the journey Arren has to travel through regions where the true name is not a secret amulet but an open passport denoting the baring of his soul before the world. The heroine of the second book, *The Tombs of Atuan,* undergoes a similar trial. In this novel we enter the shadow world of Earthsea, Atuan, which is ruled by chthonic deities known—suggestively—as the "Nameless Ones." I say *suggestively* because they aren't linked with shadows but with total, unbalanced darkness. The heroine, Arha the high priestess, bears a name signifying the "eaten one," in that her identity had to be relinquished in childhood in order for her to become high priestess. Later, through the efforts of Ged, Arha recovers her true name (after also confronting her shadow self), but she can't resume it with impunity until she has escaped the eternal darkness and the bondage of the Nameless Ones. In the trilogy,

Atuan represents uncertainty and the loss of identity.

Whereas, in Le Guin's Earthsea world, the naming process represents hegemony in the Adamite sense, a custodianship involving the upholding of balance and harmony, the act, or deed, reverberates with Faustian implications: it threatens the equilibrium. When the name—the individual entity—exerts itself on the environment, or macrocosm, in an individual act of power, the organic, cosmic equilibrium is threatened. Then the name, or identity, is, in turn, threatened as everything returns to chaos and unbalance. By the end of the trilogy we see that the secret, true name signifies the individual *and* his actions, that the individual must accept full responsibilty for his actions.

In *The Left Hand of Darkness* the shadow image is again used to focus on identity, but now with a slightly different emphasis. Instead of being, as it is in the Earthsea trilogy, an area of uncertain identity bearing the potential for choice (in that it invites the act or responsibility for the act), it becomes an area of personal integrity. In the austere monarchy of Karhide men cast their own shadows; but in effete, socialist Orgoreyn, "...each of them lacked some quality, some dimension of being; and they failed to convince. They were not quite solid. It was, I thought, as if they did not cast shadows" (*LHD,* X). (Compare this with the insubstantiality and duplicity of the Shing in *City.*) The most significant merging of shadow with integrity is in the region of *shifgrethor:*

> "I've made some mistake in shifgrethor. I'm sorry; I can't learn. I've never really understood the meaning of the word."
>
> " 'Shifgrethor?' It comes from an old word for *shadow.* " (*LHD,* XVIII)

Although *shifgrethor* has various meanings, it seems to contain both the Renaissance concept of *virtu* and the Celtic *geas,* as well as a kind of Oriental saving face. In other words, it comprises the identity by which a man wishes to be recognized by his peers. One aspect of the concept of *shifgrethor* is revealed when the extraplanetary emissary, Genly Ai, becomes aware, amid Orgothan sloth, of the lean shadowy presence of the exiled Estraven who, like Banquo's ghost, jolts Ai's conscience and opens his eyes to the peril to his integrity that is represented by Orgothan subterfuge. Genly Ai later assimilates this and goes to extreme lengths in trying to clear his friend's good name—in short, to posthumously restore his shadow. In an effort to have Estraven's exile revoked, Ai confronts the mad king, Argaven, thus putting his mission in jeopardy; but he is forced to bow to the demands of a larger plan of alliance than that of individual friendship.

In her more recent work, Le Guin adds the metaphor of the forest to that of shadow, in the sense of potential, with name or recognized identity. The forest is a well-known metaphor for the subconscious: "We all have forests in our minds. Forests unexplored, unending. Each of us gets lost in the forest, every night, alone" (*WTQ,* "Vaster"). Because it represents the unstructured, the complexities of the potential forces for action within the individual, the forest can be a dangerous zone. At the same time, however, to venture into it is a necessary journey, particularly for the fragmented personality. Even prepsychological writings recognized this (in the modern sense). In *Alice in Wonderland,* Alice says: "This must be the wood ... where things have no names. I wonder what'll become of *my* name when I go in? I shouldn't like to lose it at all."[7]

For Alice, the wood is a benevolent place where she meets and walks with the fawn. The animal doesn't fear her until they leave the wood and it remembers their names, and the prejudices associated with the names. Similarly, in *City*, Falk finds help in the forest, which appears to be an externalization of his subconscious. In the forest he dreams and locates the empathic "Listener," someone who corresponds to the Jungian archetype of the old man of wisdom, the mentor. The Listener is a receiver for all human minds in his vicinity, hence his refuge in the forest away from humanity. In turn, he transmits simple guidelines through the chaos of the subconscious, the touchstone of values that lies beneath words and names. In "A Trip to the Head"—a curious, fragmentary story written some years later—Le Guin conceptualizes, or abstracts, the imagistic coupling of forest, shadow, and name in a way that can be interpreted as a conscious, parodic exegesis on the Lewis Carroll segment quoted above, or perhaps as a parody of her own method:

> Shadow came into the eyes as Earth went round on its axis. Shadow slipped eastward and upward into the other's eyes.
>
> "I think," blank said carefully, "that we should move out from the shadow of the, this, here." He gestured to the objects near them, large things, dark below and multitudinously green above, the names of which he could no longer remember. He wondered if each one had a name, or if they were all called by the same name. What about himself and the other, did they share a name in common, or did each have one of his own? "I have a feeling I'll remember better farther away from it, from them," he said. (*WTQ,* "Trip")

In a more recent story, "The New Atlantis," Le Guin uses the image of the sea to express these linked complexities.[8] The forest metaphor in later works evolves fully into a Taoist symbol, which gives momentum to the entire world of *Word for World* discussed below in the context of holistic designs.

From the shadow and darkness as chaos, either as antilife, antiform, or the potential womb of all form, we move to the center of the spectrum and the shadow and darkness motif in connection with the recognition of the other, the alien. This falls into two categories, Jungian and Taoist. In the Jungian category is the concept of the shadow as the subconscious self, the suppressed self. It is also linked to the animus-anima polarization within each individual, which, in turn, is linked to the yin-yang interaction that is more closely related to Taoism. In Jungian terms, the shadow is the secret self:

> The shadow is not the whole of the unconscious personality. It represents unknown or little-known attributes and qualities of ego—aspects that mostly belong to the personal sphere and that could just as well be conscious. . . . It is particularly in contacts with people of the same sex that one stumbles over both one's own shadow and those of other people.[9]

In *Rocannon's World* the Fiias' "shadow," in the collective sense, are the Clayfolk. Both groups are weakened by not recognizing each other. Although the Fiia, the children of light, are associated with the healing forest, they are still children; the Clayfolk, on the other hand, are dour, subterranean toilers (similar to Wells' Morlocks and Eloi) with little appreciation of the nonmaterialistic world. Before he can become a rounded individual and grow into wisdom, Kyo (Rocannon's Fiian companion) must learn to suffer, to mix his light with his shadow or darkness. In Le Guin's early books, the Jungian shadow figure is sometimes embodied in a Cain-Abel juxtaposition. For example, in *Planet,* the alien Agat is confronted by the blond barbarian indigent: "They stood there for a moment in the firelight like day and night. Agat dark, shadowy, somber, Umaksuman fair-skinned, light-eyed, radiant" (*PE*, IV). Umaksuman later kills his kinsman, Ukwet, out of loyalty to this bond established, this mutual recognition and acceptance of the other. "Darkness Box," a very early story, deals with a similar conflict, one that ends in the darkness of death and exclusion rather than the healing of recognition and tolerance. In *City,* Falk's alter ego—or Ramarren's alter ego, for that matter—must learn to coexist with the consciousness of his other self:

> But there was no integrating or balancing the two minds and personalities that shared his skull, not yet; he must swing between them, blanking one out for the other's sake, then drawn at once back the other way. He was scarcely able to move, being plagued by the hallucination of having two bodies, of being actually physically two different men. He did not dare sleep, though he was worn out: he feared the waking too much. (*CI,* IX)

Finally he does sleep, and Ramarren experiences Falk's dreams, "like shadows and echoes in his mind." In some ways *City* explores the confrontation of shadow and self in its most extreme forms, the most traumatic bringing to consciousness of the labyrinthine minotaur of the hidden self. One feels that the struggle will never be resolved completely:

> He has not joined me yet,
> peers from no mirrors.
> My skull's my own, so far
>
> He is the other,
> smiling from friends' eyes,
> prince of the empty houses
> and the lost domains behind me
> and the last domains before me.
>
> He is the brother
> and the prince and stranger
> coming from far
> to meet me; but we have not met.
> And so I fear the darkness like a child. (*Wild Angels* p. 25)

This poem reveals that the shadow, in the sense of microcosm, recurs throughout Le Guin's work.

The testing of a name or identity in Earthsea emanates from a nihilistic darkness by means of its messenger—the shadow as hunter, as active enemy—who assumes a form opposite to the particular quarry. In the Earthsea trilogy the shadow is externalized as a hunting monster. It is a Faustian, overreaching act which unleashes the shadow, an attempt to exert identity on one's surroundings before the limits of that identity have been explored. In Earthsea the shadow self is synonymous with the inability to accept either individual or cosmic mortality.

At the beginning of *Wizard,* Ged, in a premature grasp for power and in response to wounded pride, comes close to unleashing his shadow from the Underworld. Having been saved by his teacher, he leaves on a ship named *Shadow,* seeking glory and the will to act. After all, the shadow has whispered to him. As his knowledge grows in the school of wizards, so does his thirst, which eventually leads him to breach the barrier between the worlds of death and life and loosen his own shadow on the world of Earthsea:

> Then the sallow oval between Ged's arms grew bright. It widened and spread, a rent in the darkness of the earth and night, a ripping open of the fabric of the world. Through it blazed a terrible brightness. And through the bright misshapen breach clambered something like a clot of black shadow, quick and hideous, and it leaped straight out at Ged's face. (*WE,* IV)

Throughout *Wizard,* Ged's quest is to pursue and name (hence, recognize) this shadow which was released in ignorance. Like most hunts, Ged's is ambivalent; the shadow begins by pursuing Ged, the turning point involves a reversal in which Ged turns on his hunter and eventually discovers that he is pursuing the key to his own identity. Ged names the shadow—which bears *his* name—and thus renders it powerless. This name is partly Ged's hubristic pride and partly, on a larger scale, his acceptance of his own mortality, against which identity alone can finally be measured:

> And he began to see the truth, that Ged had neither lost nor won but, naming the shadow of his death with his own name, had made himself whole: a man: who, knowing his whole true self, cannot be used or possessed by any power other than himself, and whose life therefore is lived for life's sake and never in the service of ruin, or pain, or hatred, or the dark. (*WE,* IX)

In *Tombs,* the darkness is a pervasive, cosmic power stretching through the underground labyrinth of the Nameless Ones, a labyrinth that, traditionally, is associated with loss of identity. The darkness isn't just death but a death prolonged to exclude rebirth, since the deities "eat" the souls of their victims. In the macrocosmic sense, Atuan is, indeed, the shadow self of Earthsea. Birth and life are at first equated with light, especially through the character of Ged, now Archmage and the bearer of light, or understanding. While Arha is the uneasy priestess of this life-denying realm, she fears the light as a spell that will undermine unquestioning obedience to her masters. When she is able to momentarily see the jeweled splendor of the labyrinth as illuminated by Ged, the shell of darkness surrounding her identity begins to crack:

> The darkness pressed like a bandage on her eyes. To have seen the Undertomb confused her; she was bewildered. She had known it only as a region defined by hearing, by hand's touch, by drifts of cool air in the dark; a vastness; a mystery, never to be seen. She had seen it, and the mystery had given place, not to horror, but to beauty, a mystery deeper even than that of the dark. (*TA,* "Light")

Paradoxically, her shadow self is embodied in light. When exposed to the light, the darkness, instead of becoming a shroud, becomes a cocoon presaging rebirth. Through unification with light, her darkness changes from all-consuming malevolence to creative benevolence:

> She woke. Her mouth was stopped with clay. She lay in a stone tomb, underground. Her arms and legs were bound with graveclothes and she could not move or speak. Her despair grew so great that it burst her breast open and like a bird of fire shattered the stone and broke out into the light of day—the light of day, faint in her windowless room. . . . It was not long past sunrise, a fair winter's day. The sky was yellowish, very clear. High up, so high he caught the sunlight and burned like a fleck of gold, a bird was circling, a hawk or desert eagle. "I am Tenar," she said, not aloud, and she shook with cold, and terror, and exultation, there under the open, sunwashed sky. "I have my name back. I am Tenar!" (*TA*, "Names")

Note that by the end of the book there is no longer a simple opposition of light and dark, either microcosmic or macrocosmic, but rather a mingling, or wedding (by means of the ring of Erreth-Akbe), of the two. Throughout the novel Ged is subtly portrayed as the "dark-faced" bearer of light, but Arha/Tenar, who follows the quest for identity, consistently wears black, and denies the light, until the climax of decision. When her choice is made, though still clothed in black, she is now associated with the lamp (rather than the vulnerable and ambivalent candle) and continues on to take up her role of the White Lady of Gont. Thus both light and dark are incorporated in Ged and Tenar; each has come to terms with the shadow self.

In *The Farthest Shore* the theme of the shadow self, as an analog for the acceptance of death, is amplified. There is a more pronounced split between Ged and what could loosely be called his two alter egos: the black male-figure Cob (who opens the door between life and death but who does so largely through fear of his own death), and the young neophyte, Prince Arren. (Ged draws the parallel between his own action and that of Cob. Note also that both names carry the meaning of *fish*.) Here the burden of seeking knowledge has been placed on Arren, the future temporal king of Earthsea, who must find his own identity. He must confront his shadow before he can embody the harmony of Earthsea. In contrast, Ged is the adept who grasps certainty but who must also undergo a purging of the spirit:

> You were born to power, Arren, as I was; power over men, over men's souls; and what is that but power over life and death? You are young, you stand on the borders of possibility, on the shadowland, in the realm of dream, and you hear the voice saying *Come.* But I, who am old, who have done what I must do, who stand in the daylight facing my own death, the end of all possibility, I know that there is only one power that is real and worth the having. And that is the power, not to take, but to accept. (*FS,* "Orm Embar")

Ged recognizes the boundaries of identity and assumes responsibility for his actions, for his place in the balanced whole.

The fear of death is more immediate in the characters of Arren and Cob. Because of his fear, Arren is tempted to break his oath to Ged:

> A great chill went through Arren's body. He remembered his dreams: the moor, the pit, the cliffs, the dim light. That was death; that was the horror of death. It was from death he must escape, must find the way. And on the doorsill stood the figure crowned with shadow, holding out a little light no larger than a pearl, the glimmer of immortal life. (*FS,* "Madman")

This, then, is Arren's particular shadow, rendered more virulent because it contains a false light—or false life. In effect, Ged uses Arren's fear as a decoy to lead him to the source of the evil. But at the same time, Arren must confront its crippling implications:

> The sweat broke out on Arren's face and he had to force his voice, but he went on. "I was afraid of you. I was afraid of death. I was so afraid of it I would not look at you, because you might be dying. I could think of nothing, except that there was—there was a way of not dying for me, if I could find it. But all the time life was running out, as if there were a great wound and the blood running from it—such as you had. But this was in everything. And I did nothing, nothing, but try to hide from the horror of dying." . . . He knew now why this tranquil life in sea and sunlight on the rafts seemed to him like an after-life or a dream, unreal. It was because he knew in his heart that reality was empty: without life or warmth or color or sound: without meaning. . . a playing of illusions on the shallow void. (*FS,* "Children")

Cob, the source of the evil, had once been humiliated by Ged through this same fear, and the obsession that resulted had engendered his desire to remove the barrier between life and death; hence the osmotic swallowing of light by darkness. Far from creating eternal life, however, Cob's act causes a wasteland to be created in which all identity is blurred and lost in a kind of life-in-death:

"... they must climb over the walls of stones when I bid them, all the souls, the lords, the mages, the proud women; back and forth from life to death, at my command. All must come to me, the living and the dead, I who died and live!"

"Where do they come to you, Cob? Where is it that you are?"

"Between the worlds."

"But that is neither life nor death. What is life, Cob?"

"Power."

"What is love?"

"Power," the blind man repeated heavily, hunching up his shoulders.

"What is light?"

"Darkness!"

"What is your name?"

"I have none." (*FS*, "Dry Land")

Prolonging the appearance of life-in-death is related to the death-in-life of Atuan. In both cases the unbalanced worship of either life or death is a travesty that withers both the individual and the harmony of the natural cycle. In the confusion, Ged's directive, that identity which is found when the union of life and death is maintained, illuminates the path:

> He said Arren's true name, which he had never spoken: Lebannen. Again he said it: Lebannen, this is. And thou art. There is no safety, and there is no end. The word must be heard in silence; there must be darkness to see the stars. The dance is always danced above the hollow place, above the terrible abyss. (*FS,* "Children")

Thus, albeit with a smoother transition than in *Tombs,* the connotations of darkness have again shifted from the nihilistic malevolence of thwarted pride and human irresponsibility (Cob) to the benevolence of cyclical life and death. Identity is recovered or acquired by moving from the conflicting temptations of the shadow land, where the shadow self rules in isolation, to a reassertion of the boundary between life and death, between darkness and light.

At the novel's conclusion, Cob dies fully, and Arren, like Ged earlier, learns to accept his mortality. Ged must finally expend all the power he labored to amass, in order to close the fissure which is a prototype of the one he opened in his youth. This final act of responsibility is exercised from the standpoint of the certainty of identity. As Ged returns to his homeland and a life of contemplation, the autocracy of the shadow is absorbed into the self. Throughout the trilogy the shadow, which spurs Ged's quest for certainty of identity, is the enemy only if it is isolated from the self in nonrecognition.

In the context of the yin-yang dichotomy, the shadow self has a slightly different emphasis than the acceptance of mortality which it carries in Earthsea. Here, recognition of the secret self is accentuated by sexual differences. *It isn't recognition of the self as alien, but of the alien as self.* To some extent, Genly Ai and Estraven are the best examples of this interaction; but they don't quite represent the norm, since, in his self-sufficiency, Estraven is in some ways a fusion of yin and yang within himself. This is his burden. It blinds him to the dualistic perspective of his friend. In terms of metaphysics, the fusion of male and female occurs first in *Planet* when Rolery meets the alien male, Agat: "Closing her right hand, she seemed to hold against her palm a handful of darkness, where his touch had been" (*PE*, I). Although their estrangement appears to be accentuated by the "darkness," potentially it is negated by the "handful"; this potential is, in fact, fulfilled. Just as their Winter planet foreshadows Gethen in *The Left Hand of Darkness,* so Rolery and Agat foreshadow the couple in *Planet.* Later the darkness hides their meeting as lovers, and finally, like Genly Ai and Estraven, they succeed in mindspeaking (communicating telepathically):

> She the stranger, the foreigner, of alien blood and mind, did not share his power or his conscience of his knowledge or his exile. She shared nothing at all with him, but had met him and joined with him wholly and immediately across the gulf of their great difference: *as if it were that difference, the alienness between them, that let them meet, and that in joining them together, freed them.* (*PE,* IX, my emphasis)

In *City,* there is the interesting variant of the false opposite—Estrel of the Shing, the "gray shape of grayness," whose shadowy appearance prefigures the insubstantiality and duplicity of her race. (This is similar to the earlier description of Falk, when psychologically fragmented, slipping westward.) Estrel is a false shadow self—or, in the Jungian sense, a false anima; hence, after she is recognized for what she is, she must be evaded. Throughout his quest, Falk is warned about Estrel by others; but he cannot heed the warnings because he must recognize her falseness for himself.

While it doesn't contain the shadow image (apart from the one instance mentioned), *The Lathe of Heaven* does make use of the yin-yang motif in Orr's pursuit of Heather through the various dream worlds.

The most sustained exploration of the yin-yang pattern occurs in *The Left Hand of Darkness,* in a setting which is inimical to life (as was the case with Agat and Rolery and Ged and Arha). Here Genly Ai and Estraven recognize their shadows in each other and themselves:

> . . . I drew the double curve within the circle, and blacked the yin half of the symbol, then pushed it back to my companion.
>
> "Do you know that sign?"
>
> He looked at it a long time with a strange look, but he said, "No."
>
> "It's found on Earth, and on Hain-Davenant, and on Chiffewar. It is yin and yang. *Light is the left hand of darkness*. . . how did it go? Light, dark. Fear, courage. Cold, warmth. Female, male. It is yourself, Therem. Both and one. A shadow on snow." (*LHD,* XIX)

Genly Ai tries to convince Estraven that his race may be as "obsessed with wholeness as we are with dualism," but discovers that Estraven recognizes the true entity as being a mixture of the self and the other, a recognition which Genly Ai himself must painfully work out (*LHD,* XVI). The quest isn't complete until Genly Ai visits Estraven's home after the death of his friend and encounters his "son" by his brother, and finds himself confronting not only alien sexuality but incest as well. In Genly Ai's mind this darkness has become the darkness that nurtures the seed of his friend's spirit. As with Rolery and Agat, their alienness becomes a common ground. The novel represents a consistent, consummate reversal of the shadow image as automatically suggesting negative connotations of death or insubstantiality. Along with the concept of *shifgrethor,* the yin-yang motif insures such a mythic reversal.

The end product of this reversal, however, is an emphasis on the Taoist organic whole. In Le Guin's work, the dynamic interaction of opposites is the culmination of the shadow motif. It is the celebratory other end of the shadow-darkness spectrum we have been exploring in this chapter. Without shadows there is no life. For the best illustration of this analogy we must turn again to *The Left Hand of Darkness*. Genly Ai and Estraven are traveling through the region of the "Unshadow," a twilight zone inimical to life:

> Every football was a surprise, a drop or a jolt. No shadows. An even, white, soundless sphere: we moved along inside a huge frosted-glass ball. There was nothing inside the ball, and there was nothing outside it. But there were cracks in the glass. . . "Fear's very useful. Like darkness; like shadows. . . It's queer that daylight's not enough. *We need the shadows in order to walk."* (*LHD,* XIX, my emphasis)

As in Earthsea, where the shadow incorporates death, the mixture is needed to make up the life-endowing tensions of the organic whole.

Again, there are intimations in earlier books of this particular meaning of the shadow; the place of unshadow as being synonymous with death occurs earlier. In "Darkness Box" the shadowless city and the prince's shadowless room signify a state of enchantment, of eternal conflict between brothers in an eternal moment stretched to accommodate only that conflict. When the shadows are released from the box of darkness, the conflict becomes a finite one, while at the same time, the prince finally has individuality bestowed on him. In *Rocannon's World* the first glimpse of the city of hideous, parasitic angel men is described as "a pure geometric perspective in the unshadowed clarity of dawn." From the outset this suggests their sterility. Compare this with a story written later ("The New Atlantis"), in which a city rising into new pristine life—Atlantis reemerging from the Lethean sea—is first described this way: "Planes and angles appeared. . . shadowless and clear in that even, glowing, blue-green light."[10] As it nears the surface and life, the shadows appear.

In the Earthsea trilogy Le Guin is attempting to explain the idea of the equilibrium using the macrocosmic polarities of the interaction of darkness and light, while the shadow is related to a microcosmic intermingling within the individual, particularly with respect to acceptance of individual mortality. The relationship of this equilibrium to the individual act of power is explained to Ged when he begins his apprenticeship in wizardry. Changing anything will affect the equilibrium, will reverberate throughout the cosmic whole. In *The Tombs of Atuan,* Ged seeks to absorb the shadow self of Earthsea, Atuan; that is, the microcosmic balance. But again, the effect is embodied in individuals, especially Tenar. When Tenar/Arha learns to accept the light, she personifies the coming to terms of Earthsea with its shadow world, and the balance is restored. Similarly, in *The Farthest Shore* the equilibrium restored on an even greater scale is measured through the human gauges of Ged, Arren, and Cob, since again, it is the individual act and confrontation with responsibility for an act that constitutes change and threat. It is fitting here that the lesson of the awareness of equilibrium should come from Ged whose wisdom has strained to reach this truth throughout the trilogy:

> Presently the mage said, speaking softly, "Do you see, Arren, how an act is not, as young men think, like a rock that one picks up and throws, and it hits or misses, and that's the end of it. When that rock is lifted, the earth is lighter; the hand that bears it heavier. When it is thrown, the circuits of the stars respond, and where it strikes or falls the universe is changed. On every act the balance of the whole depends. The winds and

> seas, the powers of water and earth and light, all that these do, and all that the beasts and green things do, is well done, and rightly done. All these act within the Equilibrium. From the hurricane and the great whale's sounding to the fall of a dry leaf and the gnat's flight, all they do is done within the balance of the whole. But we, insofar as we have power over the world and over one another, we must *learn* to do what the leaf and the wind do of their own nature. We must learn to keep the balance. Having intelligence, we must not act in ignorance. Having choice, we must not act without responsibility. Who am I—though I have the power to do it—to punish and reward, playing with men's destinies?...do only that which you must do, and which you cannot do in any other way." (*FS,* "Magelight")

The arena of choice, as presented to the novice, makes an interesting comparison with the passage quoted from *Wizard.* There is, I believe, more substance here, in that there is firmer control in balancing the message and the speaker's individual voice. There is a hint of humor in the older man's voice, which betrays his awareness of the impetuosity of the younger man. The humor lies in his choice of images, which embraces the extravagant whale and the equally extravagant gnat. In *The Farthest Shore* the dialogue has moved from exposition to communication involving mutual recognition.

In *Rocannon's World* the image of mingled light and dark, as indicating wisdom, is embodied in the "Dweller in the Cave," the oracle who combines the characteristics of the Fiia and the Clayfolk, the two most extremely opposed and thus necessarily connected races on that world. In *City*, the prince, who gives Falk the Taoist canon that enables him to finally balance his two selves, is described as having a "hard, shadowy face." Once again, the intermingling of darkness and light in shadow suggests wisdom. (The firecrackers set off against the Shing air-cars also suggest an awareness of the need to set light against darkness. "In the shadow of total calamity why not set off a firecracker?"—*CI,* V).

In *The Left Hand of Darkness* the interweaving of light and darkness is the basis of everything in that world. The title, in which darkness is symbolically stressed (since light connotes the bar sinister of illegitimacy), points to what may well be the central weakness of the novel, that there is a flavor of proselytizing about it. The book is sometimes almost a pamphlet for mythic iconoclasm, the acceptance of darkness and shadow as benevolent images, a rehabilitation of those images. This is particularly true in the discussion of the Handdara and Yomesh sects on Gethen. By means of the Weaver, the Handdara have gained mystical insight through the synthesization of the hysterical energy from the interaction of a group of misfits and abnormals. Their aim is the acceptance of oneself and one's environment. It is a similar lesson to that which must be learned on Earthsea:

> "You don't see yet, Genry, why we perfected and practice Foretelling?"
>
> "No—"
>
> "To exhibit the perfect uselessness of knowing the answer to the wrong question. . . . The unknown . . . the unforetold, the unproven, that is what life is based on. Ignorance is the ground of thought. Unproof is the ground of action. If it were proven that there is no God there would be no religion. No Handdara, no Yomesh, no hearthgods, nothing. But also if it were proven that there is a God, there would be no religion. . . . Tell me, Genry, what is known? What is sure, predictable, inevitable—the one certain thing you know concerning your future, and mine?"
>
> "That we shall die."
>
> "Yes. There's really only one question that can be answered, Genry, and we already know the answer. . . . The only thing that makes life possible is permanent, intolerable uncertainty: not knowing what comes next." (*LHD,* V)

Here, though, the presentation is expository rather than being enacted, as it is in the Earthsea trilogy. In contrast (in what is perhaps meant to be an uncomfortable reminder of the Christian principle of light), the rival sect of the Yomeshi view life not as past, present, and future, all coming from and returning to darkness, but as merely the present moment as illuminated by Meshe's awareness, which is analogous to the sun, in that it is pure light and thus is unbalanced in the cosmic sense. In the abstract, we are confronted with the age-old struggle between the patriarchal and the matriarchal cosmologies, with the latter, as perhaps befits the androgynous Gethenians, having the edge. Darkness becomes the womb of life, or, as Estraven says, "praise then darkness and Creation unfinished" (*LHD,* XVIII). As the reader's human counterpart in the book, Genly Ai is educated into sympathetic empathy with an alien culture and with the alien within himself, by means of this redefinition at every level, of "shadow" and "darkness." But it is in his interaction with others, rather than in these expository sequences, that this reeducation is credibly presented.

In "The Field of Vision" Le Guin has developed the idea of light alone as being too shattering for human comprehension. Two astronauts have a vision of heaven, or God, as pure light, and are henceforth unable to live through their normal senses in the world. Here, Man is an obstruction to this vision; again, the flawed microcosm is described in terms of the shadow: "A blot. A shadow. An incompleteness, a rudiment, an obstruction. Something completely unimportant. You see, it doesn't do any *good* to be a good man, even..." (*WTQ,* "Field"). The price, finally, is suicide.

It is in the interaction, stressing the boundaries and limits of each, that the balance lies; so in Le Guin's work we continuously get the interpretation, the mutual support, of light and dark. At the same time, there is the middle ground appropriate to the hybrid human (or its analogues); this is the province of the shadow. Although in earlier books the shadow was the microcosmic confluence framed in the larger macrocosmic polarities, in her later work there seems to be an elevation of the middle ground to macrocosmic levels. This occurs when the shadow is linked to the image of the forest, in which case the shadow motif incorporates the necessary interaction of the polarities. I am thinking here of the novella, *The Word for World Is Forest.* The world presented in this work is Le Guin's most consistent celebration of the holistic Taoist world, in terms of organic symbiosis. The humans in the story are a parasitic intrusion into this equilibrium, while the Athsheans are an extension of the Fiia; they are self-sufficient in their instinctive interaction with the forest. Like the Fiia, they, too, must learn to confront their collective shadow—the other—which, in an interesting reversal, is represented by the humans. The alien self is embodied both in the insane killer, Davidson, and the anthropologist, Lyubov who, through the mind of Selver, operates benevolently as shadow, in the Jungian aspect. By absorbing the shadow of the dead Lyubov, Selver attains an unwelcome severance from his race. It is a necessary step toward individuality, though, meaning that Selver learns responsibility for his actions. In the crisis of imminent genocide, the Athsheans need a leader, and that is what Selver becomes. He gains wisdom (as Kyo does in *Rocannon's World*) but at the price of changing the equilibrium:

> Lepennon laid his long hand on Selver's hand, so quickly and gently that Selver accepted the touch as if the hand were not a stranger's. The green-gold shadows of the ash leaves flickered over them.
>
> "But you must not pretend to have reasons to kill one another.

> Murder has no reason,'' Lepennon said, his face as anxious and sad as Lyubov's face.
>
> ''We shall go. Within two days we shall be gone. All of us. Forever. Then the forests of Athshe will be as they were before.''
>
> Lyubov came out of the shadows of Selver's mind and said ''I shall be here.''
>
> ''Lyubov will be here,'' Selver said. ''And Davidson will be here. Both of them. Maybe after I die people will be as they were before I was born, and before you came. But I do not think they will.'' (*WW,* VIII)

The balance of this world has been changed, first, through Davidson's initial irresponsible acts which then reverberate on a spiritual and more far-reaching level in the race's acceptance of killing when survival is at stake. Selver's recognition of Lyubov represents his race's necessary acceptance of the other. The forest full of shadows is an image of the symbiotic whole, but it is not invulnerable and not immutable.

In her use of the shadow to represent the ambiguous lessons of moral and pyschic absolutes the individual must absorb in his quest for Jungian individuation or Taoist wisdom, and in the accompanying images of light and darkness and the complexity of forests, Le Guin's work demonstrates the evolution of her mythopoeic artistry. Her increasing assurance in investing these traditional images with her own particular metaphorical implications means that she is increasingly purging her art of those early touches of jarring proselytizing. She moves now with greater subtlety and ease through images which have emerged from their petrified cocoons of obsolete symbolic meanings and are now familiar in their metamorphosed selves. The spectrum of values attached to the shadow motif demonstrates how the modern fantasist can give the traditional image new significance by uniting it with new images born of the ''waking dream'' of the aware mythopoeic artist, freed of the rigidity of naturalism.

9. Words of Binding: Patterns of Integration in the Earthsea Trilogy

JOHN H. CROW and RICHARD D. ERLICH

THE DEVELOPMENT of Ursula K. Le Guin's fantasy and science fiction displays not so much "the growth of a poet's mind" as the mastering of an artist's craft. Her published work suggests that there was never very much the matter with Ms. Le Guin's mind. She confesses, in fact, to being "an intellectual born and bred," a statement with which any attentive reader of her work can agree. Somewhat inconsistently, she confesses at the same time to a certain dismay because the critics have focused on her ideas rather than her art. This remark should be noted for the record, since it may be the first time a novelist has complained of being taken seriously. It may also be the last.

Le Guin's work demands to be taken seriously. Even in her early work, it is impossible not to respect the keen intelligence and mature vision. Her vision is essentially one of integration. Whether she develops a political theory, a philosophical perspective, or offers insights into human psychology, she depicts the possibility of unification, if not its necessity. Regardless of how many worlds she creates, she remains a firm proponent of the oneness of the world, and it is this vision that unifies her work.

According to Le Guin, her best work is the Earthsea trilogy. We believe an analysis of this trilogy will reveal its own coherence, as well as the patterns and themes which reveal the unifying vision of her work, from *Rocannon's World* to *The Dispossessed.* We begin our analysis of the trilogy with the observation that the Hero is the one who finds a way when all others have abandoned hope.

Paradoxically, perhaps, Le Guin has created in Earthsea a heroic world embodying the sort of existentialist perspectives that seem to make heroism impossible, perspectives which have generated much of the literature of despair and hopelessness in the twentieth-century West.

Although Le Guin's Earthsea novels embody these perspectives, they are not philosophical discourses. She has borrowed from philosophical systems concepts useful for the creation of the cosmologies in which she chooses to work, without obligating herself to develop a particular scheme. Her use of philosophical concepts seems assimilative rather than systematic or eclectic, while her fictional constructs remain mythological. The Earthsea trilogy presents concepts familiar to students of philosophy and psychology, primarily existentialist philosophy and Jungian psychology, that are woven with the binding spells of art, thus creating a world of fantasy which reveals the common heroism necessary to confront a world without a transcendant god, a world in in which man is thrown back on his own finite existence.

The world of Earthsea suggests that the recently disbanded Flat Earth Society may have despaired too soon. The world of Earthsea is flat, and the vertical dimension of Le Guin's cosmos lies between the depths of being and the empty sky, neither of which has much to do with the pursuits of everyday life, although both have significance. It is a world of immanence rather than transcendence, ruled by one principle, balance. A corollary of this principle is unity; for the balance to hold, two things in balance must each remain whole. The two things held in cosmic balance are the world of life and the realm of death. Light and darkness are associated with the two worlds, but it is misleading to say that light and darkness are balanced on a cosmic scale, since light and darkness are themselves a natural part of the world of life. They must find their balance there—in nature and in the lives of men.

More precisely, the world of life is a world of change and time. The realm of death is one of permanence and timelessness. As opposites, these two attract one another, and in this attraction lies the danger. While the two worlds must cohere, remaining interdependent, they must not interpenetrate, if the Equilibrium is to be maintained. The Balance is natural; nothing in nature disturbs it. Only man can destroy the natural system, and only man can restore it once it has been disturbed. Fortunately, only a few men have the power to significantly affect the Balance. But even fewer can correct the Balance once it has been disturbed, for correction requires great power and great effort, power and effort of heroic proportions. The evil that men do requires a hero to compensate for the evil. The significance of Le Guin's trilogy goes beyond this, however. Consideration of the trilogy's structure and the nature of the cosmology it presents suggests that, in an important sense, all action is heroic.

Three basic patterns of development are apparent in the trilogy. Least obtrusive is the pattern of movement from social disorder to social order. The first volume, *A Wizard of Earthsea,* opens with a raid on Gont by warriors from the Kargad lands. Such raids are a recurring threat for all the eastern islands of the Archipelago. Pirates within the Archipelago constantly prey on trade, while on the western side of Earthsea, the dragons of Pendor threaten the stability of the small communities on the Ninety Isles. In *Wizard,* Ged removes the threat of the dragons and in *Tombs* overcomes the Old Powers of darkness that hold the Kargish people in benighted superstition, resulting in a cessation of hostilities and an alliance between Kargad and the Archipelago. In *The Farthest Shore* he leads the young Prince Arren through an initiation which qualifies him to become the first king in Havnor in 800 years, an ascension that promises to end lawlessness and to restore order throughout Earthsea. Consistent with Le Guin's philosophical position in the trilogy, this pattern receives minor emphasis. For Le Guin, the individual is always primary. Society is beyond hope if the individual remains undeveloped as a human being.[1] By virtue of his consciousness, man stands outside nature and out from under the laws of nature. Consequently, he must govern himself or be governed by the laws and customs of man. More perfect societies—that is, less coercive societies—wait upon the development of the more nearly perfect man.

The theme of human development dictates a second structural pattern in the trilogy, a pattern that approximates C. G. Jung's process of individuation. Immediately after the raid by Kargish warriors in *Wizard,* Ged goes through his rite of passage into manhood. He gives up his childhood name, Duny, and receives from the wizard Ogion his true name—Ged. Ged takes for his name "Sparrowhawk" and goes with Ogion to become his apprentice. Together, Ogion and Ged manifest the archetype of the Wise Old Man and the Child, an image that suggests, among other things, both continuity with the past and the possibility of growth, as well as assurance of the future, in which the present comes to fruition.

Ged is eager for a more active life than the one he leads with Ogion, however, and he goes into the world, where circumstances eventually force him to confront his Shadow. The conquest of the Shadow, which Jung describes as the first step in the process of individuation, comprises the action that completes *Wizard*. Although Ged has by this time earned his wizard's staff and even successfully confronted the dragons on Pendor, he has not yet established his credentials as the compleat hero, at least as Jung uses the term. To do so, Ged must descend into the underworld and rescue the Anima from the Great Mother, here portrayed as the Old Powers. This takes place in *The Tombs of Atuan*, despite the pattern's being somewhat disguised by narrating the story from the Anima-figure's point of view. Besides disguising the pattern, this technique allows Le Guin to treat the woman as a person with an individuality of her own, rather than making her nothing more than an adjunct of the male, as often happens in myths and stories of this type.

In the third novel, *The Farthest Shore*, Le Guin returns to the archetype of the Wise Old Man and the Child, this time with Ged as the Wise Old Man, and Prince Arren as the Child. Arren is to be initiated into his adult role in life. This forms a circular pattern which asserts both the continuity and the unity of life. The pattern of the hero's life becomes a whole—returning to the archetype from which it began, just as Ged returns to the isle of Gont to live out his life, while Arren, the initiated child, takes up the active life that Ged must abandon. At the beginning of the trilogy, Ogion represents that which Ged must become and does become at the close of the trilogy. As Jung would say, in my beginning is my end, in my end is my beginning; or in Odo's words, true journey is return. Ged's return to Gont on the back of the ancient dragon suggests an alliance with the spirit and a completion of the Self in the final process of individuation.

The third pattern of the trilogy takes up the theme of balance and assumes a dialectical form. Each novel provides the point of view of a different character, each of whom acts in accord with a different controlling idea. The first novel presents Ged's point of view. Under the tutelege of his masters on Roke, Ged learns the value and importance of the Balance, even though, in his youthful pride and ignorance, he nearly destroys it. The plot of *Wizard* deals with the growth of the hero from a childish concern for his own preeminence to his recognition of the paramount necessity of the Balance and his achievement of balance, an achievement that is of equal importance to Ged *and* his world.

When Ged comes to the school at Roke he already has great power for his age, and he soon acquires more. He sees power as something to be used for personal benefit, believing that a wizard is "powerful enough to do what he pleased, and balance the world as seemed best to him"(*WE,* III). Ged ignores the fact that a wizard's acts have consequences that are external to himself.[2] At the same time that Ged finds it easy to dismiss external considerations, he is enormously sensitive to external definition and pressure. Proud, quick to anger, and sensitive to any scoff or slight, his particular nemesis is the noble-born Jasper who looks down on Ged and his origins as a goatherd. Thus two forces influencing Ged are an immoderate concern for his personal satisfaction and the weight of the traditional social structure outside Roke, which ascribes to Jasper a status higher than Ged's.

Attempting to humble Jasper, Ged misuses his power, rends the veil of the world, and looses an unknown thing of evil and darkness into the world. The thing is his shadow, a thing of "unlife," the negation not only of Ged's life but of all his power to do good. Ged's obligation to conquer his shadow is an obligation to himself as well as the world on which he unleashes it. Obligations are both external and internal; they must be balanced. Threatened at Low Torning by the reappearance of his shadow, Ged cannot flee from personal danger until he fulfills his responsibility to protect the islanders from the dragons on Pendor, a conflict which he resolves by sailing to Pendor and confronting the dragons. This episode is a great trial for Ged. He knows the name of the great dragon of Pendor, and true names give a wizard power over the things they name; but the dragon knows the true name of Ged's shadow and offers to reveal it if Ged will abandon his mission. Ged remains true to his social duty, however, and extracts from the dragon the oath that neither he nor his sons will ever come to the Archipelago.

Free of this responsibility, Ged turns to the problem of the shadow and finally overcomes it in the only way the shadow can be overcome, by recognizing it for his own and accepting it for what it is—his hate, his pride, his fear of death, his evil, his inhumanity. In accepting the dark side of himself, Ged achieves self-knowledge and makes himself "whole: a man: who, knowing his whole true self, cannot be used or possessed by any power other than himself, and whose life therefore is lived for life's sake and never in the service of ruin, or pain, or hatred, or the dark"(*WE,* X). The self-mastery Ged achieves gives him the power with which to challenge the forces that govern the protagonists of the succeeding novels.[3]

Tombs presents the point of view of Arha, the nameless one, who is taken as a child, dedicated to the Old Powers, and raised to be their priestess at the tombs of Atuan in the Kargad Lands. Arha's life is controlled by the darkness, the Old Powers, the forces of the unconscious, and by the weight of tradition, the dead weight of the past. The Kargish people believe in reincarnation, and Arha is chosen to become priestess because she was born the night the old priestess died and is therefore assumed to be the old priestress returned to life. Life for Arha has been extended beyond the natural limits of birth and death into ancient times. Tradition defines her duties, devotions—all the possibilities of her life. Arha gives up personal identity in the service of a social order. She must serve the powers of darkness in the undertomb, where light never comes, and in the labyrinth, a wandering maze (which Jung sees as one of the oldest images of the forces of the unconscious). Time and darkness weigh heavily on Arha, although the tradition she serves denies time altogether. The Old Powers are timeless, and the priestess herself is held to be eternal in her continual reincarnations. The worship of darkness and the denial of time contradict the Balance between the world of the living, with its time and change, and the realm of death, with its permanence and timelessness.

This contradiction is a source of disorder in the world. The discrepancy in world views makes the Kargad Lands and the Archipelago alien to one another, making hostility seemingly natural, even right. On a more personal level, disorder appears in the tension and conflict between Arha and Kossil, the priestess of the Godking, as Arha tries to maintain her authority and the timeless efficacy of the Nameless Ones against the skeptical, manipulative Kossil. The fallacy of Arha's position and the religion she serves becomes evident in the description of the setting at Atuan. The temple of the Nameless Ones is the most ancient and has been allowed to fall into disrepair. More recent but still maintained is the temple of the twin Godbrothers, and "centuries newer" and most lavishly adorned is the Temple of the Godking. The evolution of religious belief from nameless, undifferentiated powers associated with the feminine, to celestial and masculine gods, and on to the deification of the king as god denies the permanence and timelessness to which Arha's life is devoted.

This evolution, in which distant mysterious gods become more anthropomorphic and move closer to their devotees, is a cliché in religious history. Since the Kargad Lands will later join with the Archipelago and accept wizardry, the reader may suspect that wizardry is the next step in this evolutionary process which, roughly speaking, moves from transcendence to immanence. Such a view also lends support to those who wish to see in "Ged" a suggestion of "god," thereby linking him with Rocannon in *Rocannon's World* and Selver in *The Word for World Is Forest,* characters explicitly called "gods." The problem with this view is that no similar process of religious evolution seems to have ever occurred in the Archipelago. However this problem might be resolved, it is clear that the world Arha inhabits and defends is outdated even in the context of her own culture.

Into this world Ged comes, seeking the ring of Erreth-Akbe and the Lost Rune—"the Bond-Rune, the sign of dominion, the sign of peace" that allows a king to rule well and to end the quarrels and wars afflicting Earthsea. Ged, and the powers he commands, cause Arha to become dissatisfied with the unconscious life she has been living. She leaves the Tombs and returns with him to Earthsea to take up the task of creating an identity, a human consciousness to go with the name Ged returns to her. The hero overcomes the darkness and the denial of time and change implicit in the control of human life by the external force of an unchanging tradition.

The challenge presented the hero in *The Farthest Shore* is, in almost every way, the reverse of that presented in *Tombs*. *The Farthest Shore* presents the point of view of young Prince Arren, who falls victim not to the social tradition that extends life into the past, but to the intense personal desire for an immortality that would extend life into the future.[4] As conscious of his life as Arha is unconscious of hers, Arren fears his death. He loathes the thought of the inevitable end to life that rises gradually in his consciousness like the constellation of the Rune of Ending rising over the southern horizon. Gripped by this thought, Arren sinks into despair, overwhelmed by the futility of struggling against the inevitable. He loses all hope of significant action and gives up the struggle to sustain life. To become immune to the fear and hopelessness excited by the thought of death, Arren must conquer his fear by crossing the realm of the dead and must accept the pain of losing all that the world of the living can offer by scaling the Mountains of Pain. This done, Arren is fit to become king; metaphorically, he is now fit to rule life. Having accepted death and loss, he can act in accord with whatever may enhance life, rather than from irrational or illusory hopes and motivations. The contrast between Arha and Arren, then, is the contrast of being controlled by the weight of the past, embodied in public tradition, and being controlled by the fear of the future, motivated by private concern—a contrast of thoughtless action and the paralysis of thought. Both differ from Ged's thoughtful attempts, in the present moment and with due regard for both past and future, to choose between action and nonaction.

In *The Farthest Shore*, too, the problems of the protagonist have a parallel in society. The malaise that takes hold of Arren as he watches the Rune of Ending rise, is already, at the beginning of Ged's and Arren's journey, a general malaise. People lose their sense of purpose, craftsmanship suffers, trade declines, lawlessness spreads, slavery increases. People who see no value in their own lives see no value in the lives of others. Deluded by illusory hope, people take to drugs and search the misty reaches of reality, looking for an occult secret to save them from death. Le Guin's contempt for the drug culture, occult societies, and transcendental religion becomes apparent here. The sorcerer, Cob, who opens the door between life and death, appears finally as a charlatan promising what he cannot deliver; he is a false prophet. In truth, Cob symbolizes nothing more than our collective dread of death and our desire to avoid it. As Ged points out to Arren, the real traitor is in the mind: Cob can speak to us only with our own voice. The dread, nonetheless, is real, even if the voice is false. The people of Earthsea respond, and meaning seems to drain from the world. The joy goes out of living; the people lose faith in wizardry. Even the dragons call on the hero for help.

Dragons and wizards are both complex beings, although in different ways. In their complexity, dragons cannot be explained; they are an "irreducible symbol" of the spirit and can only be treated phenomenologically. Dragons are creatures of wind and fire, the spiritual elements, just as man and other animals in nature are creatures of earth and sea. Le Guin's picture of dragons is much like Jung's description of the spirit, which is collective and therefore not bounded by the limits of man's life. It has its roots in man's chthonic, or unconscious, nature and has at its command all the old powers of the unconscious. But for Jung, too, what the spirit is, in itself, remains unknown; it can be known only to the degree that it manifests itself in its operations. Spirit for Jung, like the dragons for Ged, lies mostly outside the scope of man's judgment and knowledge: "Who am I, to judge the acts of dragons?...They are wiser than men are. It is with them as with dreams, Arren. We men dream dreams, we work magic, we do good, we do evil. The dragons do not dream. They are dreams. They do not work magic: it is their substance, their being. They do not do; they are" (*FS,* "Hort Town").

This distinction between being and doing, so important for understanding dragons, is also important for understanding wizards. Le Guin's social cosmology is not as lacking in vertical dimension as her physical cosmology, and wizards and mages stand at the top. Below them are the sorcerers, then the prentices, who are somewhat better than the village witches, weatherworkers, and spell-weavers. In the hierarchy with which the story deals, each level implies different powers and capacities. Until one reaches the level of sorcerer, he learns only a few practical arts and the spells of illusion. The sorcerer, though, deals with "high arts and enchantments" and the spells of True Change, including the ability to change oneself into another creature. The spell of True Change entails the danger, however, of being caught in the shape of the other creature and so becoming that other creature in fact: "Every prentice-sorcerer learns the tale of the wizard Bordger of Way, who delighted in taking bear's shape, and did so more and more often until the bear grew in him and the man died away, and he became a bear" (*WE,* VII). The more often a wizard changes his shape or the longer he remains in another shape, the less chance he has of returning to a human condition.

Human life is the highest form of life in Earthsea. Thus the change of shape must necessarily be to a lower kind of existence. A man with the power to choose another shape has the power to destroy his own human being and become less than human. Metaphorically, then, the problem of shape-changing introduces the idea that man has the power to choose what he will, in essence, become. Shape precedes form; existence precedes essence; doing creates being. Such power, therefore, is dangerous. Because action places man's humanity in the balance, any man aware of the risk he runs in taking action may well be reluctant to act. Moreover, as is made clear in *Wizard*, men have shadows, and as a consequence, ill-considered actions may serve the powers of darkness rather than those of light. Since acts have consequences in the external world, the decision to act should follow only after these consequences have been consciously examined and weighed against considerations of self. The internal must be balanced against the external. Ged's act of summoning Elfarren to appear on Roke knoll—the act that releases Ged's shadow into the world—creates a danger for society as well as for himself.

The world of nature cannot be ignored, either. Only a few things in the world are inexhaustible, "such energies as light, and heat, and the force that draws the magnet, and those forces men perceive as weight, form, color, sound" (*WE,* IV); but to use wizardly spells on the stuff of the earth is to tamper with nature and threaten the Balance: "Rain on Roke may be drouth in Osskil. . .and a calm in the East Reach may be storm and ruin in the West" (*WE,* IV). The being of man is involved in the being of the world, and the balance must obtain on an ecological plane as well as on the human. Ged tells Arren: "From the hurricane and the great whale's sounding to the fall of a dry leaf and the gnat's flight, all they do is done within the balance of the whole. But we, insofar as we have power over the world and over one another, we must *learn* to do what the leaf and the whale and the wind do of their own nature. We must learn to keep the balance" (*FS,* "Magelight").

The Balance rules all of nature; but man, to the extent that he is conscious and intelligent, is outside of nature: lawlessness is a possibility for us as a part of the freedom we win through consciousness. The consequences of lawlessness are unavoidable, however. If the rule of balance is not observed, it at least is not mocked. As men, "we must *learn* to keep the balance." Our freedom is our responsibility.[5]

All this adds up to a very modest ethic for a heroic world: power may be dangerous and action may entail risk, but above all we expect a hero to act. This rather negative argument, however, has its obverse side. If action has the power to reshape man and deprive him of his humanity—symbolized by the danger to the wizard of *becoming* the thing he transforms himself into—it also has the power to create human being. It is, in fact, the only way to create it. Arha, who does not act, or at best, acts only in the way defined for her by the tradition, lacks human being. She has no name, and true names are names of true being. Her name is taken from her in the ceremony consecrating her to the Nameless Ones, the "name" in Atuan for the Old Powers, the powers of the unconscious. Nameless, Arha is unconscious, like the powers she serves, and she remains so until Ged brings light into the domain of the Nameless Ones and gives her identity by restoring her name: Tenar. Until then, she is woman or priestess, but she does not have personality. Until Ged awakens her into consciousness, she shows no sense of possessing the freedom to choose her acts on the basis of a personal identity unrestricted by assigned roles. Perhaps more important, she shows no sense of being free not to act, a bondage to the role of priestess most starkly apparent when Kossil goads her into sentencing to a hideous death three prisoners condemned by the Godking.

For Arha, the freedom not to act is a liberation; but Arren chafes under such restraints. To Ged's homily on the Equilibrium, he protests that "surely a man must act." Ged's reply is that an emphasis on action is an emphasis misplaced: "Never fear. It is much easier for men to act than to refrain from acting. We will continue to do good and to do evil" (*FS,* "Magelight").[6] Man not only tends to action by nature, he is bound to action by his previous acts, a truth that provides the motivation for the entire first book, where Ged's act of loosing the shadow obliges him to track down and confront it. To be free to consciously create an essence, one's own being, man must be free from bondage to his previous acts, free from being what he has been, in order to become what he would be. From this perspective, the emphasis falls not on action but choice:

> Try to choose carefully, Arren, when the great choices must be made. When I was young, I had to choose between the life of being and the life of doing. And I leapt at the latter like a trout to a fly. But each deed you do, each act, binds you to itself and to its consequences, and makes you act again and yet again. Then very seldom do you come upon a space, a time like this, between act and act, when you may stop and simply be. Or wonder who, after all, you are. (*FS,* "Hort Town").

But there is a hook in the fly of action. Man freely chooses, but having acted, he is no longer free. It would seem that freedom is possible only in being, not in doing.

Yet even in being, there is no true release from action, for the imperative to act is wholly internal, resulting from one's state of being. Ged is his own creation; he has created himself as a man of action. Like Tennyson's Ulysses, he finds it dull "to rust unburnished, not to shine in use." He leaps like a trout to a fly at the chance to engage the problem Arren brings to Roke: " 'For I am tired of safe places, and roofs, and walls around me.'...Arren saw the deep restlessness of the man, and it frightened him" (*FS,* "Masters"). Being is also a product of time, the result of being bound to past acts. Both Arren and Ged are what they are because of their past. Arren is a prince of the line of Morred and Serriadh, although it should be noted that his princely qualities are a matter of what he is—his being—rather than an accident of birth. He has accepted the obligations of a prince and thus has made himself a prince, as Ged sees when they meet: "No man had ever looked at him thus, not as Arren, Prince of Enlad, son of the Ruling Prince, but as Arren alone" (*FS,* "Rowan Tree"). Arren becomes a prince because he has acted as a prince; his statement that he has accepted the responsibility of his role draws approval from Ged: "That is what I meant. To deny the past is to deny the future. A man does not make his destiny: he accepts it or denies it" (*FS,* "Masters").

The tenor of this remark is somewhat more fatalistic than the pattern of the trilogy will support; but in context, its import seems clear: man makes his choices in terms of who he is and the particular situation he confronts, and who he is results from how he has confronted particular situations in the past. Accordingly, Ged's choice is limited by his past, for he too has a responsibility: "I've been pretending that I am free. . . . That nothing's wrong in the world. That I'm not Archmage, not even sorcerer. That I'm Hawk of Temere, without responsibilities or privileges, owing nothing to anyone. . ." (*FS,* "Hort Town"). Clearly the effect of this argument is to emphasize choice over action. Men will continue to act; there is no doubt of that. The question is, should they act? The most heroic act may be a heroic act of restraint. On the other hand, a man who has the power to act and yet refuses to act when he should, chooses to become less than he is; he chooses to change to the "shape" of a lesser creature. He denies past time by denying his being and denies the future by denying the action that creates human being. Man shapes himself for better or worse by each choice he makes. By refusing to act when he should, he refuses to create or even to sustain his own humanity.

Le Guin's formulation of the problem of being and doing arrives at something of a paradox: man exists and must create his own essence, which he can only do by acting. But to act freely, he must have choice, if he would create his own individual essence, or being. Arha, the nameless one, has no individual being because, bound by tradition, she creates only a public, or social, being—that of priestess. If man may act freely, though, he creates being and thus becomes bound to his past actions and to the being which he has created. We are free, it would seem, only to lose our freedom: "the truth is that as a man's real power grows and his knowledge widens, ever the way he can follow grows narrower: until at last he chooses nothing, but does only and wholly what he *must do*. . ." (*WE,* IV).

This restricted view of human freedom is reinforced by the description of the realm of death. In this realm those who have passed from life retain their being; all that exists in the land of the dead are names. In the confrontation with Cob in the land of the dead, Ged says that after death he will exist as a name: "And when that body dies, I will be here: but only in name, in name alone, in shadow. Do you not understand?" (*FS,* "Dry Land"). All that lives, remains in the world and partakes of the great cycle of life. Only the being that man creates passes into the timeless realm of death; only there, in timelessness and permanence, does being find freedom from action. All that is a part of nature remains in nature, leaving the ecological balance of the world undisturbed. The individual being that man creates for himself is unique and indestructible, and in that sense, timeless and without change beyond death. In the cosmological image that the trilogy provides, then, the *being* of man, his conscious human being, must maintain a balance with the being of nature.

The world of shaped matter comes into existence when Segoy says the "Words of the Making"—mythologically, the birth of consciousness. The existence of the world depends on man's consciousness, an idea that has been prevalent in Western philosophy since Kant. Therefore, man's capacity to destroy the world is twofold. To abuse the being of nature with irresponsible acts, on the one hand, or to refuse the responsibility to create one's own human being, on the other, is to place in jeopardy the whole of creation. In other words, for man, existence precedes essence. What mankind makes of itself will determine the fate of the world, and by extension, of the human race dependent on physical nature for existence. Man has it in his power to speak the Words of the Unmaking, to destroy the balance and all human life that depends on it. Human greed can bring on the apocalypse in which the islands of the Archipelago slip beneath the sea and the world returns to the unconsciousness of the Old Powers.

The Old Powers, however, are not the greatest danger to man's existence. Their "evil is of earth" (*WE,* VIII). As a consciousness emerges from the amoral chaos of the sea, it becomes aware of the opposition of the sea of unconscious as a fixed, permanent thing. Consciousness differentiates the amorality of the sea into good and evil, appropriates good and light to itself, and relegates to the earth the "chthonic powers" of evil and darkness. The amoral chaos of the sea becomes the evil of the stone, an evil most apparent in the stone tombs of Atuan and the stone of Terrenon. The greatest danger, though, is the force that produces, *ex nihilo,* the shadow Ged comes to terms with in *Wizard. The Farthest Shore* makes clearer the nature of this shadow: Cob is a gebbeth, a shell filled with the darkness of the void. Dwelling neither in the world of life nor the realm of death, he is, as Ged says, "without name, without form," without being.

> "Where do they come to you, Cob? Where is it that you are?"
> "Between the worlds."
> "But that is neither life nor death. What is life, Cob?"
> "Power."
> "What is love?"
> "Power," the blind man repeated heavily, hunching up his shoulders.
> "What is light?"
> "Darkness!"
> "What is your name?"
> "I have none." (*FS,* "Dry Land")

This passage requires that we recall the first novel of the trilogy, which establishes the realm of the dead as the realm of being. When Ged calls Elfarran out of this realm of darkness and being, he also calls his shadow, the negation of his own being. The ground of being is also the ground of unbeing; both being and unbeing can come into the world, into the realm of light and existence.[7] In the world, unbeing destroys being but not existence; one does not die, one becomes a "gebbeth." Cob's confusion of light and darkness is the confusion of existence and being, and it reflects his attempt to find in his physical, mortal existence a permanence that belongs only to being. Cob refuses to do what Ged accomplishes at the end of *Wizard:* to overcome unbeing by accepting it. Consequently, he has only a hideous, mangled existence and no being. Blind, Cob can "see" no way out of his predicament except the blind pursuit of more power.

Cob's obsession with power is much the same as the young Ged's when he arrived at the school on Roke, convinced that a wizard could do as he pleased, balancing the world according to his will. Ged's desire to display his power and humble Jasper brings the release of the shadow, and with it, the danger to himself and the world. The lesson of power misused, visible in the scars on his face, are never lost on Ged. When he and Arren set out to find what has upset the Balance, Ged explains to Arren how the Balance is destroyed by "an unmeasured desire for life": "when we crave power over life—endless wealth, unassailable safety, immortality—then desire becomes greed. And if knowledge allies itself to that greed, then comes evil. Then the balance of the world is swayed, and ruin weighs heavy in the scale'' (*FS,* ''Hort Town''). Evil comes with knowledge, with consciousness, and the birth of consciousness brings the knowledge of good and evil and the power to do each. Evil is the alliance of conscious knowledge with the greed for life inherent in the unconscious.

Good is not the opposition of the two, however. Arha represents a situation in which consciousness and unconsciousness are allied under the dominance of the unconscious and its desire for life, a desire given conscious expression in the belief in reincarnation. According to this belief, one's human being is neither new nor unique but merely an extension of past lives. Cob has opposed his conscious being, which he accepts as something unique, against the unconscious, collective life force of nature. In using the Pelnish lore, he seeks to sustain his conscious human being by opposing the return of his physical existence to the life cycle in nature. To accomplish his end, he is willing to exhaust physical nature in the process by opening the door that drains the world of light and water. But in doing so, he destroys the very thing he is trying to keep. His choice has destroyed his human being, and he has become an inhuman gebbeth, with no name, no human being, and no real power. To release him into the world of the dead, Ged must give him back his name.

Cob is an intriguing parallel to the mad scientist with the power to destroy the world, a representation of our present power to destroy the world with our technology.[8] The only force capable of halting this selfish, scientistic madness is the power of a fully developed humanity which man sees as a sufficient end in itself and values because it must eventually, but certainly, be lost in death. When he understands this, man will value his humanity too highly to surrender before death by making bad choices. Because he loves only himself, Cob tells Ged that love is power. To him, love is merely the power to prolong his own existence. Cob is afraid to lose his life and therefore values it and loves it. But we do not lose our own being in death because our being is unique and indestructible. Cob does not err in loving what he must lose; he errs in not seeing that ''the springs of being'' are ''deeper than life,'' thus in not seeing what he should love most. This lesson Arren learns from Ged when, impatient with the long trek across Selidor, he calls it a land of death:

> "Do not say that," the mage said sharply. . . . "This is your kingdom, the kingdom of life. This is your immortality. Look at the hills, the mortal hills. They do not endure forever. The hills with the living grass on them, and the streams of water running. . . . In all the world, . . . there is no other like each of those streams, rising cold out of the earth where no eye sees it, running through the sunlight and the darkness to the sea. Deep are the springs of being, deeper than life, than death. . . ."
>
> He stopped, but in his eyes as he looked at Arren and at the sunlit hills there was a great, wordless, grieving love. And Arren saw that, and in seeing it saw him, saw him for the first time whole, as he was. (*FS,* "Selidor")

The last sentence of this quotation echoes the description of Genly Ai's first really seeing Estraven as a man and woman, during their journey on the Gobrin Ice. In his discovery of Ged, Arren discovers the wonder of the world in which he lives, as well as the source of value and meaning:

> "I have given my love to what is worthy of love. Is that not the kingdom and the unperishing spring?"
>
> "Aye, lad," said Ged, gently and with pain.
>
> They went on together in silence. But Arren saw the world now with his companion's eyes and saw the living splendor that was revealed about them. . . . (*FS,* "Selidor")

At this point Arren comes to understand Ged's view of life, although perhaps without quite understanding Ged's pain. In crossing the land of the dead with the Archmage, however, he conquers the fear of losing life, and, in the Mountains of Pain, the pain of losing what he loves. In discovering that he must lose what he loves, he achieves the capacity to rule life. He becomes the king.

Having journeyed to the end of the earth and having exhausted their strength, Ged and Arren return to Roke on the dragon, Kalessin. Man can be carried by the spirit beyond the point where human strength fails. Ged's return to the isle of Gont completes the pattern in the trilogy, which presents the hero as an archetypal representative of man's psychological journey from the birth of consciousness to the complete integration of the Self at the end of the process of individuation. In *Wizard,* Ged exhibits the typically inflated ego of the newly arrived hero who must learn humility through the discovery of the Shadow—the negative, mortal fallibility which he at first denies. The discovery of the Shadow reveals the incompleteness of the hero and motivates his quest for the Anima, the lost feminine side of the Self. In *The Tombs of Atuan,* Ged descends into the labyrinth at Atuan for the integration with his anima. The "wedding with the Anima" takes place innocent of the sexuality common to such myths. Instead, it occurs symbolically in the joining of the two halves of the Ring of Erreth-Akbe. In *The Farthest Shore,* Arren, as the Child Ged follows, is a manifestation of the emerging Self, an emergence which is completed when Arren becomes king and replaces Ged as the central figure in Earthsea. As Jung points out, the ego yields place to the Self, a transition which occurs without conflict, just as Ged kneels voluntarily to Arren in fealty. The Self becomes the center of the personality that recognizes and balances all aspects of the conscious and the unconscious psyche. This balance point provides for the *conjunctio oppositorum* which reconciles the dialectic in the trilogy. Thus the dialectical structure and the Jungian structure come together at the end of the trilogy. As the king who will restore social order in Earthsea, Arren is both the culmination and the continuation of Ged's function as culture-bearer, thus integrating the social structure with the other two structures in the trilogy.

Central to the trilogy is the successful development of the individual, which is always prior to, the necessary precondition of, the improvement of society. In the Earthsea trilogy Le Guin has created a mythology which shows that heroic action is not only possible but a psychological necessity in our world, as it has been and always will be in all human worlds. The problems of freedom and being are coterminous with man.

In the preceding sections we have discussed three thematic structures in Le Guin's trilogy and explored some of her philosophical perspectives. This discussion has revealed the motifs and minor themes of the hero-savior, heroic restraint, being versus doing, consciousness versus unconsciousness, light and darkness, time and change, choice and responsibility, pain and love, and the primacy of the individual. These fictional elements of the Earthsea trilogy also appear in the Hainish cycle and *The Lathe of Heaven* with similar significance, and this similarity reveals the essential continuity of the trilogy and Le Guin's science fiction.

The integration of society, as Le Guin presents it in the trilogy, continues a thematic interest prominent in the Hainish cycle as a whole. As of 1977, the cycle has taken the shape of a galactic comedy, moving from humankind's dispersal and general ignorance of one another, through the conflict with the enemy (the Shing), to a fairly widespread integration in the Ekumen. This history encompasses the fictional time extending from *The Dispossessed* through *Planet of Exile* to *The Left Hand of Darkness*.[9] Within the cycle these three novels focus on the integration of human groups, an integration in which a larger and better society is made possible by a hero who has formed a bond with a significant Other, what Martin Buber calls an "I-Thou" relationship.[10]

It is not as clear that there has been effective integration at the end of *The Dispossessed* and *Planet,* nor is it obvious that a celibate like Ged forms the kind of relationships we see with Shevek and Jakob Agat. The cycle, however, does affirm the ultimate success of Shevek and Agat. The ansible is standard equipment by League Year 18, and references to Cetians seem to include both worlds of Tau II; and the descendants of the Exiles and the natives of Werel prosper enough to send a NAFL ship back to Terra. Even though Ged doesn't marry or enter into a sexual partnership, he does form important bonds in key places in the trilogy.

Thus in *Wizard* Ged returns to Ogion, his first master (a relationship he acknowledges all his life) and the first person for whom he feels love. From Ogion he receives the crucial advice that he must "turn clear round, and seek the very source, and that which lies before the source" if he is to cope with his shadow (*WE,* VII). In the final pursuit of his shadow Ged receives help from his friend, Vetch, who, earlier at the school on Roke, entrusts his true name to Ged and through this gift of trust restores Ged's faith in himself. In *Tombs*, Ged and Tenar must trust each other if they are to escape the Old Powers and return to the Archipelago with the Ring of Erreth-Akbe; and in *The Farthest Shore* it is Arren who must lead Ged to Cob and bring him back from the Dry Land over the Mountains of Pain.

Earthsea, then, may seem a much smaller world than that of the galaxy of the Hainish cycle, and unification under a king is indeed far from the modern anarchism of Anarres or the Ekumen. But the rules of comic romance still hold in Earthsea, and the existentialist perspective of the trilogy is, oddly enough, compatible with the Tao of Man and the principles of human solidarity which we see in the Hainish novels. What varies are the details of the heroes' quests, the nature of the cultures in which they act and suffer, and the cost of their success.

The theme of individual integration is clearest in Le Guin's two most emphatically Taoist novels, *The Lathe of Heaven* and *City of Illusions,* although it also appears in works as different as the ambiguously utopian *The Dispossessed* and the savagely satiric *The Word for World.* In *City* and *Lathe* important scenes present moments of individual integration which parallel those moments in the trilogy when Ged achieves a new stage in his process of individuation. Just as Ged's merger with his shadow at the end of *Wizard* unites the contraries of good and evil, light and darkness, being and nonbeing inherent within him, Falk-Ramarren in *City* undergoes a similar joining of opposite sides of the self. Falk—childlike, naive, given to moments of mystical experience of primal oneness in which he becomes "the word spoken in darkness with none to hear at the beginning" (*CI,* VIII)—merges with the aggressive, rationalistic Ramarren, whose instinct for control is always uppermost. These two become Falk-Ramarren, the whole man who will become a hero-savior when he warns the Exiles of Werel of the Shings' conquest of Terra. In *Lathe,* George Orr undergoes an experience in which he, like Ged, turns around to seek the "very source, and that which lies before the source," an experience recalling both Falk's moment of primal unity as he reads the first page of the Old Canon (the *Tao Te Ching*) and Ged's occasional moments of stillness that mark the intimations of his unity with nature.

Ged achieves true unity, however, only with maturity; he begins the trilogy dedicated to the pursuit of power. During the scene of his first interview with the Archmage Nemmerle, "it *seemed* to him that he himself was a word spoken by the sunlight" (*WE*, III, our emphasis). Ged soon learns that the darkness can also speak and can say a word that can not be unsaid. At the end of *Tombs*, his rescue of his anima complete, he appears to Tenar "as still as the rocks themselves." But this stillness inspires in her a dread which causes her to turn upon Ged to make one last sacrifice to her former masters. Ged does not defend himself. He simply reaches out in trust to touch the ring on Tenar's wrist, the symbol of their union. Ged's integration with the shadow and with his anima produce in him the stillness of the Taoist sage; but in the predominantly existentialist world of the trilogy, sage-like stillness is not enough to inspire love and trust or even to sustain integration. One must also reach out to the Other.

Orr, on the other hand, is ordinarily a whole man, the "uncarved block" of the Taoist philosophers. For four years he has been without his balance; but with the aid of his friends, primarily a helpful Alien, he can "set his teeth," face "Chaos and Old Night," and return to "the middle of things." For him this feeling of harmony "did not come ... as blissful or mystical, but simply as normal." Orr goes "back where he belonged," where he can effectively defy the arch-manipulator Haber and go on to save his world (*LH*, IX and XI).

In *Lathe*, then, the main dialectic is not internalized but takes place between Haber and Orr, a conflict similar to Ged's battle against Cob in *The Farthest Shore*. As the Wise Old Man of *The Farthest Shore*, Ged has learned that "on every act the balance of the whole depends," and this is precisely the lesson Orr tries to teach Haber when he tells him that "everything dreams. The play of form, of being, is the dreaming of substance. Rocks have their dreams, and the earth changes.... But when the mind becomes conscious, when the rate of evolution speeds up, then you have to be careful....You must learn the way.... A conscious mind must be part of the whole, intentionally and carefully—as the rock is part of the whole unconsciously" (*LH*, X).

Orr tries to get Haber to say the magic words *Er' perrehnne* in order to get help in dealing with effective dreaming, to keep it "where it belongs, going the right way"—following the Tao, or "Rale," as they would say on Werel. Haber, of course does not take Orr's advice or pronounce Alien formulas; nor does he resist the temptation to try effective dreaming himself. His ideas of "reason" and "benevolence" take him as far in his quest for power as Cob's grab for immortality takes him. Haber will no more give up his attempt to reshape the world as he sees fit than Cob will permit Ged to close the door between life and death if he can prevent him. Haber is too imbalanced to practice restraint; appropriately, he ends up in a madhouse. Orr, who had reshaped the world with the power of the unconscious, can be cured—with a "little help from his friends." But Haber, who would reshape the world in the pride of his rational intellect, is as empty as Cob and beyond help.

While Orr and Haber are the most striking pair of contrasted characters in Le Guin's science fiction, they aren't unique. In *Word for World*, Selver and Davidson present a similar contrast; but here the contrast is muted by Selver's doing what he must and becoming the god who brings murder into his culture. The contrast is also muted by the presence of Captain Raj Lyubov, the *tertium quid*, the "inevitable third" moderate liberal who refuses to truly commit himself.

Still, the major portion of Le Guin's science fiction parallels the dialectical pattern she uses in the trilogy to contrast psychological and philosophical extremes with the wholeness that results from the balance of extremes. This pattern, along with the themes and motifs used in developing it, reveals the overall consistency of her work.[11] Whether she draws on Taoist or existentialist philosophy for a conceptual framework, engages in a critique of Sartrean rationalism, or espouses the principles of communist anarchism, her vision is the same: the unification of man with man, man with himself, and man with nature as developed in the Earthsea trilogy.[12] The contrary extremes vary from work to work, but the movement of the work always tends toward unification of the whole, with the integration of the individual as the effective cause for the greater integration of the social and natural dimensions of Le Guin's various worlds.

Le Guin accepts Sartre's idea of the absence or practical irrelevance of God and the concept that human beings are condemned to make choices. She can tell us that after being freed from her service to the Nameless Ones, Tenar "wept in pain, because she was free" (*TA*, " Voyage"). Le Guin generally accepts the Sartrean idea of the always-alien-Other and shows, with characters such as Davidson in *Word for World* and Pilotson and Ukwet in *Planet*, that people who attempt to avoid radical isolation through the dangerous expedient of dividing the world into "us" and "others" only intensify their estrangement. But in Le Guin's view, Satre's existentialism offers only a "rootless freedom." It denies the possibility of any experience of an I-Thou relationship with some Other; it denies the existence of the unconscious and acknowledges no human connection with nature.[13]

Le Guin achieves a more comprehensive and humane philosophy by balancing the analytic rationalism of Sartre's existentialism with Taoist concepts of harmonious acceptance of a unified world, supplementing these Eastern ideas with the humane and integrative concepts of Buber's I-Thou relationship and with some of Martin Heidegger's ideas on speech and being.[14] To these philosophical structures she adds insights into human psychology which show remarkable resemblance to the depth psychology of C. G. Jung. It is as if Le Guin said to Sartre: "OK, there is no God to allow or to forbid; we're all free, and 'human life begins on the far side of despair,' as you and I and Orestes have said. There's still more to reality than that. Now we must build a culture that will help people live." In the Earthsea trilogy Le Guin does some of her clearest and most impressive building.

Early in the trilogy there is the Word—not the Word-which-is-God or even with-God, but the Word that arises out of silence and will eventually fall back into silence. The universe has gone from nonbeing into being, and from being, all things and powers come. The principle that sustains being is the Equilibrium, the Balance, the basic forces which the Chinese call *Yin-Yang* (Female-Male, Dark-Light, and so on).[15] The universe, then, is whole and in balance. Its foundations are solid, even though any one world exists perilously over the void. It is an organism in which human beings must take part, since we are here: this is our fate. It is an organism to which we may consciously adapt and find our destiny: this is our free will.

From time to time we may experience a sense of wholeness by momentarily touching "the balance-pole, the center" (*CI*, IX) and become truly ourselves, parts of the world. From time to time our own beings may be sufficiently in touch with the center that we can experience the being of another, the moment of the I-Thou relationship when we see another whole as they really are. During these moments we cease to do and "let be." They are usually just moments, however, visions or dreams, or brief times of stillness. Subjectively everlasting, they are still of short duration in the context of the world's time. Soon such moments slip into merely "Yinish" rest and we go from inactivity into activity. Even for the most accomplished of us there is no sure safety, no final rest short of death, no certainty other than our knowledge that we shall die—our knowledge that the dance of life is always danced over the abyss.

From such a view of reality comes an epistemology, an ethics, and a political philosophy. As with the Taoists, the epistemology is relativistic. It is tolerant of differing views, but not so openminded, as the saying goes, that the wind blows through. "Harmony exists, but there is no understanding it..." (*CI*, X). There is truth, but it's hard to say how truth looks to an alien creature. All men are alien to each other, at least at times. Ged notes that it is difficult to get "truth" from a dragon even if the dragon very much wants to tell one the truth. Thus he declines to judge dragons although he will resist them if he must. In addition, Le Guin gives us the most obvious aspect of her "dialectical patterns," presenting the trilogy and the majority of her other novels from different points of view. Ged's story is one story through the eyes of three different characters and with alternative endings, because "truth is a matter of the imagination."[16] It is up to the reader to provide whatever synthesis is possible in Le Guin's dialectics.

As we have noted, Le Guin's ethic is a modest one for a heroic world. It is often heroic restraint, or what the Taoist philosophers called *wu-wei*, which Le Guin translates as "Unaction" (*CI*, II; compare *nusuth* in *Left Hand*). Such a notion follows from the idea of the universe as a complex organism; it could easily be misunderstood as such "fortune-cookie ideas" as "don't meddle," don't act at all, just remain quiet somewhere off by yourself. *Wu-wei*, however, can contain the ideas of avoiding aggressive action and competition, avoiding action contrary to nature, avoiding action that "is not natural or spontaneous." *Wu-wei* does not require one to become a hermit. On the contrary, it may require the true sage to work always with and among people, taking care to avoid ambition, to avoid treating people as things. Finally, *wu-wei* can involve not only the "wordless teaching" of the sage but also self-defense and the heroic action that can save the world. Indeed, *wu-wei* can require such action.[17] For Le Guin, Unaction is all of these things, but it is primarily what Ged tells Arren: "do only that which you must do," recognizing that *must* includes actions required by the pity and love that are as natural to people as our ambition and will to power. Having fulfilled one's function, one might retire from the world of action, as Ged does at the end of the trilogy. But so long as Ged has his magic he has the responsibility to use it, to act.

With this definition it becomes clear how Le Guin's exponents of "Taoist' Unaction get around to doing at least one thing and usually manage to be quite active, indeed. Orr's one act saves his world; Selver violently resists the Terran imperialists; Falk-Ramarren brings his crucial news to Werel; Faxe enters politics; and Estraven goes from politics to a very physical kind of heroism. Even Ogion has stilled an earthquake in his time. Aside from Ogion there are only three important characters in Le Guin's major works that we might see as contemplatives, withdrawn from the world of action. Of these, however, two are empaths—the Thurro-dowist who advises Falk in *City*, and Osden at the conclusion of "Vaster than Empires and More Slow." For them contact with even small groups of people can be peculiarly painful. The third is the Ancient One of *Rocannon's World*. The Ancient One is a whole man and an archetypal Old Man, but he is also a Master of Initiation, with the decidedly nasty habit of demanding for his services the forfeit of "*That which you hold dearest and would least willingly give*" (*RW*, VIII), a standard motif which dramatizes the pain and sacrifice of giving up the old self in search of the new, but hardly the sort of thing to make us think well of hermits.

For the Taoist philosophers the political implications of *wu-wei* were condemnation of aggressive warfare and espousal of anarchism, either the primitive anarchism of primeval times or a "modern" anarchism under a ruler who let his people alone. So far in her work, Le Guin has refused to show us noble savages happily sporting in a Garden world of anarchy, peace, innocence, and collective solidarity. She knows full well that as often as not, savages follow "a tortuous and cramped Way" (*CI*, IV) that can be violent and bloody. The world of Earthsea is closer to the China of the Warring States period or to early medieval Europe than it is to any golden age. Her political common sense, her tact as a storyteller, and her concern with the symbolism of individuation bring her trilogy to an end with the coronation of King Arren. Of Arren's reign we learn nothing, although we can assume that he and his people lived more or less happily ever after (perhaps Le Guin's one concession in the trilogy to the conventions of the folktale and children's literature).

When Le Guin depicts anarchism, it is of a distinctly modern kind, with no quotation marks around *modern*. This, of course, appears in *The Dispossessed*. But we do get in the trilogy the individualistic premise of all anarchism and at least one motif we can recognize as a key theme of recent and contemporary anarchists, "the unity of means and ends."[18] In the human world of time and change, all is process. We cannot be certain that our ends will justify our means; this side of the "Word of Unmaking" there is no end. Our only responsible choice is the choice of appropriate means. So, even exhausted and bewildered, Ged resists the temptation of Serret and the Terrenon stone with the formula, "ill means, ill end" (*WE*, VII). The Ekumen, too, with its anarchistic philosophy, adopts the unity of ends and means as official doctrine.

Regardless of the conceptual framework Le Guin uses, however, she returns again and again to the primacy of the individual, an emphasis which holds together the disparate strains of existentialism, Taoism, and anarchism and which holds together her work, from *Rocannon's World* to *The Dispossessed*.

Existentialism, in all its varieties, stresses the conscious individual, one who acknowledges and accepts the glory and pain of our freedom. If Le Guin criticizes existentialism's Sartrean extremes and reminds us of our relationship with others and with nature, she is still in the mainstream of that movement, within the tradition of Heidegger and Buber. Taoism and its philosophical offshoots, with their teaching of "the wholeness of the universe" of which every human is only a part, seems a long way from individualism. But Welch, for instance, stresses Lao Tzu as a strong individualist, and Wilhelm reminds us that Chinese thought held that the creative force in nature could be made effective by both "the way of the sage" and "the way of the hero"—two standard emblems for the fully developed individual. It is such individuals that communist anarchism sees as both the way to the revolution and the justification for the revolution. In a passage of great beauty, Alexander Berkman denies that anarchy would produce a faceless, undifferentiated mass and condemns the "spirit of authority, law . . . tradition and custom" precisely because they "force us into a common groove and make a man a will-less automaton without independence or individuality."[19]

In *Rocannon's World,* Le Guin's first published novel, the hero insists that "there will be no tabus broken or wars fought on my account. There is no point to it. In times like this, Mogien, one man's fate is not important." Mogien replies, "If it is not. . . what is?" (*RW,* II, IX). The same idea is part of the doctrine of the Ekumen in *The Left Hand of Darkness,* and is stressed by Estraven's kemmering in "his" fierce denial that there could be any moral mission that "overrides all personal debts and loyalties" (*LHD,* VIII).

In *The Dispossessed,* Le Guin's most recent novel at this writing, we still have the emphasis on the individual. It is the individual who feels pain and who dies his own death beyond even human touch. It is this pain, in fact, the pain of life and death and loss, that requires collective solidarity: "We are brothers in what we share. In pain, which each of us must suffer alone. . ." (*TD,* IX). Le Guin may have changed her emphasis, as David L. Porter has argued, from existentialism to Taoism and then to anarchism, but her basic view of man's relationship to the world remains the same.

NOTES

CHAPTER 1: MARGARET P. ESMONDE

1. Robert Scholes, *Structural Fabulation: An Essay on Fiction of the* Univ. of Notre Dame Ward-Phillips Lectures in English Language and Literature, vol. 7 (Notre Dame, Ind.: Univ. of Notre Dame Press, 1975), p. 80.
2. No. 7, vol. 2, part 3 (Nov. 1975).
3. Ursula K. Le Guin, "This Fear of Dragons," in *The Thorny Paradise: Writers on Writing for Children,* ed. Edward Blishen (UK: Kestrel Books, 1975), p. 89.
4. George Slusser, *The Farthest Shores of Ursula K. Le Guin* (San Bernardino, Cal.: Borgo Press, 1976), p. 31.
5. C. G. Jung, *Aion: Researches into the Phenomenology of the Self,* trans. R.F.C. Hull, 2nd ed. rev., Bollingen Series XX, *The Collected Works of C. G. Jung,* vol. 9, part 2 (Princeton, N.J.: Princeton Univ. Press, 1968), pp.3-10.
6. Ursula K. Le Guin, "The Child and the Shadow," *Quarterly Journal of the Library of Congress,* 32 (April 1975), p. 143.
7. Ibid.
8. Ibid., p. 144.
9. Ibid., pp. 143-44.
10. Jung, *The Archetypes and the Collective Unconscious,* trans. R.F.C. Hull, 2nd ed. rev., Bollingen Series XX, *The Collected Works of C. G. Jung,* vol. 9, part 1 (Princeton, N.J.: Princeton Univ. Press, 1968), pp. 207-54.
11. Ursula K. Le Guin, *Dreams Must Explain Themselves* (New York: Algol Press, 1975), p. 13.
12. Bruno Bettelheim, *The Uses of Enchantment: The Meaning and Importance of Fairy Tales* (New York: Knopf, 1976), pp. 212-13.
13. Le Guin, *Dreams,* p. 13.

CHAPTER 2: PETER BRIGG

1. Donald F. Theall, "The Art of Social-Science Fiction: The Ambiguous Utopian Dialectics of Ursula K. Le Guin," *Science Fiction Studies,* 2 (Nov. 1975), p. 256.
2. Ursula K. Le Guin, "American SF and the Other," *Science Fiction Studies,* 2 (Nov. 1975), pp. 208-209.

CHAPTER 3: PETER S. ALTERMAN

1. Ian Watson, "The Forest as Metaphor for Mind: 'The Word for World

is Forest' and 'Vaster Than Empires and More Slow,' " *Science-Fiction Studies,* 7 (Nov. 1975), pp. 231-37.

2. Wordsworth, "Lines Composed a Few Miles Above Tintern Abbey," *Wordsworth: Poetical Works,* ed. de Selincourt (London: Oxford Univ. Press, 1966), p. 108, lines 10-11, 15-16.
3. Paul de Man, "Intentional Structure of the Romantic Image," *Romanticism and Consciousness,* ed. Bloom (New York: W. W. Norton & Co., 1970), p. 70.
4. Samuel Taylor Coleridge, "Frost at Midnight," in *Coleridge; Selected Poetry and Prose,* ed. Schneider (New York: Holt, Rinehart and Winston, 1966), p. 94, lines 11-16.
5. Coleridge, "The Eolian Harp," p. 14, lines 26-27, 44-48.
6. Coleridge, "The Eolian Harp," p. 15, line 60.
7. Peter S. Alterman, "The Surreal Translations of Samuel R. Delany," *Science Fiction Studies,* 11 (March 1977), pp. 25-34.
8. Samuel R. Delany, *Triton* (New York: Bantam Books, 1976), p. 337.
9. William Blake, "London," *The Poetry and Prose of William Blake,"* ed. Erdman (Garden City, N.Y.: Doubleday & Co., 1968), p. 26, lines 11-12.
10. Wordsworth, *Prelude,* p. 499, I, 377-84.
11. See especially Kant's *Critique of Pure Reason* and *Prolegomena to Any Future Metaphysics.*
12. Watson, *"The Forest as Metaphor for Mind,"* p. 235.
13. Blake, *The Marriage of Heaven and Hell,* p. 36.
14. Ibid., p. 44.

CHAPTER 4: PHILIP E. SMITH II

1. See also Le Guin's statement in "Science Fiction and Mrs. Brown," *Science Fiction at Large,* ed. Peter Nicholls (London: Gollancz, 1976), p. 25: "What did I know about Utopia? Scraps of More, fragments of Wells, Hudson, Morris. Nothing. It took me years of reading and pondering and muddling, and much assistance from Engels, Marx, Godwin, Goldman, Goodman, and above all Shelley and Kropotkin...."
2. See, for example, Douglas Barbour, *"The Lathe of Heaven:* Taoist Dream," *Algol,* #21 (November 1973), pp. 22-24.
3. For an account of Kropotkin's influence on Emma Goldman's work, see Richard Drinnon, *Rebel in Paradise, A Biography of Emma Goldman,* (Chicago: Univ. of Chicago Press, 1961), pp. 36-38. Goldman's anarchist writings appear in her *Anarchism and Other Essays* (New York: Mother Earth Publishing Association, 1910) and in *Red Emma Speaks: Selected Writings and Speeches,* ed. Alix Kates Shulman (New York: Random House, 1972). See also her memoirs, *Living My Life* (New York: Knopf, 1931).
4. See, for example, Paul Goodman, *Art and Social Nature* (New York: Vinco, 1946); *Communitas,* Percival Goodman, co-author (New York:

Vintage, 1960); *Utopian Essays and Practical Proposals* (New York: Random House, 1962).

5. Ursula K. Le Guin, quoted in Jonathan Ward, "Interview with Ursula K. Le Guin," *Dreams Must Explain Themselves,* by Ursula K. Le Guin (New York: Algol Press, 1975), p. 36.
6. Ursula K. Le Guin, quoted in Charles Bigelow and J. McMahon, "Science Fiction and the Future of Anarchy: Conversations with Ursula K. Le Guin," *Oregon Times,* December 1964, p. 29.
7. For more information about Kropotkin's life, see George Woodcock and Ivan Avakumović, *The Anarchist Prince* (London: Boardman, 1950; reprinted, New York: Schocken, 1971); Martin A. Miller, *Kropotkin* (Chicago: Univ. of Chicago Press, 1976); and Kropotkin's autobiography, *Memoirs of a Revolutionist* (Boston: Houghton Mifflin, 1899; reprinted, several modern editions, notably New York: Dover, 1971).
8. Peter Kropotkin, *Mutual Aid, A Factor of Evolution* (London: Heinemann, 1902, 1914; reprinted, New York: New York Univ. Press, 1972), p. 17. Further references to *Mutual Aid* are to the 1972 volume edited by Paul Avrich.
9. Huxley's essay was collected and republished as "The Struggle for Existence in Human Society," in *Evolution and Ethics and Other Essays,* vol. IX of the *Collected Essays* (London and New York: several editions; reprinted New York: Greenwood Press, 1968), pp. 195-236.
10. Kropotkin, *Ethics, Origin and Development,* L. S. Friedland and J. R. Piroshnikoff (New York: Dial Press, 1924), pp. 30-31.
11. Kropotkin's opposition to state socialism is a constant theme in his revolutionary essays; for example, see Kropotkin, "The State: Its Historic Role," in *Selected Writings on Anarchism and Revolution,* ed. M.A. Miller (Cambridge: M.I.T. Press, 1970), pp. 210-64, esp. 261-62.
12. Kropotkin, "Anarchism," *Kropotkin's Revolutionary Pamphlets,* ed. Roger N. Baldwin (New York: Vanguard Press, 1927; reprinted New York: Dover Publications, 1970), p. 284.
13. Kropotkin, *Fields, Factories, and Workshops, or Industry Combined with Agriculture and Brain Work with Manual Work,* new revised and enlarged edition (London: Thomas Nelson & Sons, 1912), p. 23.
14. See, in the Le Guin issue of *Science Fiction Studies,* #7 (November 1975), Judah Bierman, "Ambiguity in Utopia: *The Dispossessed,*" pp. 249-55; Donald F. Theall, "The Art of Social-Science Fiction: The Ambiguous Utopian Dialectics of Ursula K. Le Guin," pp. 256-64; and Darko Suvin, "Parables of De-Alienation: Le Guin's Widdershins Dance," pp. 265-74. See also, George Edgar Slusser, *The Farthest Shores of Ursula K. Le Guin* (San Bernardino: Borgo Press, 1976),pp. 46-56.
15. Slusser, *Farthest Shores,* p. 48.
16. Paul Goodman, *Growing Up Absurd* (New York: Vintage, 1960), p. 7.
17. Kropotkin, "La Commune," *Paroles d'un Révolté* (Paris: Flammarion, 1885), p. 118 passim.; English translation quoted in Woodcock

and Avakumović, *The Anarchist Prince,* p. 312.

18. Critics who have also suggested the importance of the idea of walls in *The Dispossessed* include Douglas Barbour, "Wholeness and Balance: an Addendum," *Science Fiction Studies,* #7 (Nov. 1975), p. 249; Donald F. Theall, "The Art of Social-Science Fiction. . . . ," pp. 261-62; George E. Slusser, *The Farthest Shores of Ursula K. Le Guin,* pp. 50-53. Barbour also notes the presence of the "wrapping paper/ornamentation" image system in *The Dispossessed.* I believe that its use as a way of characterizing the conspicuous consumption of A-Io's society may have been suggested to Le Guin by the section on "The Theory of Packages," in Paul and Percival Goodman's *Communitas,* pp. 180-81.
19. Kropotkin, *Fields,* pp. 417, 420.
20. Shevek's dedication to principled action was also an attribute of the man who Le Guin says inspired Shevek's character, Robert Oppenheimer. See Le Guin, "Science Fiction and Mrs. Brown," p. 25, and "Science Fiction and the Future of Anarchy," p. 28.
21. Oscar Wilde, "De Profundis," *The Letters of Oscar Wilde,* ed. Rupert Hart-Davis (New York: Harcourt, Brace & World, 1962), p. 488.
22. Wilde, "The Soul of Man Under Socialism," *Complete Works of Oscar Wilde,* new edition ed. Vyvyan Holland (London: Collins, 1966), p. 1,089. Kropotkin referred to "The Soul of Man Under Socialism" as "that article that O. Wilde wrote on Anarchism—in which there are sentences worth being engraved, like verses from the Koran are engraved in Moslem lands." Quoted in *Robert Ross, Friend of Friends,* ed. Margery Ross (London: Jonathan Cape, 1952), p. 113.

CHAPTER 5: N. B. HAYLES

1. For criticism particularly relevant to the topic of this chapter, see Douglas Barbour, "Wholeness and Balance in the Hainish Novels of Ursula K. Le Guin," *Science Fiction Studies,* 1 (1974), pp. 164-73; Le Guin's comments on the relation of Taoism to her work, *Science Fiction Studies,* 2 (1976), p. 45; Refail Nudelman, "An Approach to the Structure of Le Guin's SF," *Science Fiction Studies,* 2 (1975), pp. 210-20; and Martin Bickman, "Le Guin's *The Left Hand of Darkness:* Form and Content," *Science Fiction Studies,* 4 (March 1977), 42-47.
2. Le Guin, "Is Gender Necessary?" in *Aurora: Beyond Equality,* ed. Vonda N. McIntyre and Susan Janice Anderson (Greenwich, Conn.: Fawcett, 1976), p. 137. This entire essay is of interest, because in it Le Guin discusses her perception of how *Left Hand* came into being, as well as what she believes the book means.
3. See, for example, David Ketterer, *New Worlds for Old: The Apocalyptic Imagination, Science Fiction, and American Literature* (Bloomington: Indiana Univ. Press, 1974), pp. 76-90.
4. A complete version of the following brief account is contained in N. B.

Hayles, "The Ambivalent Ideal: The Concept of Androgyny in English Renaissance Literature," unpub. diss., Univ. of Rochester, 1976. Among the important sources consulted for the study are Marie Delcourt, *Hermaphrodite: Myths and Rites of the Bisexual Figure in Classical Antiquity,* trans. Jennifer Nicholson (London: Studio Books, 1961); L.S.A.M. von Romer, "Uber die Androgynische Idee des Lebens," in *Jahrbuch für Sexuelle Zwisschenstufen,* 2 (Leipzig, 1903), pp. 707-941; Wayne Meeks, "The Image of the Androgyne: Some Uses of the Symbol in Early Christianity," *Journal of the History of Religions,* 13 (1974), pp. 166-208; and the collected works of C. G. Jung (Princeton Univ. Press).

5. C. G. Jung, *Psychology and Alchemy,* vol. 12 of *The Collected Works,* 2nd ed., trans, R.F.C. Hull (Princeton Univ, Press, 1968).
6. Titus Livius, *Livy,* trans. Evan Sage (Cambridge: Harvard Univ. Press, 1935), vol. VII, bk. xxvii, 32, p. 359.
7. Ovid, *Shakespeare's Ovid, Being Arthur Golding's Translation of the Metamorphosis,* ed. W.H.D. Rouse (London: Centaur Press, 1961), bk. IV. The ambivalence aroused by Ovid's tale is made unmistakable in an early English translation by Thomas Peend, *The Pleasant Fable of Hermaphroditus and Salmacis* (London, 1565).
8. Barbour, passim.
9. Le Guin, *The Left Hand of Darkness* (New York: Ace Books, 1969), Chapter 5. The roman numerals in parenthesis after quotations indicate chapter numbers.
10. Le Guin, "Is Gender Necessary?" p. 132.
11. In my discussion of this aspect of *Left Hand* I am indebted to Bickman's fine article, p. 42.

CHAPTER 6: J. P. BRENNAN and M. C. DOWNS

1. *The Essential Kropotkin,* ed. Emile Capouya and Keitha Tompkins (New York: Liveright, 1975), p. 111.
2. Karl R. Popper, *The Open Society and Its Enemies,* 4th ed. (Princeton: Princeton Univ. Press, 1963), I, pp. 35-201 passim.
3. Herbert Read, *Anarchy and Order* (Boston: Beacon Press, 1971), pp. 20-23.
4. See the introductory comments to the reprint of "The Day Before the Revolution," in *The Wind's Twelve Quarters* (New York: Harper and Row, 1975), p. 232.
5. Mythological conditioning is a part of the socialization process in all societies, as any parent knows who has suffered through Saturday morning television. What should unsettle us here, though, is the violated expectation that an anarchist society should be doing without this relic of more primitive social organizations.
6. This (pre-Socratic) Zeno should not be confused with Zeno of Cyprus, the founder of Stoicism, cited above in connection with Kropotkin.

7. Because Anarres is legally quarantined by the Urrasti Council of World Governments—as well as a colony thereof, in fact if not in law—there are no diplomatic missions from the other Known Worlds on Anarres, the various embassies on Rodarred (seat of the CWG) serving as missions to the Tau Ceti system, which includes the inhabited planet of Urras and its inhabited satellite, Anarres. As it turns out, in the Terran embassy (as might be expected) is a radio receiver which constantly monitors transmissions from Anarres.
8. The term *metropolis* is chosen advisedly, not in its current meaning of the central or largest municipality within a conurbation, but rather in the etymological sense of *mother city.* Abbenay is not a *capital* in a society which has no government, but it is the largest population center, the location of the Spaceport, the Divlab computer, the PDC, and the memorial statue of Odo. Like a metropolitan see within the church, it may be only *primus inter pares,* but there is a constant danger, because of its primacy, that it will become a power center.
9. After an extended discussion of how *Gulliver's Travels* reveals Swift to be a political, religious and intellectual reactionary, George Orwell once proceeded to show how the satirist had his progressive moments. After commenting that Swift was "a kind of anarchist," Orwell points to an incident which shows that in the society of the Houyhnhnms, exhortation and public pressure take the place of legal compulsion. "This illustrates very well the totalitarian tendency which is explicit in the anarchist or pacifist vision of society. In a Society in which there is no law, and in theory no compulsion, the only arbiter of behavior is public opinion. But public opinion. . . is less tolerant than any system of law. When human beings are governed by 'thou shalt not,' the individual can practice a certain amount of eccentricity: when they are supposedly governed by 'love' or 'reason', he is under continuous pressure to make himself behave and think in exactly the same way as everyone else." See "Politics vs. Literature: An Examination of 'Gulliver's Travels,'" in *Shooting an Elephant and Other Essays* (New York: Harcourt, Brace and World, 1950), pp. 65-66. Shevek's experience seems to bear out Orwell's observation, at least in part.
10. It is a moot point whether anarchism is, in fact, a special case of functionalism within political theory. The mutual-aid associations cited by Kropotkin are all teleological; they succeed because they have been created in response to a goal perceived to be of some importance and not attainable by the individual alone: members of mutual-aid societies do not necessarily have identical backgrounds, but they must have a common purpose. See Peter Kropotkin, *Mutual Aid: A Factor of Evolution,* ed. Paul Avrich (New York Univ. Press, 1972), pp. 194-245.

    In any case, it should be noted that while Shevek's collegial relationships with other physicists leave something to be desired, those with his two early teachers remind us more of the promise of anarchism. Mitis is a close friend and advisor who gives him shrewd advice; Gvarab is much like Shevek in that she sees "a much larger universe than most people were capable of seeing" (*TD,* IV); she even seems to take a sort of maternal interest in him. Is it significant that these two physicists, who are true anarchists in that they set the intellectual discipline far above personal status or power, are both women? If it is, another side of the coin is represented by Rulag, who sets "the work" above basic human relationships and ends up, apparently out of injured vanity, charging the Syndicate of Initiative with what amounts to anarchist treason.

11. As Shevek puts it at the end of a rambling, adolescent discussion on the meaning of life and suffering: "I'm trying to say what I think brotherhood really is. It begins—it begins in shared pain" (*TD,* II). There is some historical evidence for the proposition that shared suffering can serve as a basis for solidarity and that solidarity may be destroyed by the onset of a prosperity which reduces the need for mutual aid. The history of modern Israel in relation to the Holocaust and the Arab threat is a case in point, although ideological divisions seem to overwhelm solidarity even in that small country.
12. We know from *The Left Hand of Darkness* that the ansible was later developed and did lead to the creation of the Ekumen; we know further that it did not magically solve all the problems of human communications.
13. See note 4. We remark with interest a recent display advertisement for *Liberation* which includes a 1977 testimonial from Le Guin. *Working Papers for a New Society,* 5: 2 (Summer 1977), p. 65.
14. A short account of this analysis may be consulted in Northrop Frye, *The Secular Scripture* (Harvard Univ. Press, 1976), pp. 97-98. A somewhat more detailed account can be found in the same author's *Fables of Identity: Studies in Poetic Mythology* (New York: Harcourt, Brace and World, 1963), pp. 58-66.
15. Realistic fiction has as its project (in Sartre's sense) the use of only one level, that of ordinary experience, though there is some doubt whether such a project ever had any chance of succeeding.
16. A good, recent example of the "popular technology" kind of science-fiction utopia is Al Martinez, "California 2001," first published in the Los Angeles *Times* and reprinted in *Technique: Studies in Composition,* ed. E. K. Martin and C. J. Howard (San Francisco: Canfield Press, 1977), pp. 173-80.
17. All these types may also be used for antiutopian satire, as the "sleeper" narrative was used by Woody Allen in the film of that title.
18. B. F. Skinner, *Walden Two* (New York: Macmillan Paperbacks, 1962), pp. 291-92.
19. Thomas More, *Utopia,* trans. John Dolan, in *The Essential Thomas More,* ed. J. Greene and John P. Dolan (New York: NAL Mentor, 1967), p. 53.
20. William Morris, *News from Nowhere,* ed. James Redmond (London and Boston: Routledge and Kegan Paul, 1967) p. 113.

21. Plato, *Republic,* V, 454a-457c.
22. This is a nicely ironic foreshadowing of the later stage in Shevek's life when, having come up against the wall of bureaucracy and public opinion, he learns that Tirin has suffered Public Reprimand for anti-Odonianism. Tirin has ended up in semivoluntary confinement in the Asylum on Segvina Island, a therapy which, when Shevek meets him later while on emergency posting during the drought, has led to the destruction of his personality.
23. This well illustrates the TINSTAAFL cliché ("There Is No Such Thing As A Free Lunch") beloved of certain science-fiction writers and operative in Ioti society: Chifoilisk, the Thuvian physicist, rightly warns Shevek that the government of A-Io intends to be repaid for its hospitality with Shevek's theory, and asks him to consider giving it to the "socialist" nation of Thu. An important irony, which has much to do with the novel's anarchist theme, is that Shevek ends up releasing the theory to those who have no prior claim on his loyalty—except common humanity.
24. For an interesting account of the genesis and effects of the public-private dichotomy in our own culture, see Richard Sennett, *The Fall of Public Man* (New York: Knopf, 1977), esp. chaps. 1 and 5; and Hannah Arendt, *The Human Condition* (Chicago: Univ. of Chicago Press, 1958), chaps. 1-2.
25. See the comments on games in *Utopia II*, trans. Dolan, p. 58.
26. *News from Nowhere,* ed. Redmond, p. 58.
27. Ibid., p. 149.
28. Cf. Jacques Ellul, *The Technological Society,* trans. John Wilkinson (New York: Vintage Books, 1964), pp. 79-84.
29. This view is challenged by R. S. Brumbaugh, "Plato and the History of Science," *Studium Generale,* 9 (1961), pp. 520-27.
30. This is a fair characterization of the period between the introduction of carbonized iron (sometime during the "dark age" before the Archaic period) and the great upsurge of interest in mechanical contrivances associated with Archimedes and the Museum at Alexandria in the third century B.C. The welter of modern arguments over the status of the trireme is probably a more interesting phenomenon than any technological development during that period. See Henry Hodges, *Technology in the Ancient World* (New York: Knopf, 1970), pp. 168-220; and Jean Deshayes, "Greek Technology," *A History of Technology and Invention,* ed. Maurice Daumus and trans. Eileen B. Hennessy (New York: Crown, 1969), I, pp. 181-215.
31. *Republic* II, 380 d-e.
32. *Utopia*, trans. Dolan, pp. 56, 74-76.
33. The term is borrowed from E. F. Schumacher's collection of essays, *Small Is Beautiful: Economics as if People Mattered* (New York: Harper and Row, 1973), p. 178.
34. *News from Nowhere,* pp. 80-83.
35. Chapters 2-11 of *Walden Two* deal with external cultural engineering

while 12-34 are largely an exposition of the behavioral engineering possible through positive reinforcement. The other chapters constitute the narrative framework.

36. This may be verified by examining closely an apparent counterexample. E. M. Forster's "The Machine Stops" is generally taken as an antiutopia which attacks the high-technology utopias of the sort mentioned above (see note 16). In fact, the society of Forster's story, while indeed possessed of a high technology, is decadent and noninventive; the "appropriate" technology for them is one they no longer understand well enough to effect repairs on their equipment. The obverse of stability is stagnation or living on one's intellectual capital; antiutopian writers are more likely to be concerned with that problem than with the precise technological level needed to sustain a comfortable modern lifestyle. So Forster's satire seems more directed *against* the idea of technological stability in the future, which is often a component of utopian romance.
37. *Republic* IX, 592a-b.
38. *Republic* VIII, 550e-551a; IV, 422a; IX, 586a-b.
39. *News from Nowhere,* ed. Redmond, pp. 34-35.
40. *Walden Two,* p. 311.
41. See Werner Jaeger, *Paideia: The Ideals of Greek Culture,* trans. Gilbert Highet (Oxford Univ. Press, 1944), II, pp. 200-203, and III, pp. 245-60.
42. See Edward Surtz, S.J., *The Praise of Pleasure: Philosophy, Education and Communism in More's Utopia* (Harvard Univ. Press, 1957), pp. 87-150.
43. *News from Nowhere,* pp. 21-25.
44. In this, Morris is more radical than his friend Kropotkin, who apparently envisioned educational reform as involving roughly the same kind of school as those currently existing, with more efficient methods of instruction used and integration of intellectual and manual labor introduced. Kropotkin argues the social benefits that would accrue from such reform. See Kropotkin, *Fields, Factories and Workshops* [1898], reprint (New York: Greenwood Press, 1968), pp. 186-203.
45. Our statement of the problem is oversimplified. For an overly complicated discussion see Robert C. Elliott, *The Shape of Utopia: Studies in a Literary Genre* (Univ. of Chicago Press, 1970), pp. 102-128.
46. Robert M. Pirsig, *Zen and the Art of Motorcycle Maintenance: An Inquiry into Values* (New York: Bantam Books, 1975), p. 291.
47. George Woodcock, *Anarchism: A History of Libertarian Ideas and Movements* (Cleveland: Meridian Books, 1962), p. 24. The phrases of Woodcock in what follows may be found on the same page.
48. Elliott, *The Shape of Utopia,* p. 109. There is no evidence whatsoever that Morris was unhappy with Old Hammond's discourse. Elliott bases his observation on the fact that Morris varies the format from question-and-answer exposition to philosophical dialogue. Aside from the fact that many ordinary teacher-pupil conversations are structured this way,

we notice that the same phenomenon may be observed in medieval dream vision (cf. *Pearl* and Chaucer's *House of Fame*). For a better assessment of Morris's motives and aesthetic doctrines, see the introduction by James Redmond to the edition we have been citing, esp. pp. xix-xl.

CHAPTER 7: THOMAS J. REMINGTON

1. See, for example, Douglas Barbour, "Wholeness and Balance in the Hainish Novels of Ursula K. Le Guin," *Science Fiction Studies,* 1 (1974), p. 164; George Edgar Slusser, *The Farthest Shores of Ursula K. Le Guin* (San Bernardino, Cal.: Borgo Press, 1976), p. 31; and James W. Bittner, "The Roots of Le Guin's Earthsea Trilogy and the Hainish Novels," paper presented at the Le Guin seminar of the Science Fiction Research Association's National Convention in Evanston, Ill., June 18, 1977.
2. An argument for this view is presented by Slusser in his chapter, "The Early Hainish Novels," in *The Farthest Shores of Ursula K. Le Guin,* pp. 5-16.
3. Slusser, *The Farthest Shores of Ursula K. Le Guin,* p. 31. Bittner offers an outline of Le Guin's writing career, which "indicates that we cannot separate the Earthsea trilogy from Le Guin's other writing," adding "at the same time she was exploring Earthsea and the Hainish worlds, Le Guin was writing the stories she calls 'psychomyths,' and she was also writing and rewriting stories set in Orsinia."
4. See Ian Watson, "Le Guin's *Lathe of Heaven* and the Role of Dick: The False Reality as Mediator," *Science Fiction Studies,* 5 (1975), 67-75.
5. Barbour, "Wholeness and Balance in the Hainish Novels."
6. Barbour, "On Ursula Le Guin's *A Wizard of Earthsea,*" in *Riverside Quarterly,* 6 (April 1976), 121-122.
7. Remington, "A Touch of Difference, a Touch of Love: Theme in Three Stories by Ursula K. Le Guin," *Extrapolation,* 18 (Dec. 1976), 28-41.
8. Ibid.
9. Slusser, *The Farthest Shores of Ursula K. Le Guin,* p. 11.
10. The chapter heading is significant in recalling that, for Le Guin, neither pure light nor absolute darkness is associated with good; but shadow and twilight are so associated. Barbour discusses Le Guin's light-dark imagery extensively in "Wholeness and Balance." But I feel that he places too little emphasis on her insistence on a mixture of light and dark; instead, he says, "good emerges from ambiguous darkness, evil from blinding light" (p. 164). Nevertheless, his treatment of light-dark imagery in Le Guin's novels recognizes the importance of shadow and is seminal to a study of this element in her work. See also Barbour's "On Ursula K. Le Guin's *A Wizard of Earthsea*" for his comments on light-dark imagery in the first novel of the Earthsea trilogy.

11. The centrality of touching opposites to *City of Illusions* is undoubtedly related to the emergence of overt references to the Tao in that work. Direct references to the Tao are continued in *The Lathe of Heaven,* and the yang-yin mandala is alluded to in *The Left Hand of Darkness* and, if we may assume that the mandala is the "Circle of Life" with which Anarresti books are imprinted, in *The Dispossessed.* In this context it is also worth noting that the mandala is used as the logo in *The Wind's Twelve Quarters* and that in the passage from Housman, which Le Guin uses for the book's epigraph, occur the lines, "Take my hand quick and tell me,/What have you in your heart." The idea of "touching opposites" is central to the Tao. In the two articles referred to above, Barbour discusses the significance of the Tao to the Hainish novels (through *The Left Hand of Darkness*) and in *A Wizard of Earthsea.* He also touches on the mandala's significance in *The Dispossessed,* in "Wholeness and Balance: An Addendum," *Science Fiction Studies,* 2 (1975), pp. 248-49, although he does not suggest that the "Circle of Life" is the Yang-Yin mandala. In addition, Barbour has treated Le Guin's use of the Tao in *The Lathe of Heaven,* in "*The Lathe of Heaven*—Taoist Dream," *Algol,* 21 (Nov. 1973), pp. 22-24.
12. For the internal chronology of the Hainish novels, see Watson's "Le Guin's *Lathe of Heaven* and the Role of Dick: The False Reality as Mediator."
13. Darko Suvin, "Parables of De-Alienation: Le Guin's Widdershins Dance," *Science Fiction Studies,* 2 (1975), p. 265; and Scholes, "Science Fiction as Conscience: John Brunner and Ursula K. Le Guin," *New Republic,* 175 (Oct. 30, 1976), p. 38.
14. The reader unfamiliar with *The Left Hand of Darkness* should note that, despite the identity of names, the Estraven and Arek of the legend "Estraven the Traitor" are not the same characters as those in the novel's main narrative.
15. Scholes and Rabkin, *Science Fiction: History, Science, Vision* (New York: Oxford Univ. Press, 1977), p. 229.
16. I suspect that Delany has made this point in print; but here I am referring to his remarks made from the floor at a symposium on science fiction and literary criticism in which Robert Scholes and I participated. The symposium was held as part of the Science Fiction Research Association national conference in Missoula, Montana, June 1976.
17. The allusion to Gulliver's revulsion at mankind on his return from the land of the Houyhnhnms, in Ai's response to his fellow bisexual humans, was suggested by Scholes and Rabkin, p. 230.
18. Watson, "Le Guin's *Lathe of Heaven,*" pp. 67, 71.
19. Ibid, pp. 68-69.
20. Barbour, "Wholeness and Balance: An Addendum," p. 248.
21. The fertility of Jakob's and Rolery's marriage seems to have been overlooked by Suvin in "Parables of De-Alienation: Le Guin's Widdershins Dance," where he writes that Le Guin's "heroes pay a stiff price for their victories, though the price decreases through Le Guin's

opus down to Shevek, the first Founding Father who is also a biological father and whose collective or *comitatus* is not destroyed at the end of the story—another way of saying he can live on to enjoy his victory" (p. 271). Unless we view matters through Pilotson's eyes. Jakob's *comitatus* survives in *Planet of Exile;* we are told in *City of Illusions* that Ramarren is descended from Jakob (*CI,* VII). Estraven doesn't survive, but he does have a child—although one could quibble about the constitution of his *comitatus* and about either his "Founding Fatherhood" or his "biological fatherhood."

22. Text cited is that of Hobbe's *Leviathan Reprinted from the Edition of 1651*, 1909 (reprinted, New York: Oxford Univ. Press, 1962), p. 97.
23. Ibid. p. 121

CHAPTER 8: SNEJA GUNEW

1. Although I was interested to read Douglas Barbour "Wholeness and Balance in the Hainish Novels of Ursula K. Le Guin," *Science Fiction Studies,* ed. Mullen and Suvin (Boston: Gregg Press, 1976), pp. 146-54, and agree that the dark-light imagery is a linking device of the various books, I persevere in my distinction between this body of imagery as relating to the macrocosmic, while the shadow is related more to the microcosmic, the individual.
2. See Alan Watts, *Tao: The Watercourse Way* (New York: Pantheon, 1975), pp. 20, 26.
3. In Le Guin's work, light is often related to learning or knowledge in the scientific sense, for example the image of the candle. But this deserves a full-scale article on its own. Note the story "The Stars Below," in *The Wind's Twelve Quarters.*
4. Compare this with Ged's imprisonment in *The Tombs of Atuan* or the children playing at prisons in *The Dispossessed.*
5. Compare this treatment of the shadow of madness with "Winter's King" in *The Wind's Twelve Quarters.*
6. The implications of the act in a Faustian sense is a theme examined at length in the Earthsea trilogy.
7. Lewis Carroll, *The Annotated Alice* (Harmondsworth, Herts: Penguin, 1972), ed. Martin Gardner, pp. 225-27.
8. Robert Silverberg, ed., *The New Atlantis* (New York: Hawthorn Books, 1975), p. 71.
9. C.G. Jung, ed., *Man and His Symbols* (London: Aldus Books, 1974), pp. 168-69.
10. Silverberg, *New Atlantis,* p. 83.

CHAPTER 9: JOHN H. CROW and RICHARD D. ERLICH

1. In his *The Farthest Shores of Ursula K. Le Guin,* George E. Slusser discusses "the power of one man. . . to disturb the balance" (San Bernardino, Cal.: Borgo Press, 1976), p. 35. But he asserts "the primacy

of the social realm'' in the trilogy, where we see the primacy of the individual (p. 46).

2. Judah Bierman notes the theme of ''actions have consequences'' as central to Le Guin's view of humans in the universe: ''Ambiguity in Utopia: *The Dispossessed,'' Science Fiction Studies*—cited hereafter as *SFS*—2 (Nov. 1975), p. 253.
3. Le Guin discusses the Jungian shadow in her essay, ''The Child and the Shadow,'' *Quarterly Journal of the Library of Congress,* 32 (April 1975), pp. 139-48. In her ''Response to the Le Guin Issue'' (*SFS* #7), Le Guin says that ''Jung's Shadow'' is, indeed, in *Wizard,* though she had ''never read a word of Jung'' when she wrote the book: *SFS*, 3 (March 1976), p. 45. In our citations we refer to this essay by the short title, ''Response.''
4. Cob's desire for immortality and Ged's resistance to that desire may be additional support for the Taoist reading of Le Guin's work, developed in our third section and in two essays and a note by Douglas Barbour: ''On Ursula Le Guin's *A Wizard of Earthsea,'' Riverside Quarterly,* v. 6, pp. 119-23; ''Wholeness and Balance in the Hainish Novels of Ursula K. Le Guin,'' *SFS,* 1 (Spring 1974), pp. 164-73; and ''Wholeness and Balance: An Addendum,'' *SFS,* 3 (Nov. 1975), pp. 238-49. Holmes Welch emphasizes that ''the philosophical Taoists were distinguished from all other schools of Taoism by their rejection of the pursuit of immortality''; this quest for immortality led the Taoist Church away from the subtle philosophies of Lao Tzu and Chuang Tzu and into ''moribund superstition.'' See Welch's *The Parting of the Way: Lao Tzu and the Taoist Movement* (Boston: Beacon Press, 1957), pp. 95, 162-63. (Le Guin refers to Welch's book in her ''Response'' essay.) Note that Chuang Tzu suggests that we might well look forward with some joy even to the decomposition of our bodies after death: the process whereby we return to the cycles of nature (for example, see the speech of Tzu Yu in *Chuang Tzu,* ch. 6). In opposition to the Taoist philosophers, we find Cob and the Yomesh of *The Left Hand of Darkness,* who assert that ''there is neither darkness nor death'' (*LHD,* XII).
5. In *Word for World* Le Guin examines the relationship of psychology, culture, and ecological balance, combining the heterogeneous ideas of ecology and ontology. The power-mad *doers* upset the ecological balance of Athshe, a household in which the native humans have found a place to *be.*
6. Compare ''Ambitious men love change. Thus, men are always doing something; inaction is to them impossible'' *(Chuang Tzu,* ch. 24, ''Hsü Wu Kuei''); we use the translation by Herbert A. Giles, 2nd rev. edn. (London: Allen & Unwin, 1926), p. 237.
7. Lao Tzu's formulation is slightly different: ''For though all creatures under heaven are the products of Being,/Being itself is the product of Not-Being'' (*Tao Te Ching,* ch. 40). We use the translation of Arthur Waley, *The Way and Its Power* (London: Allen & Unwin, 1934), p.

192. Martin Heidegger's views on Being and Not-Being are similar to Lao Tzu's.

8. Magic as a science in Earthsea is asserted by Judah Bierman (p. 254) and Robert Scholes, *Structural Fabulation* (Notre Dame and London: Univ. of Notre Dame Press, 1975), p. 82. Elsewhere, we have argued the truth of this assertion (note 12 in "The Three Voyages of the Archmage Sparrowhawk," a paper delivered at the Heroic Fantasy Seminar at the Seventh Annual Convention of the Popular Culture Association, Baltimore, 29 April 1977).
9. Ian Watson provides a chronology of the Hainish cycle in "Le Guin's *Lathe of Heaven* and the Role of Dick: The False Reality as Mediator," *SFS*, 2 (March 1975), pp. 67-75. We depend on Watson's tables and discussion for the dating of events in the cycle.
10. Le Guin uses the phrase "I and Thou" (a literal translation of Buber's title, *Ich and Du*) in *The Left Hand of Darkness*. For discussions of significant bonds in Le Guin's fiction, see Rafail Nudelman, "An Approach to the Structure of Le Guin's SF," trans. Alan G. Myers, *SFS*, 2 (Nov. 1975), pp. 210-20; and Thomas J. Remington, "A Touch of Difference, A Touch of Love," *Extrapolation*, 18 (Dec. 1976), pp. 28-41.
11. Le Guin's consistency in "themes and values" is asserted by Robert Scholes and Eric S. Rabkin in *Science Fiction: History, Science, Vision* (London and New York: Oxford Univ. Press, 1977), p. 78; also see David L. Porter, "The Politics of Le Guin's Opus," *SFS*, 2 (Nov. 1975), p. 243. Barbour's Taoist reading of Le Guin's works also works toward demonstrating the unity of her canon.
12. Holmes Welch presents the thought of Lao Tzu as a complete philosophical system, lacking only a logic (*Parting of the Way*, pp. 86-87). Note also Welch's Part IV, "Tao Today," with its presentation of the *Tao Te Ching* as a critique of the excesses of Americanism. Welch's book seems to have had a profound effect on Le Guin, from matters of philosophy to suggesting the title of and theme for a short story ("Field of Vision") and the scene in *Lathe* in which Orr and Haber discuss giving or withholding snakebite serum; see Welch, pp. 50, 61, and 46. (Citations of Welch in our text refer to *Parting of the Way*.) A critique of Sartrean existentialism quite useful for a study of Le Guin appears in William Barrett, *Irrational Man* (1958; reprinted Garden City: Doubleday, 1962), ch. 10, section 3 pp. 254-63.
13. Barrett, *Irrational Man*, pp. 255, 257, 261.
14. Most modern anarchists also stress the importance of men living in harmony with nature in a unified world. See Marshall S. Shatz's introduction to *The Essential Works of Anarchism* (New York: Bantam, 1971), pp. xvii-xix.
15. This process is schematically presented in the Diagram of the Supreme Pole, the *T'ai chi t'u* Le Guin mentions in her "Response" essay, p. 45, and which is discussed by Joseph Needham, *Science and Civilization in China* (Cambridge: Cambridge Univ. Press, 1956), II, pp.

460-67; Le Guin makes a general reference to Needham in her "Response."

16. The quotation on truth is from *The Left Hand of Darkness,* introduction to the 1976 Ace edition and p. 1; see also p. 2.
17. See Welch, *The Parting of the Way,* pp. 25, 33-34, 82; see also, Hellmut Wilhelm, *Change: Eight Lectures on the I Ching,* trans. Cary F. Baynes (New York: Pantheon, 1960), p. 34. Le Guin mentions Wilhelm's book in her "Response."
18. The unity of means and ends was discussed by Victor Urbanowicz, "Personal and Political Development in *The Dispossessed,*" a paper delivered at the Le Guin Seminar at the Seventh Annual Convention of the Popular Culture Association, Baltimore, 28 April 1977. See also Alexander Berkman, *What Is Communist Anarchism?* (original title: *Now and After: The ABC of Communist Anarchism*), introduction by Paul Avrich (1929; reprinted New York: Dover, 1972), p. 168 and *passim.* Berkman's *Communist Anarchism* also shows us modern anarchism's stress on the importance of individual freedom and responsibility, the ultimate unity of the human race, and the necessity to manage only things, never people.
19. Berkman, *What Is Communist Anarchism?* p. 206.

Ursula K. Le Guin: A Bibliography

Compiled by MARSHALL B. TYMN

ALTHOUGH not intended to be definitive, this bibliography is comprehensive in its scope and coverage and is representative of Ursula K. Le Guin's total output. All items are listed in alphabetical order. The last section gives a list of important critical articles about her work.

Books and Pamphlets

City of Illusions [novel]. New York: Ace Books, 1967 pb; London: Gollancz, 1971.

The Dispossessed [novel]. New York: Harper & Row, 1974; Avon Books, 1975 pb.

Dreams Must Explain Themselves [essay collection]. New York: Algol Press, 1975 pb.

The Earthsea Trilogy [novels: *A Wizard of Earthsea, The Tombs of Atuan,* and *The Farthest Shore*]. London: Gollancz, 1977.

The Farthest Shore [third novel of the Earthsea trilogy]. New York: Atheneum, 1972; UK: Penguin/Puffin, 1974 pb.

From Elfland to Poughkeepsie [speech]. Portland, OR: Pendragon Press, 1973 pb.

The Lathe of Heaven [novel]. In *Amazing Stories* (March & May, 1971); New York: Charles Scribner's Sons, 1971; Avon Books, 1973 pb.

The Left Hand of Darkness [novel]. New York: Ace Books, 1969 pb; Walker, 1969.

Nebula Award Stories Eleven [anthology]. London: Gollancz, 1976.

Orsinian Tales [short story collection]. New York: Harper & Row, 1976; Bantam, 1977 pb.

Planet of Exile [novel]. New York: Ace Books, 1966 pb [bound with Thomas M. Disch's *Mankind Under the Lease*]; Garland, 1975.

Rocannon's World [novel]. New York: Ace: Books, 1966 pb [bound with Avram Davidson's *The Kar-Chee Reign*]; Garland, 1975.

Three Hainish Novels [*Rocannon's World, Planet of Exile,* and *City of Illusions*]. Garden City: Nelson Doubleday [Science Fiction Book Club], 1978.

The Tombs of Atuan [second novel of the *Earthsea* trilogy]. In *Worlds of Fantasy* (Winter 1970-71];

New York: Atheneum, 1971; UK: Penguin/Puffin, 1974 pb.
Very Far Away from Anywhere Else [novel]. New York: Atheneum, 1976; Bantam, 1978 pb.
The Water Is Wide [short story]. Portland, OR: Pendragon Press, 1976.
Wild Angels [poems]. Santa Barbara, CA: Capra Press, 1975 pb.
The Wind's Twelve Quarters [short story collection]. New York: Harper & Row, 1975; Bantam, 1976 pb.
A Wizard of Earthsea [first novel of the Earthsea trilogy]. New York: Parnassus Press, 1968; Ace Books, 1970 pb.
The Word for World Is Forest [novella]. In *Again, Dangerous Visions,* ed., Harlan Ellison. Garden City: Doubleday, 1972; New York: Putnam, 1976; Berkley, 1976 pb.

Short Fiction

"An die Music." *Western Humanities Review* (Summer 1961).
"April in Paris." *Fantastic Stories of Imagination* (September 1962). Collected in *The Wind's Twelve Quarters* [hereinafter referred to as *Winds*].
"The Author of the Acacia Seeds and Other Extracts from the *Journal of the Association of Therolinguistics.*" In *Fellowship of the Stars,* ed., Terry Carr. New York: Simon & Schuster, 1974.
"The Barrow." *Fantasy and Science Fiction* (October 1976).
"Cake & Ice Cream." *Playgirl* (February-March 1973).
"Darkness Box." *Fantastic Stories of Imagination* (November 1963). Collected in *Winds.*
"The Day Before the Revolution." *Galaxy Science Fiction Magazine* (August 1974). Collected in *Winds.*
"The Diary of the Rose." In *Future Power,* eds., Jack Dann and Gardner Dozois. New York: Random House, 1976.
"Direction of the Road." In *Orbit 12,* ed., Damon Knight. New York: Putnam, 1973. Collected in *Winds.*
"The Dowry of Angyar." *Amazing Fact and Science Fiction Stories* (September 1964). Collected in *Winds* as "Semley's Necklace" [author's title].
"The End." In *Orbit 6,* ed., Damon Knight. New York: Putnam, 1970. Collected in *Winds* as "Things" [author's title].
"The Eye Altering." In *The Altered I: An Encounter with Science Fiction by Ursula K. Le Guin and Others,* ed., Lee Harding. Carlton, Victoria, Australia: Norstrilia Press, 1976.
"The Eye of the Heron." In *Millennial Women,* ed., Virginia Kidd. New York: Delacorte, 1978.
"Field of Vision." *Galaxy Science Fiction Magazine* (October 1973). Collected in *Winds* as "The Field of Vision."
"Fifteen Vultures, the Strop, and the Old Lady." In *Clarion II,* ed., Robin Scott Wilson. New York: Signet, 1972.
"The Good Trip." *Fantastic Stories* (August 1970). Collected in *Winds.*

"Gwilan's Harp." *Redbook* (May 1977).
"Imaginary Countries." *The Harvard Advocate* (Winter 1973).
"Intracom." In *Stop Watch,* ed., George Hay. UK: New English Library, 1974.
"The Masters." *Fantastic Stories of Imagination* (February 1963). Collected in *Winds.*
"Mazes." In *Epoch,* eds., Robert Silverberg and Roger Elwood. New York: Berkley Medallion, 1975.
"The New Atlantis." In *The New Atlantis and Other Novellas of Science Fiction,* ed., Robert Silverberg. New York: Hawthorn Books, 1975.
"Nine Lives." *Playboy* (November 1969). Collected in *Winds.*
"The Ones Who Walk Away from Omelas (Variations on a Theme by William James)." In *New Dimensions 3,* ed., Robert Silverberg. Garden City: Nelson Doubleday (Science Fiction Book Club), 1973. Collected in *Winds.*
"The Rule of Names." *Fantastic Stories of Imagination* (April 1964). Collected in *Winds.*
"Schrodinger's Cat." In *Universe 5,* ed., Terry Carr. New York: Random House, 1974.
"Selection." *Amazing Fact and Science Fiction Stories* (August 1964).
"Semley's Necklace." *See* "The Dowry of Angyar."
"The Stars Below." In *Orbit 14,* ed., Damon Knight. New York: Harper & Row, 1974. Collected in *Winds.*
"Things." *See* "The End."
"A Trip to the Head." In *Quark/#1,* eds., Samuel R. Delany and Marilyn Hacker. New York: Paperback Library, 1970. Collected in *Winds.*
"The Ursula Major Construct; Or, a Far Greater Horror Loomed." In *Clarion III,* ed., Robin Scott Wilson. New York: Signet, 1973.
"Vaster Than Empires and More Slow." In *New Dimensions 1,* ed., Robert Silverberg. Garden City: Doubleday, 1971. Collected in *Winds.*
"Winter's King." In *Orbit 5,* ed., Damon Knight. New York: Putnam, 1969. Emended version collected in *Winds.*
"The Word of Unbinding." *Fantastic Stories of Imagination* (January 1964). Collected in *Winds.*

Articles and Essays

"American SF and the Other." *Science-Fiction Studies* (November 1975).
"The Child and the Shadow." *The Quarterly Journal of the Library of Congress,* (April 1975).
"A Citizen of Mondath." *Foundation* (July 1973).
"The Crab Nebula, the Paramecium, and Tolstoy." *Riverside Quarterly* (February 1972).
"Dreams Must Explain Themselves." *Algol* (November 1973).

"Escape Routes." *Galaxy Science Fiction Magazine* (December 1974).
"Is Gender Necessary?" In *Aurora: Beyond Equality,* eds., Susan J. Anderson and Vonda McIntyre. New York: Fawcett Gold Medal, 1976.
"Ketterer on *The Left Hand of Darkness.*" *Science-Fiction Studies* (July 1975).
"National Book Award Acceptance Speech." *Horn Book* (June 1973).
"On Theme." In *Those Who Can,* ed., Robin Scott Wilson. New York: Mentor, 1973.
"Prophets and Mirrors." *The Living Light* (Fall 1970).
"A Response to the Le Guin Issue (SFS #7)." *Science-Fiction Studies* (March 1976).
"Science Fiction and Mrs. Brown." In *Science Fiction at Large,* ed., Peter Nicholls. New York: Harper & Row, 1976.
"Science Fiction and Prophesy: Philip K. Dick." *The New Republic* (October 30, 1976).
"The Stalin in the Soul." In *The Future Now,* ed., Robert Hoskins. Greenwhich, CT: Fawcett Crest, 1977.
"The Staring Eye." *Vector* (Spring 1974).
"Surveying the Battlefield." *Science-Fiction Studies* (Fall 1973).
"Why Are Americans Afraid of Dragons?" *Pacific Northwest Library Association Quarterly* (Winter 1974).

General

"European SF: Rottensteiner's Anthology, the Strugatskys, and Lem" [review]. *Science-Fiction Studies* (Spring 1974).
"Introduction." In *The Altered I: An Encounter with Science Fiction by Ursula K. Le Guin and Others,* ed., Lee Harding. Carlton, Victoria, Australia: Norstrilia Press, 1976.
"A New Book by the Strugatskys" [review]. *Science-Fiction Studies* (July 1977).
"No Use to Talk to Me" [play]. In *The Altered I: An Encounter with Science Fiction by Ursula K. Le Guin and Others,* ed., Lee Harding. Carlton, Victoria, Australia: Norstrilla Press, 1976.
"On Norman Spinrad's *The Iron Dream*" [review]. *Science-Fiction Studies* (Spring 1973).
"Science Fiction and the Future of Anarchy" [interview by Charles Bigelow and J. McMahon]. *Oregon Times* (December 1974).
"Tricks, anthropology create new worlds" [interview by Barry Barth]. *Portland Scribe,* May 17-24, 1975.
"Ursula K. Le Guin" [interview by Jonathan Ward]. *Algol* (Summer 1975).
"Ursula K. Le Guin: An Interview" [by Paul Walker]. *Luna Monthly* (March 1976).

Criticism

Barbour, Douglas. *"The Lathe of Heaven:* Taoist Dream." *Algol* (November 1973).

———. "On Ursula Le Guin's *A Wizard of Earthsea.*" *Riverside Quarterly* (April 1974).

______. "Wholeness and Balance in the Hainish Novels of Ursula K. Le Guin." *Science-Fiction Studies* (Spring 1974).

______. "Wholeness and Balance: An Addendum." *Science-Fiction Studies* (November 1975).

Bickman, Martin. "Le Guin's *The Left Hand of Darkness:* Form and Content." *Science-Fiction Studies* (March 1977).

Bierman, Judah. "Ambiguity in Utopia: The Dispossessed." *Science-Fiction Studies* (November 1975).

Cameron, Eleanor. "High Fantasy: *A Wizard of Earthsea.*" *Horn Book Magazine* (April 1971).

Cogell, Elizabeth C. "Setting as Analogue to Characterization in Ursula K. Le Guin." *Extrapolation* (May 1977).

Elliott, Robert C. "A New Utopian Novel." *Yale Review* (Winter 1976).

Fox, Geoff, ed. "Notes on 'teaching' *A Wizard of Earthsea.*" *Children's Literature in Education* (May 1973).

Huntington, John. "Public and Private Imperatives in Le Guin's Novels." *Science-Fiction Studies* (November 1975).

Jago, Wendy. " 'A Wizard of Earthsea' and the charge of escapism." *Children's Literature in Education* (July 1972).

Jameson, Fredric. "World-Reduction in Le Guin: The Emergence of Utopian Narrative." *Science-Fiction Studies* (November 1975).

Ketterer, David. "*The Left Hand of Darkness:* Ursula Le Guin's Archetypal Winter Journey." *Riverside Quarterly* (April 1973).

Klein, Gerard. "Le Guin's 'Aberrant' Opus: Escaping the Trap of Discount." *Science-Fiction Studies* (November 1977).

Levin, Jeff. "Ursula K. LeGuin: A Select Bibliography." *Science-Fiction Studies* (November 1975).

Nudelman, Rafail. "An Approach to the Structure of Le Guin's SF." *Science-Fiction Studies* (November 1975).

Plank, Robert, "Ursula K. Le Guin and the Decline of Romantic Love." *Science-Fiction Studies* (March 1976).

Porter, David L. "The Politics of Le Guin's Opus." *Science-Fiction Studies* (November 1975).

Remington, Thomas J. "A Touch of Difference, A Touch of Love: Theme in Three Stories by Ursula K. Le Guin." *Extrapolation* (December 1976).

Scholes, Robert. "The Good Witch of the West." *Hollins Critic* (April 1974). Rpt. in *Structural Fabulation.* Notre Dame and London: University of Notre Dame Press, 1975.

———. "Science Fiction as Conscience: John Brunner and Ursula K. Le Guin" *The New Republic* (October 30, 1976).

Shippey, T. A. "The Magic Art and the Evolution of Works: Ursula Le Guin's *Earthsea* Trilogy." *Mosaic* (Winter 1977).

Siciliano, Sam Joseph. "The Fictional Universe in Four Science Fiction Novels: Anthony Burgess's *A Clockwork Orange,* Ursula Le Guin's

The Word for World is Forest, Walter Miller's *A Canticle for Leibowitz,* and Roger Zelazny's *Creatures of Light and Darkness.*" Ph.D. dissertation, University of Iowa, 1975.

Slusser, George Edgar. *The Farthest Shores of Ursula K. Le Guin.* San Bernardino, CA: Borgo Press, 1976.

Suvin, Darko. "Parables of De-Alienation: Le Guin's Widdershins Dance." *Science-Fiction Studies* (November 1975).

Taylor, Angus. "The Politics of Space, Time and Entropy." *SF Commentary* (December 1975).

Theall, Donald F. "The Art of Social-Science Fiction: The Ambiguous Utopian Dialectics of Ursula K. Le Guin." *Science-Fiction Studies* (November 1975).

Turner, George. "Paradigm and Pattern: Form and Meaning in *The Dispossessed.*" *SF Commentary* (February 1975).

Watson, Ian. "The Forest as Metaphor for Mind: 'The Word for World is Forest' and 'Vaster Than Empires and More Slow.' " *Science-Fiction Studies* (November 1975).

______. "Le Guin's *Lathe of Heaven* and the Role of Dick: The False Reality as Mediator." *Science-Fiction Studies* (March 1975).

Wood, Susan. "Discovering Worlds: The Fiction of Ursula K. Le Guin." In *Voices for the Future,* Vol. II, ed., Thomas D. Clareson. Bowling Green, OH: Bowling Green University Popular Press, 1978.

Ursula K. Le Guin: A Biographical Note*

URSULA K. LE GUIN is one of the most highly regarded of contemporary science fiction writers. She was born in 1929 in Berkeley, California, and is the daughter of anthropologist A. L. Kroeber and author Theodora Kroeber. She attended Radcliffe and Columbia, and she married C. A. Le Guin in Paris in 1951. They have three children and live in Portland, Oregon.

Mrs. Le Guin's contributions to the science fiction and fantasy field have all been made during the last sixteen years, but in that time she has garnered an impressive array of awards. She began fairly conventionally with a superior space opera in *Rocannon's World* (1966) and with accounts of conflicts with aliens in *Planet of Exile* (1966) and *City of Illusions* (1967). With the publication of *A Wizard of Earthsea* (1968), the first volume of her *Earthsea* trilogy, she was on her way to national recognition. For that novel she received the *Boston Globe–Horn* Award.

Her major breakthrough came in 1969 with *The Left Hand of Darkness,* a richly imaginative story of an extraterrestrial world called "Winter" and of the lifestyle and sexual cycle of its inhabitants. An outstanding illustration of one of science fiction's most important features—the creation of total and consistent secondary universes—this novel won the Nebula Award in 1969 and the Hugo Award in 1970. The Newberry Silver Medal Award was hers for *The Tombs of Atuan* (1971), the second volume of the *Earthsea* trilogy, and the final volume, *The Farthest Shore* (1972), brought her the National Book Award.

The Lathe of Heaven appeared in 1971 and *The Dispossessed* in 1974, the latter a striking study of alienation, anarchy, and reconciliation set against the background of a future Earth–like planet and its moon colony. Both novels fit into the "Hainish" concept in Le Guin's work which postulates that an ancient race

---

*Portions of this biographical note are adapted with permission from Brian Ash, *Who's Who in Science Fiction* (Taplinger Publishing Company and Elm Tree Books, 1976).

"seeded" the galaxy, including Earth. *The Dispossessed* won a Nebula in 1974 and a Hugo in 1975. Other award–winning works include "The Word for World Is Forest" (a 1973 Hugo and a 1974 Nebula for best novella) and "The Day Before the Revolution" (a 1974 Nebula for best short story).

Contributors

PETER S. ALTERMAN lives in Denver, Colorado, and works for the U. S. Office of Education. His Ph.D. is in science fiction and English Romanticism, and he has published several pieces, including "The Surreal Translations of Samuel R. Delany," "Introduction: Flashforward to 2076" in *2076: The American Tricentennial,* "From Aptor to Bellona; The Novels of Samuel R. Delany" in *Voices for the Future, Vol. 2,* and a novelette, "Binding Energy," in *New Dimensions 9.* He is a member of the Science Fiction Research Association and Science Fiction Writers of America.

JOHN P. BRENNAN is an assistant professor in the Department of English and Linguistics at Indiana University–Purdue University at Fort Wayne. His Ph.D. is in Old and Middle English Literature and he has published several articles in this area. He is currently working on a theoretical analysis of utopian literature.

PETER BRIGG is an assistant professor who teaches modern drama, the modern novel, and science fiction in the Department of English at the University of Guelph, Guelph, Ontario, Canada. He has published articles in *Science-Fiction Studies* and *English Studies in Canada.* Forthcoming articles include theater history work on the Birmingham (England) Repertory, where he is theatrical archivist. He is also a contributor to the *Arthur C. Clarke* volume in the Writers of the 21st Century Series.

JOHN H. CROW is an assistant professor in English at Miami University in Oxford, Ohio. His main area is nineteenth–century British and American literature. He has published one essay on science fiction, with Richard D. Erlich, "Mythic Patterns in Ellison's *A Boy and His Dog*" in *Extrapolation.*

MICHAEL C. DOWNS is an associate professor of political science at Indiana University–Purdue University at Fort Wayne. He received his Ph.D. from Notre Dame and teaches courses in political philosophy. His interest and research has resulted in a monograph, "James Harrington" concerning early utopia of "The Commonwealth Oceana," as well as his collaboration with John P. Brennan on the work of Ursula K. Le Guin.

RICHARD D. ERLICH is an assistant professor in English at Miami University in Oxford, Ohio. His main area is Shakespeare and the Elizabethan and Jacobean drama. He has published two essays on science fiction, "Strange Odyssey: From Dart and Ardrey to Kubrick and Clarke" in *Extrapolation,* and, with John H. Crow, "Mythic Patterns in Ellison's *A Boy and His Dog*," a discussion of Ellison's novella and L. Q. Jones' motion picture in *Extrapolation.*

MARGARET P. ESMONDE is an assistant professor in the Department of English at Villanova University. She is the President of the Children's Literature Association and editor-in-chief of the Association's Newsletter. A charter member of the Fantasy Association, she is also the children's editor of the Association's Newsletter, to which she contributes regular critical essays. She has written for the Science Fiction Research Association's Newsletter, for the journal *Children's Literature,* and for *Luna Quarterly.*

SNEJA GUNEW teaches literature at Newcastle University in New South Wales, Australia. Her major interest is in genre critical theory as it relates to science fiction and modern fantasy. She is planning a book developing the critical theories on fantasy which she developed in the course of writing a dissertation on two Irish exponents of the fantasy genre, James Stephens and Flann O'Brien.

N. B. HAYLES holds degrees in chemistry and English. An assistant professor of English at Dartmouth College, she teaches Renaissance literature and science fiction.

THOMAS J. REMINGTON is the Coordinator of Graduate Studies for the English Department of the University of Northern Iowa, where he is an associate professor. His doctoral dissertation was in Shakespeare studies, and he continues to have a scholarly interest in English renaissance drama. Remington regularly reviews science fiction for *The North American Review* and has published articles in *Extrapolation* and in *Science-Fiction Studies.* He has also contributed reviews to *English Language Notes* and to *Library Journal.* He chaired the symposia on Ursula K. Le Guin for the Popular Culture Association in 1977 and 1978 and was the director of the 1978 Science Fiction Research Association National Conference. He is currently at work on a book on Le Guin.

PHILIP E. SMITH II teaches in the English Department at the University of Pittsburgh. He has published articles in *Modern Poetry Studies, Victorian Poetry,* and *Studies in Humanities.* His essay on social Darwinism in the fiction of Robert Heinlein appears in the *Robert A. Heinlein* volume of the Writers of the 21st Century Series.

MARSHALL B. TYMN, associate professor of English at Eastern Michigan University, has taught science fiction there since 1974, and is director of the largest conference on teaching science fiction held in the United States. Dr. Tymn is an active researcher in the science fiction field, and has edited several bibliographic works. His publications include *A Research Guide to Science Fiction Studies* (co-editor), *The Year's Scholarship in Science Fiction and Fantasy: 1972–1975* (co-editor), and *American Fantasy and Science Fiction: A Bibliography of Works Published in the United States, 1948–1973,* as well as numerous articles. Dr. Tymn is also general editor of four science fiction series and serves as bibliographer for the Writers of the 21st Century Series. He is an officer of the Science Fiction Research Association, a former president of Instructors of Science Fiction in Higher Education (which gives the annual Jupiter Awards), and a member of the Advisory Board of the Science Fiction Oral History Association. He is currently at work on several projects, *The Science Fiction Reference Book, The Fantasy Handbook,* and *A Historical Guide to the Science Fiction and Fantasy Magazines.* A scholar in the field of American culture, he has also published two volumes on the American landscape painter, Thomas Cole.

Index